SERENITY

FREE TO FORGIVE

Daily Devotions for Adult Children of Abuse

Dr. Paul Meir &
Dr. Frank Minirth

THOMAS NELSON PUBLISHERS
Nashville

Published in Nashville, Tennessee, by Thomas Nelson, Inc., and distributed in Canada by Lawson Falle, Ltd., Cambridge, Ontario.

Scripture quotations are from the NEW KING JAMES VERSION of the Bible. Copyright © 1979, 1980, 1982, Thomas Nelson, Inc., Publishers.

Scripture quotations noted NIV are from The Holy Bible: NEW INTERNATIONAL VERSION. Copyright © 1978 by the New York International Bible Society. Used by permission of Zondervan Bible Publishers.

Library of Congress Cataloging-in-Publication Data

Meier, Paul D.
    Free to forgive / by Paul Meier and Frank Minirth.
      p. cm. — (Serenity meditation series)
     ISBN 0-8407-3223-6 (pbk.)
    1. Adult children of dysfunctional families—Prayer-books and devotions—English. 2. Adult child abuse victims—Prayer-books and devotions—English. 3. Codependents—Prayer books and devotions—English. 4. Forgiveness—Religious aspects—Christianity—Prayer-books and devotions—English. 5. Devotional calendars.
I. Minirth, Frank B. II. Title. III. Series.
BV4596.A274M45   1991
649'.4—dc20
                                     90-21106
                                            CIP

Printed in the United States of America
3 4 5 6 7 — 96 95 94 93 92 91

Acknowledgments

Drs. Meier and Minirth wish to express their appreciation to Mark and Marie Verkler for their research, typing, and editorial assistance. We also would like to thank our fellow faculty members at Dallas Theological Seminary for producing *The Bible Knowledge Commentary* (ed. John F. Walvoord and Roy B. Zuck, Victor Books, 1987). It was a great study help in the preparation of this devotional book. Also, Dr. Meier would like to thank the members of the growth group to which he and his wife belong for their moral support, suggestions, interactions, and prayers for this project: Judy and Dick Knox, Mary Anne and Joe Merwin, and Ev and John Schroeder.

Introduction

As we prepare ourselves to cope well in the third millennium A.D., we come to grips with the realization that we are living in a morally depraved world. We desire to reach out—to love and be loved—but we are also afraid of being hurt again. What a dilemma!

Sanity is impossible without emotional bonding to some fellow human beings, to ourselves, and to God. And yet reality tells us that any human we bond to will eventually hurt us from time to time. We often are our own worst enemies, and we have doubts and fears about turning control of our lives over to a God who allows so much suffering to occur.

As we enter the third millennium A.D., there are approximately six billion of us here on planet earth, and all of us, in some way or another, have abused and been abused—some worse than others. Things have not really changed much since Eve blamed the devil, Adam blamed Eve, and Cain killed Abel. Moses recorded (Gen. 6:5) that when God looked down to study the motives and behaviors of our earliest ancestors, God saw "that the wickedness of man was great in the earth, and that every intent of the thoughts of his heart was only evil continually." People were basically using and abusing one another in their vain search for significance.

God decided to wipe them out with a flood and start over again with one very moral (but not perfect) family: Noah, his wife, three sons, and three daughters-in-law.

As I stood on Mt. Ararat in eastern Turkey in August

1985, I kept thinking one thought over and over again as I visualized Noah's descendants migrating from that huge mountain to various places throughout the world: We are all brothers and sisters; every man, woman and child is my relative. We are all sons and daughters of Noah. Why can't we live in peace, love and harmony with each other?

I was there at Mt. Ararat for only two weeks, and during that time some Kurds killed some Turks and terrorists chased my expedition team off the mountain, only to be killed themselves the next day by Turkish soldiers. So, as I was visualizing world peace and love, reality raised its ugly head again and made faces at me.

On my way home, I was sitting in the airport at Frankfort, Germany, analyzing the faces of the Germans and tourists of many different nationalities who were sitting there talking. I felt empathy with them and was wishing I had the time to get to know each of them better.

Then I heard the announcement of the last call for boarding my flight back to America and I boarded. Ten minutes later our plane took off and a few minutes after that a bomb exploded in a trash can only ten feet from where I had been sitting. It killed many of those fellow human beings whom I had just been analyzing and feeling empathy for.

I returned to my psychiatric practice in America and, for some reason or another, Frank Minirth and I were referred one hospital patient after another who had been brutally terrorized and abused as children by their own parents. Then a month later, Frank and I felt very emotionally hurt by the decisions and actions of a few of our close friends. Let's just say that 1985 was one of those vintage, maturing years of my life.

We are all adult children of abuse in many ways. We all have holes in our souls. We all experience painful moments of loneliness, abandonment, or simply feeling like a nobody. We all have abused ourselves from time to time with self-critical messages from deep within our own minds. We need coping skills to continue to love and be loved.

We need to discover the holes in our souls and fill them in positive, constructive ways. If we don't, these holes will be filled with food addictions, drug addictions, sexual addictions, control addictions, workaholism, alcoholism, codependency, or other maladaptive behaviors in an attempt to avoid looking our negative motives and emotions square in the face.

Frank Minirth and I wrote this devotional book, *Free to Forgive,* as a love offering. It is our contribution to our brothers and sisters who have been hurt and victimized. God's wisdom is far above our human reasoning. We would like to share with you 365 nuggets of God's wisdom from His love letter to us, the Bible. These are passages that have helped us to fill the holes in our own souls, and that we have shared with many of our beloved patients down through the years.

Paul Meier, M.D.

Therefore, whatever you want men to do to you, do also to them, for this is the Law and the Prophets.
—MATT. 7:12

I had a psychiatric patient whose father was an abusive alcoholic. As a teenager, she had crushes only on abusive alcoholics. Later, she married one.

She didn't understand her patterns of behavior. She didn't know she was addicted to alcoholics who were abusive. She blamed everything on bad luck. But she finally looked at the truth, began long-term therapy and joined an ACA (Adult Children of Abuse) group. She quit *enabling* her husband. By "enabling," I mean she gave him money she earned so he could buy whiskey. She would think for him, bail him out of jail, and nag him about his drinking.

She and their friends eventually did an intervention. He went into therapy, joined an AA group, and they have both had ups and downs but progressive improvement ever since. It doesn't always turn out that nice.

Our passage for today is the first rule we should learn if we want to break out of our codependency cycles. It does not say, "Do unto others whatever they want you to—anything to prevent a hassle or rejection." It does say that, given all the insight you now have, what you would want that other person to do to help you mature, become independent, and become responsible for your own behaviors and feelings.

What percentage of time do you actually live the golden rule and avoid codependency?

> *Bear one another's burdens, and so fulfill the law*
> *of Christ. . . . For each one shall bear his own load.*
> —GAL. 6:2, 5

Our passage for today was written by the apostle Paul nearly two thousand years ago, and yet it gives excellent guidelines for avoiding codependency if you study these words in the original Greek that Paul wrote them in. The English language just doesn't do them justice.

In Galatians 6:2, Paul encourages us to "bear one another's burdens." This could easily be misunderstood and become the theme song for enablers. The Greek word for "burdens" is *barē*, which actually means "overburdens." It implies a heavy, crushing load that is more than a man or woman could carry without help.

In Galatians 6:5, Paul appears to be contradicting what he had just said in 6:2. In 6:5, Paul tells us matter-of-factly that each one of us "shall bear his own load." This verse, if misapplied, could become the masochist's theme song—"I'll do it all by myself with no help from anyone, thank you!"

But the Greek word for "load" or "burden" here is *phortion*. It means a "normal emotional load." It implies a load that is equivalent to a backpack carried by a soldier.

If we are true soldiers of Christ, we will carry our own phortion (backpack), expect others to do the same, ask for help for our barē (overloads), and help others with their barē as well.

*Make it your ambition to lead a quiet life, to mind
your own business and to work with your hands,
. . . so that you will not be dependent on anybody.*
—1 THESS. 4:11–12 (NIV)

My wife and I are currently rearing six teenagers. We love them, hug them, provide them with food and clothes, help them with carpools, cheer for them at their games and activities, give them advice when they ask for it and sometimes when they don't ask for it. We provide them with authority to make most of their own decisions, boundaries they cannot cross while living under our roof, and insights into our family dynamics.

They know that when they graduate from high school (two already have), they either move out and become financially independent by that fall, or move into a college dorm and continue to get reasonable financial support until they graduate.

They will either obey today's passage or starve. I've observed our children for many years now, and their motivational level and survival instincts go up dramatically whenever they are hungry.

Our passage for today tells us each human must grow emotionally to a point where he or she can lead a quiet life, mind his own business, work to survive, live a respectably independent life, and not be dependent on anybody for his *phortion* (his normal emotional load). Paul, who wrote this passage, told us we should be dependent on others for our *barē* (overburdens).

May God help us to love our children enough to enable them to become self-reliant.

> *For even when we were with you, we commanded you this: If anyone will not work, neither shall he eat.*
>
> —2 THESS. 3:10

Many years ago, two different men in our church lost their jobs, and both came to me as a friend. One came, asking for our prayers that he would rapidly find more work—any kind of work. I persuaded him to take a small amount of money from me to buy groceries for his family for a week or so. By the end of a week, he found work. It wasn't a very pleasant job, but he did it anyway. He later moved up to a better job, then an even better one. Today, he and his family are quite well off.

The other man in our church was a secret alcoholic. I didn't know it. He asked directly for money, and I gave it to him. He didn't find another job to his satisfaction, so he came back for more, and I foolishly loaned him a larger sum of money, which he still has never paid back. I was an "enabler" and a "rescuer." Getting fooled the first time was OK. But I had my blinders on the second time.

The alcoholic's marriage ended in divorce. The children suffered dramatically. It was all a tragedy.

Confrontation may or may not have helped. But it sure would have been more loving than being an enabler. I learned much that year. I also learned that Paul was right.

———————

May God grant me the courage and wisdom to give when I should give and confront when I should confront.

*Direct my steps by Your word, And let no iniquity
have dominion over me.* —PS. 119:133

Addictions are basically shame-driven. If you search
hard enough, every human being has some shame,
every human has some addictive tendencies, and
every human came from a somewhat dysfunctional
family—including my own children. None of us are
perfect parents. It's all a matter of degree. I try to be
the best father I can be. I think about it. I read about
ways to do it well. I plan. I make "contracts" with my
children. But I also blow it sometimes. I say things I
shouldn't say—both verbally and nonverbally. I enable
at times. I'm overly critical at times. I set a bad example at times. But overall, I'm a pretty good dad.

If we were abused growing up (and we all were to
some extent or another) then we have shame. As children, we thought we must really be bad kids to deserve this kind of treatment. This is false guilt.

We carry that pain until we see the truth and forgive
not only ourselves but the abuser. But we have shame.
We stuff our feelings. We develop addictive behaviors
to keep our minds off them.

Meditating on God's Word helps us to gradually
break through our defenses and see the truth about
our feelings. It is powerful. It helps us to keep "addictive iniquities" from having dominion over us.

---

*Come up with your own plan for daily meditation on God's Word.
The truth will set you free from addictive tendencies.*

> *Stand fast therefore in the liberty by which Christ has made us free, and do not be entangled again with a yoke of bondage.*   —GAL. 5:1

If your father ignored you when you were growing up, you probably developed a father-vacuum. If your mother ignored you, you would tend to have a mother-vacuum. These are like holes in our souls that cause us to crave love or attention.

We base much of our self-concept on what our parents thought of us. Ideally, we shouldn't base *any* of it on their opinion. We want to idealize our parents, and we often remember them as being better than they really were. We put them on a pedestal. We erroneously think they ignored or rejected us because we weren't "good enough." We deny our rage toward them and toward ourselves. But we have anxiety whenever the truth threatens to emerge about our repressed rage and shame.

You don't need your parents' approval. Other people can fill the vacuum. If your parents happen to love you, that's a bonus. If they reject you, you will need to cut them loose. You cannot depend on them for your self-worth or cling to the fantasy that they will change someday and finally come through for you.

Jesus set us free so we would "not be entangled again with a yoke of bondage." Love Him. Love healthy peers. Let Christ cut your umbilical cord.

Regardless of how your parents treated you, Christ decided you were worth dying for . . . and setting free.

For a righteous man *may fall seven times And rise
again, But the wicked shall fall by calamity.*
—PROV. 24:16

We have treated thousands of people for various addictions at Minirth-Meier Clinics and one of the most common problems we see is "black/white thinking."

It occurs when you think you are all bad or all good, a total failure or a total success, an addict or a nonaddict, a total sociopath or a total saint. People think they ought to be able to simply quit their addictions and never be tempted again to fail. They think that by trusting Christ to save their soul, they will immediately enter heaven on earth with no more sins or temptations or failures.

But the truth of the matter is that when an addict becomes a Christian, he becomes a Christian addict. Peter the apostle was a hysterical, impulsive fisherman before he became a Christian, and a hysterical, impulsive apostle after he became a Christian. But he grew. He kept sticking his foot in his mouth, but he grew.

You need Christ to give you the power to overcome addictions. When you trust Christ, you begin a lifelong process of spiritual and emotional growth toward Christ-likeness. You will still fail from time to time.

Our scripture for today shows us what God calls someone who fails seven times, but gets up each time to keep growing: a "righteous man."

My recovery from addictions will have ups and downs. I won't let my "black/white thinking" defeat me.

> *Do not look on the wine when it is red, when it*
> *sparkles in the cup, when it swirls around*
> *smoothly; At the last it bites like a serpent, and*
> *stings like a viper.*   —PROV. 23:31–32

Solomon may have been the wisest man who ever lived, but he had no idea how much future scientific research would prove him true. We know now from medical research that alcohol lowers the serotonin level in the brain.

To put it simply, serotonin is one of the brain chemicals that controls all our brain and nerve cells. We think and move chemically. When our serotonin level is normal, we have energy, vitality, motivation, good concentration; we feel happy, we sleep well each night, and our appetite and sex drive are normal.

When serotonin is lowered (depleted), we become like an eight-cylinder car running on three or four cylinders. We have decreased energy and motivation, decreased concentration; we feel sad, we wake up in the middle of the night and have trouble falling back to sleep, we have bad dreams, and our appetite, sex drive, and weight change noticeably.

Alcohol abusers have a suicide rate seven times higher than those who don't drink. Many were depressed before they drank and they drank to kill the pain of their depression. But part of it is the physiological result of alcohol itself on the brain's serotonin level.

Those who linger long at the wine . . ./At the last it bites like a serpent,/And stings like a viper."

> *"They have struck me, but I was not hurt; They have beaten me, but I did not feel it. When shall I awake, that I may ask another drink?"*
> —PROV. 23:35

When someone you love drinks alcohol excessively, then decides to quit, be sure they don't go "cold turkey" without medical attention. When people quit excessive drinking all at once, they are likely to develop delirium tremens. They may black out, have seizures, become psychotic and see bugs crawling on the walls or on their bodies—just like Solomon said they would in verse thirty-three. Their brains will swell and, without medication to help them withdraw, fifty percent will die.

I have seen some alcoholics and drug addicts become believers, then think they can just quit and not get medical attention and God will somehow spare them from the laws of nature. They die and go to heaven, but they could have lived productive Christian lives if they had listened to Jesus instead of some idealist. Jesus said those who are sick need a physician.

"Bad genes" don't make anyone drink, but genetic predisposition can make one person become addicted more easily than another. Alcoholism is a spiritual and emotional and medical problem all rolled into one. Faith in Christ gives an alcoholic power—power to begin a long, hard growth process that lasts the rest of his life. People want easy answers, but there aren't any.

Alcoholism is a choice, and overcoming it is a lifelong process.

> *Have you found honey? Eat only as much as you
> need, lest you be filled with it and vomit.*
> —PROV. 25:16

We have a hospital unit where we treat three types of eating disorders. Anorexia nervosa is a disorder usually found in young women in their teens or twenties. They have found dieting to be one of the few things they think they can control, but they become addicted to dieting and become thinner and thinner. Fifteen percent who go untreated die of starvation. Nearly all who get good hospital therapy will recover and live normal lives.

Bulimia is another addiction. Many bulimics will eat ten to twenty thousand calories per day, but use vomiting, laxatives, diuretics, diet pills, and excessive exercise to stay beautiful. Nearly all want to die because they feel hopelessly out of control. Hospitalization is nearly always required to overcome this tough addiction. We also do family therapy to help worried, frustrated parents know how to help break this addiction. Some bulimics die from a chemical imbalance, even though they look healthy. Again, nearly all who get good hospital therapy recover and live very normal lives.

Overeating is also a food addiction. Outpatient therapy to resolve the root problem, along with proper dieting habits, and follow-up with support groups will usually resolve this problem.

---

*Specialists are available today who can combine the psychological
and spiritual help you need to overcome your love hunger.*

*Do not overwork to be rich; Because of your own
understanding, cease! Will you set your eyes on that
which is not? For riches certainly make themselves
wings; they fly away like an eagle toward heaven.*
—PROV. 13:7, 23:4–5

There are nearly six billion people on planet earth,
and all of us have inferiority feelings. We feel, deep
down inside ourselves, like a nobody, and we go
through life dedicating our efforts to proving that we
are not a nobody.

Some do this through sexual affairs, others through
power struggles. Many strive to prove their significance through money. A lot depends on what you
based your self-worth on when you were growing up.
Was it good looks, family wealth, academics, athletics
or popularity and social skills?

We bought a poster for our home that said, "All I
want in life is a little more than I will ever have." It
reminded us of the fact that the part of our insecure
personalities that is money-addicted is never satisfied.

As psychiatrists, we treat many millionaires who
come into our office with every material thing the
world has to offer, but they are suicidally depressed.
They are so busy earning money that they never take
time to love or be loved. Some of them miss out on the
joys of parenting their own children. Then it suddenly
dawns on them that they worked eighty hours a week
for "fool's gold" and lost the real nuggets.

*When you are older, and look back on your life, what do you think
you will wish you had done differently? Why not act wisely now?*

> *"He will also go before Him in the spirit and power of Elijah, 'to turn the hearts of the fathers to the children.'"*
>
> —MAL. 4:5

My father was a hardworking German carpenter. I heard him tell me over and over when I was growing up, "Arbeit macht das leben süss!" (Work makes life sweet). I was also taught that I should do everything anybody asked me to do.

When I was thirty years old and completed my psychiatry residency at Duke University, I moved to Chicago where I promptly became a workaholic. I taught pastoral counseling at a seminary, started my own seminary training, saw students for free therapy, had a part-time private practice in psychiatry, conducted seminars on Sunday mornings at churches, and worked for free with poor people who needed psychiatric help on Saturdays. I was a first-class codependent rescuer, "suffering for Jesus," and ignoring my own wife and children.

Studying the Bible changed me. I saw how important it was to God for fathers to spend time loving their children, and vice versa.

I reprioritized my life when I was thirty, putting God first, my own mental health second, my wife third, my children fourth, helping others fifth, my career sixth, and everything else seventh.

Do I have my priorities in order making sure that God is first in my life? Is my family a higher priority than my career?

For the lips of an immoral woman drip honey, And her mouth is smoother than oil; But in the end she is bitter as wormwood, sharp as a two-edged sword. —PROV. 5:3–4

If a woman grows up without proper love and attention from her father, she will have a "father-vacuum." She will crave male attention, and will learn to become a performer—whatever it takes to fill the hole in her soul left by an absent father. If her father sexually abuses her on top of all this, she will have repressed rage and bitterness toward him and toward herself.

The shame leads to low self-esteem and the feeling that she is trash. It becomes a self-fulfilling prophecy. She really just wants to love and be loved, but doesn't know how and confuses it with sexuality.

As a married woman, she still has a "father addiction." She has crushes on her pastor, her doctor, her boss—older men in particular. She falls into an affair, feels ashamed, quits it, falls into another one, and the cycle continues.

She loves and hates men. She craves their affection but feels guilty for having so much unconscious rage toward her father. But Jesus loves her like He loved the woman caught in adultery. He understands. She can learn to love and be loved. She doesn't need her earthly father to fill her father-vacuum, but she does need her heavenly Father's bonding.

I know that people-addictions are curable with God's help and painful, hard work.

> *And you mourn at last, when your flesh and your*
> *body are consumed, And say: "How I have hated*
> *instruction, And my heart despised reproof!"*
> —PROV. 5:11–12

Sexual addictions in men and women are more likely if they had certain types of dysfunctional families. Father absence, for example, results in a father-vacuum in both sons and daughters. Daughters will tend to be heterosexual but promiscuous. Sons will tend to identify with mom and develop homosexual urges.

If there is a good dad present, but mother-absence, then the children will have a mother-vacuum and identify with dad.

Both parents may do a great job, but the teenager may make poor choices, like purchasing pornographic magazines or watching pornographic movies. Pornography is very addictive, and can eventually lead to rape or even murder.

If a child of either sex is treated like a substitute mate by the parent of the opposite sex, this also leads to increased tendencies toward sexual addictions. The child grows up feeling he (or she) deserves the attention of all other members of the opposite sex.

Sexual addictions are overcome by insight-oriented therapy, looking closely at all significant past relationships. Accountability and confession are helpful and healing; filling those father- and mother-vacuums and bonding with our heavenly Father is a must.

Dear God, please grant me the wisdom to see myself and love myself as You see and love me.

Therefore, if you died with Christ from the basic principles of the world, why, as though living in the world, do you subject yourselves to regulations . . . which all concern things which perish with the using?

—COL. 2:20–21

Some people are so afraid of their sexuality that they become extremely legalistic on themselves or their children. They may avoid the opposite sex by burying themselves in work or books or music. They may wait for God to send a fantasy mate while wearing blindfolds and missing the ones He already provided.

They may make their teenagers miss out on the joys of dating. They may even demand that their children wear ridiculous clothing, or never swim on beaches with mixed company.

Extramarital sex is definitely a sin, and psychologically damaging. Pregnancy out of wedlock can also be quite devastating. We are told to control all of our body parts, including hands and eyes.

So, too much liberalism and permissiveness is dangerous, and too much legalism is equally dangerous. God leaves many of the inbetween decisions (when to hold hands, when to give a good-night kiss) up to the individual, but it should be a sincere matter of prayer.

What is important in decreasing sexual temptations is loving and being loved by God, family, and friends, confessing temptations to a trusted pastor or friend, and praying and meditating daily on Scripture.

Fill the holes in your soul in biblical ways, not through promiscuity or legalism.

> *Then Jesus said to His disciples, "Assuredly, I say*
> *to you that it is hard for a rich man to enter the*
> *kingdom of heaven."* —MATT. 19:23

I read about an interesting tribe in Africa that likes to eat monkeys. They have gotten good at catching a monkey whenever they are hungry, because they discovered that monkeys are very greedy.

This tribe cuts a hole in the side of a large pumpkin —just big enough for an adult monkey to squeeze his empty hand and arm through it. Then they fill the pumpkin with good smelling nuts that the monkey will like, and tie it down and leave it. They come back to check it every few hours.

When a monkey smells the nuts, he will squeeze his hands in and grab as big a handful as he can. He will stay there for hours, trying to get his full hand out, but he will not let go of the nuts.

Some rich people are kind and godly; others are greedy like the monkeys. They grab hold of worldliness and go to hell because they won't let go. Without the Holy Spirit's conviction, no rich man or poor man would ever trust Christ as Savior, but Jesus is clearly saying that rich people have a much tougher time humbling themselves before Almighty God and saying, "God, be merciful to me, a sinner." They are more used to getting what they want. Impossible? With God, all things are possible.

May God grant our wealthy friends the wisdom to let go of the nuts of
worldliness before they end up in the stew.

*But godliness with contentment is great gain. For
we brought nothing into this world, and it is certain
we can carry nothing out.* —1 TIM. 6:6

Many adult children of abuse become addicted to money. There are valid reasons for this, too. One reason is because abused children feel like their family situation is out of control. They cannot trust their parents.

They learn rapidly to take control of every situation. They even hate to take a Tylenol® for a severe headache because they are so afraid of losing control. They develop side effects to every medicine their doctor gives them, even placebos.

With money, too, control becomes a bigger issue than big spending. They may be quite stingy and hoard it all. They want enough money to feel in control of any emergency, and, of course, no amount is enough.

The pursuit of money can lead to all kinds of other evils. It can lead to white lies, then outright lies. It can lead to compromised morals. It can puff up the ego and lead to sexual entitlement. It can lead to ignoring the real gold you are missing out on—a bonding relationship with God, your mate, your children, and with godly friends.

We have seen many suicidal millionaires who have nothing worthwhile. They have "pierced themselves through with many sorrows."

May God grant us realistic expectations of what pays off in life and what corrupts.

> *Come now, you rich, weep and howl for your*
> *miseries that are coming upon you! Your riches are*
> *corrupted, and your garments are moth-eaten. Your*
> *gold and silver are corroded, and their corrosion*
> *will be a witness against you and will eat your*
> *flesh like fire. You have heaped up treasure in the*
> *last days.*
> —JAMES 5:1–3

It is truly better to give than to receive.

Don't get me wrong. I like to get presents as much as the next guy does, but I honestly enjoy it much more when I see the sparkle of surprise in the eyes of one of my children.

God loves to give too. He gave us His Only Son, Jesus, to die on the cross for our sins, so we can depend on what He did for us to obtain eternal life. And God wants us to give like He gives.

We are living in the "last days" before Christ returns to earth. Millions don't know Christ the Savior. Millions are starving. Millions need medical treatment. We need to all pitch in.

But the Bible says many in the last days will hoard all their riches and not give money to these urgent causes. God promises that He will get even with them for that. He promises to give a hundred-fold increase in blessings (not necessarily money) for what we do give. There is no set amount for New Testament believers to give. God just wants us to give with a cheerful heart.

May God grant me the joy of giving and a glimpse of the various
blessings I will receive for doing so, both now and in heaven.

*Each one should test his own actions. Then he can
take pride in himself, without comparing himself to
somebody else.*
                              —GAL. 6:4 (NIV)

In this important passage, the apostle Paul commands
us to take a careful inventory of our lives. He wants us
to examine our own psychology. He wants us to see
where we have been, where we are now, and where
we are going emotionally and spiritually. He wants us
to be involved in the "sanctification" (spiritual growth
toward Christ-likeness) process. He wants us to compare ourselves now to where we used to be, but not
compare ourselves to others. And lastly, Paul wants us
to be proud of ourselves for cooperating with God in
our growth process.

He doesn't want us to have false or arrogant pride.
The original Greek word here is *kauchēma*, which implies personal exultation over what you and God are
doing as a team in your life.

If you have been abused as a child, you especially
need to do this. List every significant person in your
life since birth and describe them in great detail. Get in
touch with repressed grudges or even rage, and forgive them one at a time.

Forgiving them, even if they don't deserve it, frees
you up from the psychological grip they hold over you.

---

*A personal inventory may take several hours to do correctly the first
time. But then you can put it in a safe place and update it once a year
in a matter of minutes.*

> *You have set our iniquities before You, Our secret sins in the light of Your countenance. Where there is no counsel, the people fall; But in the multitude of counselors there is safety.*
> —PS. 90:8, PROV. 11:14

After writing a detailed inventory of every significant personal relationship you can remember, the next therapeutic step is "exploration and discovery." That requires careful analyzing of your own role in each of those relationships. Are you usually a victim, a rescuer or a persecutor?

Pray for insights. Remember that God sees through you like an X-ray machine. He knows all your thoughts, feelings, motives, and drives. There are no secret sins from Him—only from yourself.

Don't be embarrassed to see a professional counselor either. An objective, trained therapist can see patterns in your interrelationships with others that are obvious to him or her, but you may not get those insights on your own for several more years. "In a multitude of counselors there is safety," wise King Solomon taught us.

Don't just look at facts, either. Carefully examine your own emotions. You may even want to keep a temporary diary of your emotions when you talk about dad, or mom, or a friend.

May God give me insight into my secret sins, so I can eliminate some of the unnecessary pain I suffer and grow more like Christ.

The wisdom of the prudent is to understand his way, but the folly of fools is deceit. Without counsel, plans go awry, But in the multitude of counselors they are established.
—PROV. 14:8, 15:22

My wife and I went to the beautiful state of Alaska and saw some large icebergs. About one-eighth of the iceberg sticks up out of the water and seven-eighths is under water. If you dynamited the part sticking out of the water so it blew off, another eighth of the iceberg would emerge from the water.

Our thoughts, feelings and motives are like an iceberg. We are only aware of about twenty percent of them. Eighty percent are unconscious. As we deal with conscious conflicts and forgive those involved, more repressed conflicts come up to conscious awareness.

If you have trusted Christ to save you and forgive your sins, then the Holy Spirit lives within you. He "pushes" truth from your unconscious to your conscious, because He wants to set you free and the truth sets you free. But your depraved brain hates the truth. It pushes the truth back down through about forty self-deceiving defense mechanisms. The tension between the Holy Spirit pushing truth up and your depraved brain pushing the truth down is known as anxiety—the fear of the unknown.

If we can accept our "badness" the way God accepts our "badness" and loves us anyway, then looking at the truth is not quite so scary.

One of the scariest things I will ever do in my life is to look at the truth about myself.

When my father and my mother forsake me, Then the LORD will take care of me. —PS. 27:10

Many children have been forsaken by their parents. Some parents abandoned their children to run off and have a sexual affair. Some abandoned their children by committing suicide, and some by excessive smoking, drinking and/or eating. Some abandoned children because the children did not comply perfectly to the unrealistic demands placed on them by perfectionistic parents. Some abandoned children for love of work or money. Some abandoned children for fear of intimacy.

But even worse than abandoning children is abusing children. Abandonment proves relative disregard for the child, but physical and sexual abuse reveals severe disregard for the dignity and rights of that child. The child is merely an object to be used or abused to satisfy animal-like impulses.

It hurts to look at the truth, but it also heals. Leaving home psychologically means independence from your parents. Take them off that phony pedestal. Get in touch with the rage you have felt toward them. Verbalize the rage with God, with your mate, a trusted friend, or a professional counselor.

You can't forgive them until you get in touch with the truth about your anger or bitterness. Ask God to help you forgive.

———

There are six billion people on earth—my parents are just two of them. My self-worth does not depend on their acceptance or rejection. God loves me and will help me find godly parent substitutes in a healthy local church and support groups.

My son, hear the instruction of your father, And do not forsake the law of your mother; . . . When you roam, they will lead you; When you sleep, they will keep you; And when you awake, they will speak with you.
                                        —PROV. 1:8, 6:20–22

Sometimes psychiatrists get a bad rap. Sometimes the parents of our patients—even our adult patients—feel like we are trying to create animosity between parent and child. I know that is not the case at our clinics. We want adult children of abuse to get in touch with the anger toward parents that has festered subconsciously for years, so the patients can forgive their parents. But some parents had control of their adult abused children. Therapy broke these adult children of abuse free from parental control. Abusive parents get angry when they lose control. So be it!

On the other hand, as today's passages illustrate, it is important to God that we honor father and mother, and treasure whatever biblical principles they may have taught us. We need not obey our parents at all. The original Greek tells us only that "little children" should obey their parents—not adult children.

It's time to grow up and leave the nest. If your parents want you to be a lawyer but you feel God wants you to go to a Christian college and become a missionary, then you had better do what God wants. Honor your parents, listen to their opinion, be polite, but live your own life in subjection to the Lord.

Honor your parents today. Consider calling, writing, or sending flowers. Love them unconditionally even if they love you conditionally.

> *"He who loves father or mother more than Me is
> not worthy of Me. And he who loves son or
> daughter more than Me is not worthy of Me."*
> —MATT. 10:37

Jesus is saying quite strongly here that we need to "cut the codependency." My goal in life is to serve Christ the most effective way I can. God never told me out loud where to live, who to marry, what career to choose, how many children to have, what church to attend, etc. I had to make guesses all along the way. I pray about it, I get counsel, then I guess where I will be most effective for Him. My loyalty is to Christ.

My parents wish I lived in their city. I'm glad they love me that much. I miss living near them. They are my friends, but I think I can serve God better living near Los Angeles. I have to please God rather than parents.

Jesus isn't telling, in today's message, to ignore our parents. He is saying that our loyalty to Him must come first. I know of many Christians who missed out on having a godly mate because selfish parents manipulated them into staying home. Others missed out on God's call to full-time Christian work because they were pressured into staying in the family business. Parental control over adult offspring is child abuse—depriving the child of God's freedom.

May my loyalty to Jesus Christ come first, above all others.

> *"But whoever causes one of these little ones who believe in Me to sin, it would be better for him if a millstone were hung around his neck, and he were drowned in the depth of the sea."*
> —MATT. 18:6–7

Today's passage is very clear about how God looks at the abused children of the world. They are extremely important to Him. He doesn't want any of us to look down on any child. Every child has dignity. Every child and adult has a guardian angel, who keeps God informed somehow about everything that affects the child.

God is furious with child abusers. They will burn in hell unless they genuinely repent and trust Christ for forgiveness. But very few repent. Most are sociopathic and have little if any guilt. Most abusers would be better off if someone put a cement millstone around their necks and threw them into the ocean, than for them to receive the terrible vengeance of Almighty God for abusing an innocent child.

I cannot understand why God allows child abuse. I know it infuriates Him. I know He never wants it to happen and never tempts anyone to sin. I know it grieves Him. He says in verse 7, "For offenses must come, but woe to that man by whom the offense comes." So why doesn't God prevent it? I don't know. I'll find out when I get to heaven, but in the meantime I just simply do not know.

Jesus said child abuse is inevitable in this age, but that He will avenge all who have been abused.

> *Then another of His disciples said to Him, "Lord, let me first go and bury my father." But Jesus said to him, "Follow Me, and let the dead bury their own dead."*
> —MATT. 8:21–22

When it comes to the psychological process of leaving home, we must again seek balance and common sense. We have responsibilities to parents and responsibilities to God. Our highest loyalty must be to God.

But God's Word also tells us that if we don't take care of the needs of our own families, including parents, then we are worse than infidels (atheists). So we have to interpret Scripture in light of other Scriptures. The Bible never actually contradicts itself, even though it looks that way at times.

So God wants us to love our parents, honor them, and help provide financially for their care. But He also wants us to put our loyalty to Him first, even if that means disobeying their wishes, facing their rejection, or moving away from them. We must be absolutely certain they have food, clothing, housing, *and* medical care. We should also strive to provide psychological and spiritual support. But supplying basic needs is very different from meeting all their wants. Obey God. Seek balance.

We must love them unconditionally even if they love us conditionally or even if they absolutely reject us altogether. God's love within you will help you do this.

May God grant me the wisdom to find a godly balance in my relationship with my parents. May I treat them right before God without depending on them for anything financially or psychologically.

"How long, you simple ones, will you love simplicity? For scorners delight in their scorning, and fools hate knowledge." —PROV. 1:22

It took thirteen years of college, graduate school, medical school and psychiatry residency to become a psychiatrist. Seminary training came later. But during those thirteen years, one of the main issues we studied was the defense mechanisms—the ways we deceive ourselves every day.

Part of us is wise and wants to know the truth. Part of us is foolish and fears the truth. After all, the truth hurts.

Whenever someone is abused as a child, he or she suffers a tremendous loss. Some parents never allow their children to enjoy being a child and have fun growing up. Or the child may even be expected to function as a substitute parent from youth, thus experiencing a lost childhood. The abused child also suffers a loss of self-esteem, a lost healthy relationship with the abusive parent, a loss of energy and motivation from the depression that comes from abuse, and often even a loss of the will to live. The losses are tremendous.

The adult child of abuse should never deny those losses. He should own them, face them and grieve them. He should weep over them both alone and with somebody. Don't love simplicity. Don't hate knowledge. Love the truth and grieve it, then forgive. It will set you free.

The first stage of grief is denial. I must break through denial to facilitate healthy grieving over all my losses.

> *Even in laughter the heart may sorrow, And the*
> *end of mirth may be grief.* —PROV. 14:13

Many times Dr. Minirth and I have treated people who were hospitalized for serious clinical depressions, often even to suicidal proportions, but the patient had a smile on his or her face, and denied feeling depressed.

They may have overdosed the day before or had a gun to their heads, but they deny depression and smile nonstop. This is known as a "smiling depression." It occurs when a person uses so much denial that his rage, bitterness, shame and guilt, and even his sadness and death wishes are repressed—but sneak out once in awhile.

Our passage for today describes a "smiling depression" very well. These patients get well, too, but it takes a little longer to strip away their defensive wall, brick by brick—their wall of denial, to protect them from intimacy and awareness of emotions.

In the 14th Century, the Chinese built a wall about thirty feet high, and more than a thousand feet long, to keep foreigners out. There is also a wall inside each of us—a defensive wall that keeps people out. Learning to love and be loved requires us to tear down our walls—one brick at a time.

―――――――――

May God grant me the courage to break down my defensive walls of denial and the wisdom to find a good therapist to help me do so.

Rejoice with those who rejoice, and weep with those who weep.
                                      —ROM. 12:15

It was a cold day in Michigan and the snow was blowing. The eight-year-old girl was alone in the kitchen while mom was on the phone in the living room. The girl saw her pet cat shivering in the snow outside the kitchen window. So she went out the kitchen door, hugged her cat, brought it in the house, and put it in the microwave oven. She accidently loved her cat to death.

Fortunately, this is not a true story. But many well-intentioned adults want to help friends who are suffering but end up "killing them" with love like the little girl with her cat.

When people get in touch with grief, they need to break the denial and go ahead and weep. Some well-intentioned believers see a grieving person weeping, and instead of weeping with them, they tell them things like, "Don't cry. Everything will work together for good. Don't grieve like nonbelievers." These people mean well but are taking biblical principles out of context.

Christians need not grieve like those who have no hope, but they do need to grieve. Jesus wept at Lazarus' death. Things will work out for good in the long run, but sharing Romans 8:28 at the peak of tears is not the appropriate time for that verse.

When someone I love begins to grieve, help me break through his denial and obey Romans 12:15 by giving that person a warm hug and by weeping with those who weep.

Then Peter came to Him and said, "Lord, how often shall my brother sin against me, and I forgive him? Up to seven times?" Jesus said to him, "I do not say to you, up to seven times, but up to seventy times seven."

—MATT. 18:21–22

The second stage of grief, after denial, is anger toward others. Whenever we suffer a loss, we deny it at first, then when the reality of the loss hits us between the eyes, we get angry at others.

Who is to blame for the loss? Why couldn't the doctor save his life? Why this? Why that? Anger! Maybe even rage! Forgive? What do you mean forgive? Forget it! How many times am I expected to forgive him?

Peter asked Jesus that question. Peter thought he was really being pious when he asked Jesus if he should forgive his offender up to seven times. But Jesus embarrassed Peter when He suggested seventy times seven. In other words, we must always forgive.

When friends you love are grieving a loss, whether it is a current loss or the severe loss that comes from childhood abuses, help them break through denial, weep with them when they weep, then help them talk about their anger and rage. They can't forgive until they get in touch with and verbalize their anger. The healing is in the forgiving. They need to turn vengeance over to God.

The second stage of grief is anger toward others, so I should help the grieving person to verbalize and to forgive the offenders.

Our Father in heaven, Hallowed be Your name.
Your kingdom come. Your will be done On earth as
it is in heaven. Give us this day our daily bread.
And forgive us our debts, As we forgive our
debtors. And do not lead us into temptation, but
deliver us from the evil one. For Yours is the
kingdom and the power and the glory forever
Amen.
—MATT. 6:9–13

This famous passage is known popularly as "the Lord's Prayer." It is actually a prayer the Lord created as a model prayer for His disciples, so some call it "the disciples' prayer." We are to create our own prayers based on the principles found here.

We are to pray to the heavenly Father. We are to honor Him. We are to live in expectation of His kingdom on earth, His eventual messianic kingdom (one thousand year kingdom with Christ returning to earth to rule), and His eternal kingdom in heaven. We are also to rely on the Father for daily needs and protection from temptation.

But at the heart of this model prayer is the request for God to forgive us as much as we forgive our debtors (or our abusers). Now that takes a lot of humility to pray that part. Forgive me as much as I forgive my abusers? Are you kidding, Lord? No, He's not kidding. But He will also help you forgive, because forgiving abusers requires supernatural help.

May God grant me the humility to forgive my abusers with His help, turning vengeance over to Him.

> . . . *It is a righteous thing with God to repay with*
> *tribulation those who trouble you.*
> —2 THESS. 1:6

When God asks us to forgive our abusers, sometimes we misunderstand Him to mean they will get off scott-free for abusing you. That's what makes you want to say, "No way, Lord. I won't forgive him to the day I die! He/She doesn't deserve my forgiveness."

But God loves you. Grudges are bad for your physiology. They cause decreased serotonin and clinical depression. God does not want you to suffer. He wants to get even with the jerk Himself! He'll do a better job than you could, anyway.

Vengeance is God's business. He promises in today's passage to "repay with tribulation those who trouble you." He also promises revenge in Romans 12. He will do a perfect job of revenge, both in this life, and with eternal hell.

If your abuser humbles himself before God and genuinely repents, God will love him and forgive him just like He loves you and forgives you for all of your sins. Jesus took the vengeance of all mankind on the cross, but only those who depend on Christ's substitution in their place will be forgiven. All others will have to pay for their own sins.

I will leave vengeance for the Lord to take care of. And I will ask Him to strengthen me when I am threatened and comfort me when I am hurt. But I will forgive, no matter what, with God's help.

"If you do well, will you not be accepted? And if you do not do well, sin lies at the door. And its desire is for you, but you should rule over it."
—GEN. 4:5-7

Many thousands of years ago, Cain killed Abel and committed the first murder. The apostle John wrote that Cain "belonged to the evil one" (see 1 John 3:12). God wanted blood sacrifices to start teaching mankind that He would send His Son, the Messiah, to shed His blood for the sins of mankind. But Cain wanted to play God and do things his own way. He insisted on using plants and refused to sacrifice animals. God blessed Abel, who obeyed God, and refused to bless Cain, who rebelled.

So Cain got very angry at God. His serotonin got depleted. He got clinically depressed and more irritable, then killed his brother in rage. Satan won the victory in Cain, even with God Himself counseling Cain how to get over his depression.

Today, people still want to play God, make fun of His rules for living, and yet expect Him to come through with all their desires. Their sadness turns into a clinical depression with insomnia often the first sign, followed by tiredness, lack of motivation, decreased sex drive, trouble concentrating, and increased irritability. Frequently, "serotonin dumping" from the brain also causes migraine headaches.

God tells us we can avoid sinning when we get angry (see Leviticus 19:17-18 and Ephesians 4:26). But it is a sin to harbor grudges, bitterness and vengeful motives. Vengeance is God's business. I will mind my own business.

> "I, even I, am *He who blots out your transgressions*
> *for My own sake; And I will not remember your*
> *sins.*"
>
> —ISA. 43:25

The five general stages of grief are: denial; anger turned outward, toward others, toward God; anger turned inward; true guilt *if* some is involved; false guilt, taking too much responsibility for the "bad things" that happened; genuine grief (weeping over the losses—a vitally important stage for healing); resolution (sorting it all out in your mind and learning and growing from the sad experience and the pain).

True guilt is frequently, but not always, involved in grief. If you were speeding down a city street and had an accident, damaging both cars and injuring both yourself and the other driver, you would grieve the injuries, the embarrassment, the financial losses, the increased insurance rates, and the hassle of waiting to get your car repaired. You would also experience some true guilt for having given yourself the ungodly entitlement to violate the laws designed to keep you from such accidents.

Hopefully, you would apologize immediately to the other driver, ask God to forgive you, and forgive yourself.

As a true believer, I have no right to hold grudges against any of God's children, not even myself. I will grieve my losses.

He is despised and rejected by men, A Man of sorrows and acquainted with grief. And we hid, as it were, our faces from Him; He was despised, and we did not esteem Him. Surely He has borne our griefs and carried our sorrows. —ISA. 53:3–4

All humans grieve from time to time. It's healthy. It's moral. It cleanses the soul of pain from losses. But only about half of the people go through so much bitterness that a clinical depression follows. Some people have genetic depressions even when they are not bitter about things.

In our passage for today, we see that Jesus Himself was well acquainted with personal griefs. We have a Messiah who empathizes with our grief reactions.

He was wounded and bruised to relieve our true guilt. The chastisement for our peace from true guilt was upon Him. By His stripes, our true guilt can be healed. All of us, like sheep, go astray from time to time, resulting in true guilt. But the Father laid on Jesus the Messiah all of our true guilt.

If we don't forgive ourselves for all of our past sins and failures, and ask God the Father to also forgive us for all past, present and future sins and failures, we are wasting an awful lot of effort by the loving Son of God to save us and relieve us of all true guilt.

Jesus, I'm depending on your death and resurrection to pay for all my true guilt and to give me eternal life. Please help me to forgive myself as well.

> *For the wages of sin is death, but the gift of God is*
> *eternal life in Christ Jesus our Lord.*
> —ROM. 6:23

There are four vital developmental areas of growing up. We refer to them as "the Four B's" and we will discuss them in more detail later in this book: bonding, boundaries, "badness" and becoming boss of our lives.

Badness has to do with taking a realistic look at, and dealing with, our true guilt—our sinful conscious and unconscious motives. Somehow, we have to see it, accept it, love ourselves anyway (like God loves us), and develop plans for gradually improving it all our lives, realizing we will never be perfect.

The apostle Paul tells us we are all in the same boat. Every human except Christ, the God-Man, has sinned (see Rom. 3:23). One sin makes a sinner. We all fall short of God's righteous demands for perfection. Paul also said we all deserve spiritual death for our sins. God the Father's righteousness demands it.

Fortunately, God is not only righteous, but very loving. He provided us with the gift of eternal life in heaven but only if we accept the gift. Then all your true guilt (past, present and future) is paid for, once, for eternity. God promises to never retract that gift. The gift was Christ, Who was perfect. His shed blood paid the debt. His resurrection proved He was God and gave us life.

Are you depending on your couch or your chair to hold you up right now? Depend in the same way on Christ's gift of life and freedom from guilt.

All things are lawful for me, but all things are not helpful; all things are lawful for me, but all things do not edify.
—1 COR. 10:23

Now that you have received the free gift of eternal life, you are free to live by grace. This does not mean we should look for ways to sin so grace can abound in our lives. We can no longer lose our salvation and go to hell, but we can still experience plenty of personal hell on earth. Sin has consequences in our daily lives. All sins hurt someone in the long run, even though they may feel good in the short run.

The apostle Paul said there is nothing we are not permitted to do, but not all things are good for us. Paradoxically, the most "selfish" thing I can do is totally commit my life to Christ, because that is the nicest thing I can do for myself. It helps me love myself, and I can love and be loved better by others. There are eternal rewards. I also have a clear conscience.

In the 1 Corinthians 10:27–29 passage, Paul describes an example of false guilt. If you were living in an idol-worshipping area, and they sold the meat that had been offered to idols cheaper than supermarket meat, it would be fine to buy it and eat it to save money. If you felt guilty, it would be false guilt. But if your neighbor is more legalistic and offended, it would be better to pay more and get the regular meat at regular prices. Your neighbor is more important than saving money. Don't flaunt your liberty.

God gave me grace (unmerited favor) and liberty. He wants me to enjoy it but not flaunt it.

> *Stand fast therefore in the liberty by which Christ*
> *has made us free, and do not be entangled again*
> *with a yoke of bondage.* —GAL. 5:1

Most people choose a lifestyle first, and then pick a religion that will permit and reinforce that lifestyle. They design a god (a "designer god"), then claim their imagined god as their own. They magically think the real God will have to fall in line with their imagined god. Then they get angry when He doesn't.

Our Higher Power is a real God—the God of the amazing, prophetically accurate, historically perfect Bible. He makes His own rules. We can accept them (and Him) or reject them (and Him). He makes His own consequences, too; He made us, so He has that right.

He wants us to live in total liberty so we can choose to obey Him. Paul says legalists will try to take that away from you to make you codependent on them— don't let them! If you have to obey legalistic rules for salvation, then what good was Christ's death? It will profit you nothing.

Baptism is important, like putting on a ring at the wedding, but you don't need it for salvation any more than you need a wedding ring to be legally married.

God wants us to be baptized after we trust Him, even though it is not required for salvation. If you feel guilty for never getting baptized, that is still true guilt, because you are violating God's recommendation.

God wants us to live by His principles, by our own choice, because that's what is best for us in the long run.

I waited patiently for the Lord; And He inclined to me, And heard my cry. —PS. 40:1

When I get the flu, I feel terrible. I would choose death during the flu were it not for the fact that I know it is temporary. I know that in a few days, I will be laughing, loving, playing, and serving.

When a person has suffered a tremendous loss, such as a "lost childhood" as a result of child abuse, that person can have a degree of clinical depression (partial serotonin depletion) that feels like having a mild to severe case of the flu for years. Some never get therapy to correct it and spend their entire lives in that kind of pain. The pain is simply the result of unresolved grief. That person got "hung up" in the stages of grief.

Any real grieving they do at this point is *good grief*. It will gradually correct their chemical imbalance. Remember that the main healing comes from *forgiving*. You are free to forgive, as this devotional teaches you, and forgiving will set you free—free from the abuser's effect on your life. Why in the world should *you* suffer for what some jerk did to you. It's senseless. It's such a waste. You can enjoy a meaningful life. Get a professional to help you finish grieving. Check into a hospital and get it over with in six weeks or so, even after twenty to thirty years of depression. Cry out to God for help. He promises to pull us out of the mire. Grab His hand and follow His steps to finish forgiving and finish grieving.

I grieve as soon as I become aware of any grudges, because I want to have maximum energy, peace, and joy in my life

> *But I do not want you to be ignorant, brethren,*
> *concerning those who have fallen asleep, lest you*
> *sorrow as others who have no hope.*
> —1 THESS. 4:13–14

A person can experience chronic emotional "flu"—depression from unresolved grief from past abuse or from current losses. Divorce can be worse than death sometimes because divorce is a chosen abandonment.

If we live long enough, we will all experience grief reactions from the death of loved ones. Jesus wept when his friend Lazarus died. Joseph wept for a month when his father, Jacob, died. And our passage for today tells us we should grieve, but not as those who have no hope.

When a Christian dies, his or her soul is immediately with God in heaven, in a new body. She or he is actually better off. There is no more pain or sorrow. There is total joy. Believers in heaven are surrounded by love from God, fellow saints, and even angels.

But that doesn't ease the sense of loss *we* feel. We will miss that person until we join her or him. We feel angry and sad about our loss and the others who will miss that person. For this we weep and mourn. This is godly and proper and respectful.

Nonbelievers have double grief. They grieve their own loss as well as the imagined "end" of their loved one. Believers grieve only our own loss, but celebrate the new beginning of our beloved who is now happy in heaven.

Grieve your losses as they occur. But remember that the Lord has promised better things in heaven.

Precious in the sight of the LORD Is the death of His saints.
—PS. 116:15

When a believer dies, it is a precious time for the LORD. That's because He has an eternal perspective that we finite humans don't have. God knows that a dying believer will immediately be with Him, in a perfect new body, with no more depravity or psychological garbage to carry around from past abuses or sins. He will be set free to join God and other deceased believers in heaven for eternity.

But God should choose when that time should come to join Him. Suicide should never be an option. If you are alive today, it is because God still has some chores for you to do. Your good times in heaven will last forever. Don't be in a hurry. Enjoy life on earth the best you can in this corrupt world and serve God.

When a Christian friend dies, we know he is in heaven, but we still go through all five stages of grief: Denial; Anger turned Outward; Anger turned Inward (such as wishing we had spent more time with him or said "I love you" one more time); Genuine (Good) Grief; and Resolution.

Resolution is the fifth and final stage of grief. It is whatever time it takes to sort out our thoughts and feelings about that particular loss. It is a time to grow and become a more mature person, better equipped to handle future losses.

The "resolution" stage of grief is a positive time, even though it may still hurt. I look forward to rejoining my loved ones some day.

Rejoice always, pray without ceasing.
—1 THESS. 5:16–17

Once upon a time there existed a nice couple with identical twins who were not identical. They were ten years old and looked exactly alike, but one was too pessimistic and the other was too optimistic.

The parents took their twins to an eccentric therapist who suggested curing them by putting the pessimist in a room full of new toys, and putting the optimist in a shed full of horse manure with a shovel and telling him to dig it. So they did.

The pessimist cried and cried, saying, "Look at all these new toys; they will all break or wear out some day!" The parents gave up on him. Then they went to the shed full of horse manure where they had left their optimistic twin an hour earlier. He was whistling a happy tune, shoveling away in the manure, and saying, "With all this horse manure, there must be a pony here somewhere!"

There is a balance between pessimism and optimism: positive thinking with realistic expectations. In psychiatry, we call it cognitive restructuring. It means getting rid of lies we tell ourselves and replacing them with biblical truths.

Paul told us to rejoice always. He didn't mean don't grieve, because he also told us to weep with those who weep. But even in grief, we can rejoice in the resolution stage.

May God grant me a sense of fellowship with Him and an attitude of prayer all day.

*Now therefore, if you will indeed obey My voice
and keep My covenant, then you shall be a special
treasure to Me above all people; for all the earth is
Mine. And you shall be to Me a kingdom of priests
and a holy nation.* —EX. 19:5–6

There are six billion people on planet earth; all of us
have self-concept problems. The more abused a person
is throughout his or her life the lower the self-concept.

All psychological problems (except severe brain
damage or severe inherited psychiatric disorders) are
resolvable. No one becomes perfect, but I've never met
a patient who couldn't eventually develop joy, peace
and a reasonable self-concept.

I have inferiority feelings myself, but my self-
concept is reasonably functional. I had loving parents. I
had discipline. I had bonding with my siblings. I have
had one good wife for twenty-five years and six loving
teenagers. Life has been good to me.

And then I see so many hospital patients who were
abused as children and have severe self-concept problems. I go home after work and weep. I get angry at
God for allowing human suffering and then I talk with
Him about it, realizing He loves them a million times
more than I could.

It feels so good to see them grow and release their
negative emotions. The reward is worth the pain.

May God help me to love myself as He loves me.

> *I* am *poor and needy;* Yet *the* LORD *thinks upon
> me.* You are *my help and my deliverer; Do not
> delay, O my God.*
> —PS. 40:17

When a person is abused, especially as a child—but even as an adult—he tends to blame himself. He thinks it is somehow his fault.

As an adult, he has very low self-esteem. He may become an angry abuser himself, figuring he's no good and no one else is, either. Or, he may value his children, but lose his temper. When his son's behavior reminds him of something he hates in himself, he may beat his son in a fit of rage, then be apologetic later.

A more likely course is that the abused child grows up to be a masochist, looking unconsciously for a substitute abusive parent. He thus tends to marry an abusive mate; find an abusive boss; or find a church with an abusive, controlling pastor.

But who are you going to believe, your abusive parent or God? Who knows your value best? Most adult children of abuse who have not had the benefit of ACA groups and/or therapy, tend to believe their abusive parents. Even as adults, those verbal and nonverbal messages about the child's nonworth ring in the brain of the adult child.

We must reprogram our brain—not to believe a lie, but to believe the truth. The truth is that God thinks we are worth helping, worth delivering, and worth thinking about innumerable times daily.

He who knows me best, loves me most!

O LORD, You have searched me and known me.
You know my sitting down and my rising up; You
understand my thought afar off.

—PS. 139: 1–2

The most beautiful chapter in the entire Bible on self-concept is Psalm 139. King David had suffered a clinical depression earlier as a result of his own shame and self-hatred. I have taken hundreds of patients to this passage, and have seen the beneficial effects it has on people who meditate on it. I have meditated on it often, especially when I am down on myself.

Therefore, we will take this chapter apart and look at exactly how God, who knows you best, sees you. We will examine five sections of this vital chapter over five days, starting today.

In today's passage, we see that our heavenly Father has "searched us" and knows us inside and out. He knows every time we stand up or sit down. He is omniscient (all-knowing). We have no idea how He can do this. He reads our minds—our conscious and unconscious thoughts, our emotions, our motives, our defensive mechanisms (methods of self-deceit)—and keeps on loving us in spite of what He sees. He watches the paths we walk during the day and the dreams we dream and every word that we speak.

This old hymn says it well for us:

> *Amazing love! How can it be?*
> *That Thou, My God*
> *Should'st die for me.*

You have hedged me behind and before, And laid Your hand upon me. Such knowledge is too wonderful for me; It is high, I cannot attain it. Where can I go from Your Spirit? Or where can I flee from Your presence?

—PS. 139:5–7

God always encourages healthy spiritual interdependence, not codependence, in our relationship with Him. He could do His work alone, since He is God, but does much of His work through human hands. He tells us to live in liberty and make our own decisions, but to trust Him for subtle guidance and protection.

In John 10:27–30, Jesus said He holds us in His hand, and no one can snatch us out of His hand (not even ourselves). He says that the Father's hand is wrapped around Jesus' hand, and no one can snatch us out of the Father's hand. It's a beautiful word-picture of His love and protection.

The Holy Spirit told the authors of the Bible what to write—a team effort again—using the author's style and vocabulary but with no errors. When the Holy Spirit moved David to write today's passage, David also exclaimed that He could not comprehend all this omniscience *and* omnipresence. It was too wonderful to believe. David could go anywhere in the universe and still be in the hands of His Lord (the Messiah) and His Lord (the heavenly Father, Yahweh).

My favorite male singer is George Beverly Shea of the Billy Graham Association, and for many years I have loved to hear him sing, "He's got the whole world, in His hands."

> If *I take the wings of the morning,* And *dwell in the
> uttermost parts of the sea,* Even there Your hand
> shall lead me, And Your right hand shall hold me.
> *If I say, "Surely the darkness shall fall on me," Even
> the night shall be light about me; Indeed, the
> darkness shall not hide from You, But the night
> shines as the day; The darkness and the light* are
> *both alike* to You.
>
> —PS. 139:9–12

Isn't it funny to observe people, especially when they
think no one is noticing them? You see someone cup
his hands around someone's ear and they think no one
hears their secret. They sneak off to a motel and think
no one sees their affair. They have sex with their mate
but fantasize about another and think no one knows
their thoughts. They make a dishonest business deal or
cheat the IRS and think they will never get caught.

David said we can't hide from God in the daytime,
and we can't hide from God at night. It makes no difference. We can't hide from Him no matter where we go,
even if we take the "wings" of the morning and fly to
the farthest part of the ocean.

Here, again, in this passage is the word-picture of
God's hands. God tells us through David that with His
left hand He leads us, and with His strong right hand
He holds or hugs us. You and God are walking through
life together. He leads, but He gives you a lot of rope.
He even lets *you* decide whether to walk through life
with Him at all.

*The next time I feel insecure, I will visualize God hugging me with
one arm and leading me through life's rough spots with the other.*

> *For You have formed my inward parts; You have*
> *covered me in my mother's womb. I will praise*
> *You, for I am fearfully and wonderfully made.*
> —PS. 139:13

As a physician, I particularly like this passage. I delivered twenty-two babies before I went into psychiatry and it was unbelievably exciting to see the emergence of new life into the world.

Many of my patients have shared with me confidentially that they feel inferior about their physical appearance. I have found that the more beautiful a woman is, the more inferior she tends to feel about her appearance. We tend to base our self-worth on what we get praised for the most as children, so it is actually harmful to often tell your young daughters how beautiful they are. It's better to praise them for godly character traits.

People may also feel inferior about their IQ, or about their lack of creativity. All of us have brains that are talented in some areas but not others. I love sports, but I can't walk and chew gum at the same time. But God made me very creative, so I use my creativity for God and my fellow man.

Our passage for today says that when *you* were in your mother's womb, God designed your particular features, strengths, and weaknesses. All the results were written in His book before conception. At the creation of the world, God could look into the future and know you intimately. Jesus had you in mind somehow when He died for you on the cross.

God does not make junk and He does not make any mistakes.

How precious also are Your thoughts to me, O God!
How great is the sum of them!   —PS. 139:17

People who get lots of hugs and attention growing up make good listeners. Their "love tanks" were filled by parents whose "love tanks" were also filled. As adults now, they feel loved and have love left over to give out to others.

A child who is abused by being ignored has an empty "love tank." He or she may crave attention like a bottomless pit. He may develop strong codependency and look for masochists who will listen to him several times a day for hours on end. If you talk with someone with an empty love tank for several hours straight, he or she will still get angry at you whenever you leave. The tank is still empty. Those who crave this much attention feel frustrated and lonely. They can't figure out why everyone except the masochists try to avoid them.

But God loves people with empty love tanks too. He gives them more attention than they could ever hope for. He thinks about them so many times each day that his thoughts toward them outnumber the grains of sand on the seashore.

With proper long-term outpatient therapy people with empty love tanks can learn to fill their own tanks through healthy, non-codependent relationships with God and peers. They can even become good listeners.

I now know that low self-esteem affects people in different ways.

> *"Are not two sparrows sold for a copper coin? And not one of them falls to the ground apart from your Father's will. But the very hairs of your head are all numbered. Do not fear therefore; you are of more value than many sparrows."*
>
> —MATT. 10:29–31

I had a phone call today from a woman who was concerned about her daughter who had just gone off to college. Her daughter was spending lots of time volunteering for an animal rights group and not emphasizing academics as much as her mother wished she would.

I explained to the mother that animals are important to God, too, and that at this stage in life, she needs to let go. I told her to be her daughter's friend now and not try to control her; accept her the way she is.

Animals *are* important to God. He hates it when people hurt animals needlessly. Our passage for today says a sparrow doesn't fall to the ground without God knowing it, even though sparrows are numerous.

God tells us not to be afraid of being a nobody. We are more important to Him than "many sparrows." In fact, we are so important to God that even the hairs on our head are numbered. He is intimately acquainted with every detail of our lives. And yet He gives us grace and freedom to take authority over our own lives.

As a child of Christ, I must be significant to Him because even the hairs of my head are numbered.

> *"What do you think? If a man has a hundred sheep, and one of them goes astray, does he not leave the ninety-nine and go to the mountains to seek the one that is straying? And if he should find it, assuredly, I say to you, he rejoices more over that sheep than over the ninety-nine that did not go astray."*
>
> —MATT. 18:12–13

My father grew up in a German village in Russia, prior to the revolution. He used to get up at 4:00 A.M. to help tend sheep each day before going to school. He led them to food and water and protected them from wolves and other wild animals. Several of the sheep became pets.

Jesus says we are much more than pets, and we become His sheep by trusting Him as our Savior. We are children of the heavenly Father, and Jesus is the first-born among many brothers and sisters.

Jesus said if He had a hundred sheep, He would love every one of them. But if one sheep (believer) wandered off for awhile, Jesus would pay special attention to that one to convince him to come back to the fold (fellowship with Him). If he refuses to come back, he will perish (die physically and go to heaven).

Jesus also loves lost sheep who are not His children—enough to die for them—and wants them to join His fold by faith. Jesus is especially concerned with "little" lambs. In verses 6 and 10 He refers specifically to *mikrōn toutōn*, or "little children."

If my past sins make me feel so worthless that I am ashamed to ask Christ to save me, then I am just the sheep He is looking for.

> *"In My Father's house are many mansions; if it*
> *were not so, I would have told you. I go to prepare*
> *a place for you. And if I go and prepare a place for*
> *you, I will come again and receive you to Myself;*
> *that where I am, there you may be also."*
> —JOHN 14:2–3

All of us are troubled from time to time with feelings of insecurity, loneliness, and inferiority. Part of our problem is that we see things from a narrow point of view. If we have a few bad days in a row, we tend to get into negative self-talk. We amplify and exaggerate in our own minds how bad things really are. We "catastrophize" and think things not only will get worse, but that there is no light at the end of the tunnel, so things will never get better.

Teenagers do that even more than adults, because they have less experience to draw on. Suicide is the second leading cause of death in teenagers, and the narrow perspective is a major factor.

In our passage for today, we see the *broad* perspective. We don't need to be troubled by a few bad days. We believers will live forever, with God and other believers, in heaven. A mansion specially designed by Jesus Himself is waiting for you with your name on it. If you die, you will be there immediately. If you live until the Rapture (see 1 Thess. 4:13–18) then Jesus says in today's passage, "I will come again and receive you to Myself; that where I am, there you may be also."

Jesus has designed and built a mansion with my name on it. He wants me in His neighborhood.

For I say, through the grace given to me, to everyone who is among you, not to think of himself more highly than he ought to think, but to think soberly, as God has dealt to each one a measure of faith.
—ROM. 12:3

This may surprise you, but the more inferior a person feels, the more arrogantly he will usually behave. Conversely, the more arrogantly a person behaves, the more inferior he feels on a deep, subconscious level.

Stop right now for a moment and think about the two or three most arrogant people you know. Can you believe that they feel insecure on the inside? Look at your own children when they are about thirteen years old and they think they know everything and you know nothing. The older they get, the nicer they get. And the more they like themselves, the more they respect you.

God wants us to think highly of every single human being's dignity, even if we hate their behavior. God hates every sin because all sins hurt somebody, somehow; but God loves every sinner.

God wants us to look at ourselves soberly. He has given each of us a measure of faith, implying different spiritual and mental gifts to use for His service. Why should we think we are better than someone else just because He gave certain gifts to us and other gifts to others? We are not superior or inferior—just different. And we were designed by Him in our mother's wombs.

May God grant me the wisdom to not compare myself with others, but to be proud of myself for cooperating with God.

*And because you are sons, God has sent forth the
Spirit of His Son into your hearts, crying out,
"Abba, Father!" Therefore you are no longer a
slave but a son, and if a son, then an heir of God
through Christ.*
—GAL. 4:6–7

When you were a three-year-old child, you said
your bedtime prayers and prayed, "Dear heavenly
Father. . . ." But you were probably thinking, "Dear
heavenly version of my earthly father." This is *usually*
the case as research shows. I have seen it over and
over again in my patients. I have even done some unof-
ficial research on hundreds of patients over the years.

They almost always had the greatest doubts about
God in the same areas that their earthly fathers were
weak: no dad—atheism; workaholic dad—agnosticism;
harsh dad—harsh God; spoiling dad—"sugar-daddy
God"; and the list goes on. We see God through sunglasses colored the color of our parents.

To build an accurate self-concept, we need to see
God as He *really is* (by studying the Bible), and then
see ourselves as He sees us (since He knows us best). In
our passage for today, we see that we have an inheritance coming as sons of God if we have trusted Christ.
Not only that, but God the Father loves us so much, and
feels so comfortable with us, that He tells us to call Him
"Daddy." The word *Abba* is an Aramaic word used by
small children to address their "daddies." It implies
familiarity and affection.

---

*Some people miss out on intimacy with God because of a poor
earthly example.*

So husbands ought to love their own wives as their own bodies; he who loves his wife loves himself.
—EPH. 5:28

Another reason we should all work on developing healthy, accurate self-concepts is because it affects the way we behave toward all others humans, especially the ones we love the most.

Eighty percent of our faults are out of our conscious awareness. The Bible calls them "secret sins." We fear being aware of them, because that would temporarily hurt our self-concept. We must accept our "badness" and develop a plan for patiently, gradually improving our faults, realizing we won't ever reach perfection in this life.

When we gain insights into our own faults and love ourselves biblically, anyway (dealing with them biblically), then we can love other people with faults even if their faults are similar to ours.

If I had one hundred faults and my wife had one hundred faults, but only five of them were the same, then ninety-five of her faults would not bother me much. But I would feel rage toward her for having the five faults that make me anxious because I don't know I have those five, too.

That's why the Holy Spirit told Paul to write in today's passage that he who loves his wife loves himself. We can only love our mate as much as we love ourselves in a biblical (not arrogant) sense.

I can improve my love for my mate by getting over my fear of seeing all my faults.

> Let *nothing* be done *through selfish ambition or*
> *conceit, but in lowliness of mind let each esteem*
> *others better than himself.*   —PHIL. 2:3

Whenever two people meet, there are actually *six* people present: 2 people as they see themselves; 2 people as they see each other; and 2 people as God sees them.

An excellent book on self-concept is *His Image—My Image,* by Josh McDowell. Josh encourages us to see ourselves—the good, the bad and the ugly—just as God sees us. That may be scary to some, but it won't be based on a bunch of phony information that pumps you up emotionally but leaves you high and dry in the long run.

In today's passage, the apostle Paul again encourages balance in our quest for a healthy but not arrogant self-concept. We should treat others *as though they were* better than ourselves, even though we are equal. And think about things you can do to help other people, especially secret things that they don't even know you are doing for them. Desire their benefit. Pray for God to bless them, especially with the greatest gift in the world—Christ-likeness (and Christ Himself in their lives).

I love myself the most when I put others first, without codependency or masochism, and without ignoring my own God-given needs.

> *But you* are *a chosen generation, a royal*
> *priesthood, a holy nation, His own special people.*
> —1 PETER 2:9

Do you really desire to see yourself as God sees you? Let's take a look at what He says about you if you have trusted Christ to save you.

A *chosen generation.* The original Greek word for "chosen" here is *eklekton*—elected (by God). We won't understand the concept of predestination completely until we get to heaven and have God explain it to us. It is foolish to argue over it. Suffice it to say that somehow, in some way, God *elected* you to be His child. He picked you out for adoption.

A *royal priesthood.* (see 1 Peter 2:5, 9 and Revelation 1:6.)

A *holy nation.* We will act as a nation of believers in the one thousand year millennial kingdom in particular, along with *believing* Israelites who trust Christ as their Messiah.

His own special people.

Ambassadors—to proclaim the good news about Christ to others.

Called out of spiritual darkness into spiritual light.

Called, as *people of God,* to obtain mercy (and eternal forgiveness).

Now, ask yourself an honest question that demands an honest answer. How can you have low self-esteem if you believe those seven things about yourself?

We are *these seven things God says about us today. But we only have a glimpse of what we are going to be in eternity.*

> *Behold what manner of love the Father has bestowed on us, that we should be called children of God! Therefore the world does not know us, because it did not know Him.*
> —1 JOHN 3:1

If you are a committed Christian, please do not look to the people of this world to give you self-esteem. Committed believers are one of the most hated, most discriminated against subcultures in America today, especially in *academic* circles, in the *media*, and among the *jet set* in-crowd.

There are certainly exceptions to this rule, and I thank God for those brave men and women within these circles who gently and lovingly but courageously take a stand for Christ. We may be priests and kings and sons of God (which we are), but in the world we are often the butt of jokes.

I encourage Christian college students not to mention their Christianity whatsoever on applications to graduate schools, medical schools, psychiatry residencies, gynecology residencies, etc. There are even many seminary students and young pastors in some mainline denominations who have to keep their faith in the Bible to themselves for fear of being weeded out, until they have tenure—then they preach what they want and get sent to the smallest churches.

Jesus lived the most committed, loving life a person could live. He helped people everywhere. He never hurt anyone, except when He whipped the Pharisees for ripping people off in the temple. But society nailed Him to a tree. I will get my self-esteem from Jesus, definitely not from the world.

> *"He who has an ear, let him hear what the Spirit says to the churches. To him who overcomes I will give some of the hidden manna to eat. And I will give him a white stone, and on the stone a new name written which no one knows except him who receives it."*
> —REV. 1:6, 2:17

When my self-esteem takes a temporary dip, I love to dig out my *Bible Knowledge Commentary* (Ed. John F. Walvoord and Roy B. Zuck, Victor Books, 1987), and I love to study Bible prophecy, especially about my own future. I sometimes long for the future. I hate all the suffering and evil I see in our world. And I hate the selfishness that sometimes creeps up in myself. I'll be happy to be relieved of my own depravity *and* the depravity of the world.

Jesus is the firstborn from the dead, and His resurrection makes my resurrection a certainty. Jesus loves us. He washes us in His own blood. He made us priests (we can pray directly to God the Father and don't need any human to do it for us). He made us kings (we'll get our kingdoms later).

Jesus Himself will also give each of us a beautiful and special white stone in heaven. It will have a private and personal name written on it, which Jesus will call us in personal conversations. It's just something else He wants to do to show each of us how special we are to Him.

Thinking about God's plans for my eternal future helps me to feel better about myself. It also gets me real excited!

> *As a dog returns to his own vomit, so a fool*
> *repeats his folly.*
> —PROV. 26:11

I treated a movie actress one time who was clinically depressed because she had just divorced her fifth husband. I asked her what he was like, and she told me he repeatedly ran around on her. He physically abused her. He was an alcoholic. But he was good-looking.

I asked her about her other four husbands and they were all very similar to the fifth one. She thought all men were alike, and I told her none of my friends were like that.

I asked her if kind, loving, Christian men had ever asked her out, and she admitted that they had, but she turned them down because she found them boring. I asked her if I could guess what her father was like without offending her and she told me to try.

It was really quite easy. I guessed that he ignored her, that he ran around on her mom, that he was an alcoholic, and that he molested her when she was a teenager. She was astounded and thought I must have talked to her mother before I met her. I assured her I hadn't talked to anyone about her.

Eighty-five percent of people marry someone who is very similar psychologically (sometimes even physically) to the parent of the opposite sex, whether the family of origin was functional or dysfunctional.

I need not continually repeat destructive behavior patterns and will develop new life experiences free of codependency.

Seldom set foot in your neighbor's house, Lest he become weary of you and hate you.
—PROV. 25:17

Although there are many exceptions to the rule, we tend to see common patterns of personality development based on a person's birth order. Parents expect too much out of the first child. So he strives for perfection. Fifteen of the first sixteen American astronauts were firstborn, for example.

Middle children have to learn good communication and manipulation skills, so they become more histrionic and make excellent salespersons.

Most mothers hate to see their youngest child grow up. They think too much for him, pamper him, spoil him, bail him out of trouble. Youngest children tend to be more prone to alcohol and/or drug addictions. They also tend to be more "passive-aggressive"—they pout, procrastinate, are usually late to meetings, ask others to make decisions for them then fail when they follow the advice.

As Solomon said in today's passage some people tend to keep going to their neighbor's house for his tools, sugar, lawnmower, money, and sometimes his wife. He depends too much on others and sets himself up for failure. He has low self-esteem and lots of unconscious shame for being so dependent.

I will strive to recognize my passive-aggressive codependency so that I can overcome it with God's help (and a good therapist, if needed).

> *She seeks wool and flax, And willingly works with*
> *her hands. She is like the merchant ships, She*
> *brings her food from afar. She also rises while it is*
> *yet night, And provides food for her household.*
> —PROV. 31:13–14

Three thousand years ago, in the middle of one of the worst periods of male chauvinism in world history, God inspired King Lemuel to write a disclosure on "the wise woman." Please read the entire chapter. During the next three days, beginning today, we will see some surprising things that God taught three thousand years ago about the role of women.

In today's passage, we see that the wise, non-codependent woman is not lazy and dependent on others. She "works willingly with her hands." She is a wise shopper. She gets the best wool and flax to use not only for her family, but also for a clothing business she runs (verse 24).

She is not afraid to go to distant stores to purchase quality foods for her family. She has servants, showing that it is not a sin to be rich and have servants if God happens to choose to bless you in that way. Some reactionary children of wealthy workaholics rebel by self-righteously criticizing all believers who don't live near the poverty level and give all the rest of their money away. We'll look at what God advised on money quite extensively later in this book.

I know that the opposite of codependence is not total independence. I need bonding and a healthy interdependence on others.

She extends her hand to the poor, Yes, she reaches out her hands to the needy. She is not afraid of snow for her household, For all her household is clothed with scarlet. She makes tapestry for herself; Her clothing is fine linen and purple. Her husband is known in the gates. —PROV. 31:20–23

This is our second day to look at what the Holy Spirit told King Lemuel to write three thousand years ago to condemn the codependent abuse of women. Male chauvinism has been a problem throughout human history.

In today's passage, we see that "the wise woman" of Proverbs 31 is also a caring and compassionate woman. She's not a cold, cruel executive trying to "out-con" other executives. Some women today are just getting into the misery selfish men have *already* suffered for thousands of years. The wise woman reaches out her hand to help the poor and genuinely needy—not to help codependent moochers. She is a helper, not an enabler.

She wasn't afraid of cold weather. Her family wore expensive and warm clothing. She wasn't afraid of the criticism of "pious" citizens who think wearing nice clothes is a sin.

Her husband had his independent business life and she had hers. They had independent business lives, but interdependent family lives. They were family-oriented and highly regarded each other.

God intended some male/female differences in responsibilities and authority within the family, but he called for an end to codependence.

> *Strength and honor are her clothing; She shall rejoice in time to come. She opens her mouth with wisdom, And on her tongue is the law of kindness. She watches over the ways of her household, and does not eat the bread of idleness. Her children rise up and call her blessed; Her husband also, and he praises her.*
> —PROV. 31:25–31

This is the third in a series of observations of God's plan for ending the codependent abuse of women in marriage and business. In some parts of Asia, even today, groups of women follow their husbands around, not speaking a single word, while their husbands laugh and talk to each other. The women even have their faces covered.

In today's passage, King Lemuel describes a woman who is physically, emotionally, and spiritually strong, honorable, and "rejoicing." She speaks openly and wisely, and when she speaks, people listen. She speaks the truth in love and kindness.

She is not lazy. She keeps close tabs on all the activities of her children in spite of her home-centered industries. Her children are her top priority. She doesn't ignore them.

In fact, her children rise up in the mornings and call her blessed. Her husband also highly regards her and praises her.

The Bible tells us that in heaven there will be no inequalities or codependency between men and women.

> *"So then, they are no longer two but one flesh. Therefore what God has joined together, let not man separate."*
>
> —MATT. 19:6

Ideally, it would be nice if newlyweds could move at least five hundred miles away from both sets of parents for several years. The ideal couple would wait three to five years to have their first child so they could adjust to each other. Then they could move back near their parents so the babies would have the wonderful experience of being loved and cared for periodically by healthy grandparents. But it seldom works out that way.

Many parents feel too insecure to let go of their young adult children when they get married. They use various "hooks" to keep controlling them, like money or manipulation through guilt. The newlywed may fear parental rejection. Or the newlywed may choose to continue codependence for financial reasons, even though he or she hates it.

Newlyweds need to continue to honor parents and maintain a good relationship as much as possible. But they need to develop friendships in their own local church and neighborhood with couples their own age.

God says "no man" should separate or drive a wedge between any married couple. That also means no parent, no counselor, no lawyer. There are no perfect marriages, but for most people the advantages of marriage far outweigh the disadvantages.

The happiest marriage is not a codependent marriage or a totally independent coexistence. It is healthy interdependence.

> *"For whoever does the will of My Father in heaven
> is My brother and sister and mother."*
>
> MATT. 12:50

In this beautiful passage of Scripture, Jesus was not insulting His own mother and younger brothers who were waiting outside. He was teaching us the value and importance of reparenting.

You see, none of us had perfect parents. None of us will be perfect parents. We all have some developmental "holes in our souls." All of our children will have some developmental holes in their souls too.

We can go through life suffering the loneliness and pain from those holes and blame it on our parents, or we can assume responsibility for our own needs. We can gain insights into our own root problems. We can figure out how God wants to meet those emotional and spiritual needs. We can find love, joy, and peace with meaning—not heaven on earth, not perfection, but a great life.

The best place to look for loving but imperfect people to bond to is in a healthy local church. Find a church that believes in the *inerrancy* of Scripture. Look for one that has small groups of about six to sixteen people who meet together once every couple of weeks to eat together, share fellowship and personal concerns, and have Bible study and prayer. Remember, you don't have to have your parents. A substitute mother, father, brother, or sister will do just fine.

I need a support group for good mental health and reparenting and will regularly attend a growth group at a local church.

He who covers his sins will not prosper, But whoever confesses and forsakes them *will have mercy.*
—PROV. 28:13

Every human alive needs to be accountable to God and to at least one other human. We all have to answer to God whether we want to or not, so we might as well do it voluntarily. It's not a matter of ritualistic, meaningless confession, paying penance, or repeating the same prayer over and over. God's Word tells us He does not want us to do these things.

What God wants from us is a personal relationship. He runs His areas of responsibility (vengeance on our abusers, protection for us, observation, supervision of angelic activities, etc.) and He wants us to own our areas of responsibilities (self-control, helping others, parenting, being a good mate, etc.). He is always waiting to help us with our overburdens and with our areas of temptation. He also wants us to meditate on His Word daily to strengthen ourselves.

When we feel tempted, we should tell the Father about it. He already knows, but it helps *us* to tell Him.

The temptation is filling some hole in our soul. So if we figure it out and fill that particular hole in our soul in biblically acceptable ways (such as a gut-level friendship with a friend of the same sex, for example), then the temptation level will decrease significantly. We also *must* be accountable to at least one other human.

I can decrease my temptation level by meditating on Scripture and being accountable to a friend or support group.

March 9 – ACCOUNTABILITY

> *Confess your trespasses to one another, and pray*
> *for one another, that you may be healed. The*
> *effective, fervent prayer of a righteous man*
> *avails much.*
> —JAMES 5:16

Every human alive should be accountable to at least one other human. Whoever thinks he doesn't need accountability needs it the most.

The apostle Paul was an outstanding believer, but he was always accountable and never traveled alone. He usually took Dr. Luke along with him, but also Silas or Barnabas and others as well. Paul said that we should really worry when we think we can't fail because that's exactly when we will fail. It was also Paul who said he sometimes did what he didn't want to do and didn't do some things he wished he would have done. He had to live with his "badness" just like we do.

As a psychiatrist, I have seen human-to-human accountability in individual therapy situations, in group therapy, in growth groups, in AA, in ACA, in Overeaters Anonymous, and in mini-church settings. I have also seen it friend-to-friend. It's one of the most *powerful* healing forces for overcoming addictions known to man.

Confessing our sins and failures promotes physiological changes in our bodies also, resulting in physical and emotional healing. It restores our serotonin by helping us forgive ourselves and others, decreasing our grudges and vengeful motives.

May God grant me the courage to overcome shame and introduce a powerful force in my life: confession and accountability.

Blessed is the man Who walks not in the counsel of the ungodly, Nor stands in the path of sinners, Nor sits in the seat of the scornful; But his delight is in the law of the LORD, And in His law he meditates day and night.
                                          —PS. 1:1–2

When I was ten years old, my loving mother helped me memorize Psalm 1. I have thought about that psalm, and about her doing that hundreds of times.

We had family devotions all my life. My parents would share a few verses at the supper table every night and we would pray for each other. I trusted Christ to save me when I was six years old.

I started having daily devotions when I was ten. I have done it ever since, even in graduate school when I reexamined whether I even believed in Christianity. Daily devotions gave me the strength to pull through that doubting period.

If I have extended daily devotions, I won't have nearly as much time to accomplish other worthwhile things. But what's more important, what I accomplish or who I really am on the inside? I think the latter. In reality, I actually accomplish much more in much less time by working on who I am. God promises that we will bear fruit and prosper in various ways if we meditate on His Word day and night.

Start rethinking your own devotional habits. Think of a way to have a brief devotion at least twice a day, morning and evening.

Your word I have hidden in my heart, That I might not sin against You. —PS. 119:11

We need to work at decreasing our temptation level through *meditation* on Scripture daily.

Consciously, we want to succeed in life. But part of us, usually at a deeply unconscious level, wants to fail.

Failure has its payoffs. If you were abused as a child, it has even greater payoffs. Failure gets vengeance on parents, on yourself, on your mate, and on God. It's also a way to rationalize giving up the hard work it takes to succeed in life. You can blame it on someone else or you can say, "I knew I couldn't do it!"

That's why we need to meditate on Scripture daily. Hiding God's Word in our heart (mind, emotions, and will) helps reduce our failure script. His principles are our daily counselors.

I often tell our young therapists that they will usually only get to see each patient once a week for about nine months or so, then they will seldom see them after that. But, if they can convince their patients to meditate on Scripture daily, those beloved patients will have a counselor with them *daily* for the rest of their lives.

The Bible is God's love letter to me.

One who turns away his ear from hearing the law,
Even his prayer shall be *an abomination.*
—PROV. 28:9

God saves us unconditionally by faith in Christ's death on the cross in our place. It's not of works (see Eph. 2:8–9). God's love for us is unconditional. (see Rom. 5:8). But God's blessings in our life are conditional.

If you owned a business, would you reward the workers who showed up for your training seminars? Or would you reward the arrogant employees who think they already know everything, but keep making the same mistakes? I know I would reward those who were willing to learn the rules for success. God does too.

Today's passage is another one of those conditions. If we refuse to meditate regularly on the "laws" or principles of God, then our prayers will be an abomination to Him.

What if your child was in college and you wrote a loving letter every day, and he threw them all in the trash unopened, and you knew he was doing that? Would you send him money when he left a message requesting it on your answering machine? You'd be a masochistic enabler if you did. God says He won't. If we do meditate on His principles, He will bless us like a tree planted by the waters. If we don't, our prayers will be an abomination to Him.

God will bless me if I learn and practice His rules for success.

For as the rain comes down, and the snow from heaven, And do not return there, But water the earth, And make it bring forth and bud . . . So shall My word be that goes forth from My mouth; It shall not return to Me void. . . .

—ISA. 55:10–11

All humans have negative addiction tendencies. Abused children grow into adults with more shame and bigger vacuums. They are more prone to addictions. By following a Twelve-step program, or the ten steps from our book, *Love Is a Choice*, addictions can be overcome. But lifetime maintenance is required.

Daily devotions is a vital part of that lifetime maintenance. It is part of what we call "cognitive restructuring." It is the reprogramming of our brains. What a privilege to develop the mind of Christ!

God promises in today's passage that His Word never returns to Him void. It will accomplish in our lives what He wants it to accomplish. It will enable us to prosper emotionally and spiritually.

Each of us needs to design our own devotional program. One possibility to consider would be a devotional from a book like this every morning, and reading consecutively through your Bible every evening. When you really love a verse, write it on a three-by-five card and carry it with you for a long time with other special verses on cards. When you get a coffee break, memorize it and meditate on it—think about ways you can change your behavior to fit in with the principles in the passage.

God has a plan to improve my life, using His Word.

*"For assuredly, I say to you, till heaven and earth
pass away, one jot or one tittle will by no means
pass from the law till all is fulfilled."*

—MATT. 5:18

If we all had perfect parents, and none of us did, we
would still resent authority because by nature we are
rebellious. If you don't believe me—if you believe all
that garbage about the basic goodness of mankind—
then borrow your neighbor's two-year-old and baby-sit
him or her for one day. You'll believe me!

The more abuse we suffer growing up, the harder it
is to trust authority and the more we want to rebel
deep down on the inside. That's why people don't like
the real God—He places demands on them. That's why
they laugh at the idea of a literal hell—an eternal place
of torment. They don't want to think that it could happen to them.

That is also why humans reject God's Word. They
don't like what it says about their depravity. Jesus said
that not even the punctuation points were in error (one
"jot" or one "tittle"). He says all prophecy will be fulfilled some day. People laugh at that, too. They think a
literal Rapture is ridiculous, but I'm looking forward to
it personally. Jesus said believers who don't honor and
obey God's Word will have lower positions in God's
Kingdom. Believers who honor and obey and teach
God's principles to others will be honored in the Kingdom.

---

*Jesus said His Word is perfect and there are overwhelming proofs for
the veracity of Scripture, so I submit myself to live by its guidelines.*

"Heaven and earth will pass away, but My words will by no means pass away." —MATT. 24:35

There are only three things that will last forever: God, God's Word, and God's created beings—people and angels. A wise person will invest his time, efforts and money on things that last forever.

The savings and loan crisis in America brought many people, millionaires included, to bankruptcy. Some had invested their whole lives into building a financial empire, then lost it all overnight. Can you imagine how someone would feel if he worked eighty hours per week for forty years to build a financial empire only to lose it all overnight?

A believer is to invest his life in 1) knowing God and becoming more like Christ, 2) knowing God's Word, applying what it says to our lives, teaching it to our children and others, 3) knowing and loving people—building eternal friendships, helping each other in crisis, etc. If a wise millionaire believer lost all his wealth, he would only grieve a little, because he would only have lost a little. But he would still have everything that will last forever. He would still have intimacy with God. He would still have God's Word and principles to live by. He would still have his family and friends. All he would have lost is a million dollars!

Begin your plan today for investing in God, God's Word, and people.

*For the word of God is living and powerful, and
sharp than any two-edged sword, piercing even
to the division of soul and spirit, and of joints
and marrow, and is a discerner of the thoughts
and intents of the heart.* —HEB. 4:12

We see thousands of patients each year who have so
many scars from past abuses that they have been clinically depressed or phobic for years. And yet in four to
six weeks, if they cooperate, our trained therapists are
able to strip away their defense mechanisms; face
them with the truth about their unconscious, emotional wounds; and build their healthy defenses up to a
point where they are emotionally stronger. Our therapists are able to do this because they integrate scrip-
tural principles into their therapy—sometimes openly
and sometimes subtly, depending on which is best for
that individual patient. We also use medical and psychiatric knowledge, a thorough medical evaluation,
and appropriate therapeutic techniques. But the real
power comes from applying God's Word. The God who
inspired the Bible created our brain's physiology and
psychology.

Paul said God's Word is living, powerful, sharp,
piercing the unconscious, and reveals our innermost
thoughts, feelings and intents. I have seen it in action
for many years on thousands of patients. There is absolutely nothing like it.

---

*I will not overlook the Book that can deliver what I am searching
for—the Book that pierces to the depths of all my problems.*

> *Therefore, laying aside all malice, all guile,*
> *hypocrisy, envy, and all evil speaking, as newborn*
> *babes, desire the pure milk of the word, that you*
> *may grow thereby, if indeed you have tasted that*
> *the Lord is gracious.*   —1 PETER 2:1–3

Try to imagine a sane adult planning his coming month and saying to himself, "Well, I'm going to be pretty busy this month. I have bills to pay, work to do around the house, the kids' carpools, and, of course, my work. I guess I simply won't have any time to eat this month, so I'll skip all my meals so I'll have time to do these more important things."

Someone simply would not do this unless he was grossly overweight, under a doctor's care, and taking all sorts of vitamin supplements so he wouldn't die of a chemical imbalance. And yet, millions of believers go a month or more at a time spiritually starving themselves by having no devotions. And there aren't any believers who are genuinely spiritually overweight! There are plenty who are superficially "superspiritual," but they need God's Word even more.

The apostle Peter told us to see ourselves as starving, dependent, newborn babies who need milk. Then consider God's Word to be that milk and drink it several times each day, like a newborn baby drinks milk, so you can grow spiritually.

God loves each new believer. His Word is the best possible drink for spiritual development and maturation.

The steps of a good man are ordered by the LORD, and He delights in his way. Though he fall, he shall not be utterly cast down; For the LORD upholds him with His hand.
— PS. 37:23–24

If good men and good women didn't fall, they would never need follow-up therapy, support groups, or reexamination. But our passage for today tells us good men do fall. And it was written by David who should know. He was an extremely godly man most of his life, but committed adultery with Bathsheba and had her godly husband Uriah killed in battle. But David repented and went on to serve God the rest of his life.

David said when a good man falls, he should not assume all is lost and give up. He should not be "utterly cast down." He should prayerfully reexamine his life, like David did, accept the Lord's forgiveness, and go on with life. The Lord will uphold the fallen with His hand.

It was David who also wrote another "hand" illustration in Psalm 139. David said God holds us with his right arm and leads us through the tough times in life with His left hand.

The apostle John told us (see John 10:27–31) that we are held secure in Jesus' hand, with the heavenly Father's hand wrapped around His. He said no one can pluck us out. We can't even pluck ourselves out of His hand.

What does God call a believer who falls but reexamines himself? A "good man."

March 19 – SUPPORT GROUPS

> 'If you walk in My statutes and keep My
> commandments, and perform them, Five of you
> shall chase a hundred, and a hundred of you shall
> put ten thousand to flight; your enemies shall fall
> by the sword before you.   —LEV. 26:3, 8

No man is an island. No man can stand alone. We need each other. There *is* strength in numbers. Group therapy is a powerful tool. Support groups work. When we treat men and women for alcoholism or drug addiction, for example, the insurance companies actually call up the psychiatrist to be sure that the patients will be in an AA group when they get out. They want to save money, and they know support groups are the best hope.

Churches around America have rapidly developed support groups themselves. They are usually called "mini-churches" or "growth groups."

James told us to confess our faults to one another for emotional, spiritual and physical healing. The apostle Paul told us to speak the truth in love to one another, and to exhort and even rebuke one another.

Five believers who obey God's principles and work together can put a hundred to flight (20:1 ratio). A hundred can defeat ten thousand (100:1 ratio). There is definitely strength in numbers. Moses said it would work thousands of years ago.

Start praying that God will guide you to the appropriate support group.

God sets the solitary in families; He brings out those who are bound into prosperity; But the rebellious dwell in a dry land. —PS. 68:6

Many millions of adults were abused as children. Many have kept it a family secret. They feel guilt if they "betray" their abusive family by talking about it.

Their feelings of rage and false guilt and low self-esteem and loneliness are stuffed deep inside. They feel bound for life by these buried emotions. They think they will never experience the love and joy of a normal family. They cling to the fantasy that their abusers will repent and make their family of origin normal.

God has a better plan. He says you don't need your mother or your father. You can fill your father-vacuum or mother-vacuum with Him and other believers. He is a Father of the fatherless. He is a defender of widows. God "sets the solitary in families"—spiritual families, growth groups, mini-churches, ACA groups. He brings those who feel "bound" into emotional and spiritual prosperity.

But if you rebel—if you keep your feelings stuffed—if you keep defending your abusers—if you stay isolated—if you rebel against God's outstretched hand to help you—then you will continue to "dwell in a dry land." Happiness is a choice.

Be your own best friend and choose God's plan for you—the support of friends in a new, loving and meaningful family.

> *"For where two or three are gathered together in My name, I am there in the midst of them."*
>
> —MATT. 18:20

Whether you join a minichurch, a growth group, a Bible-study group, an ACA group, or an AA group, there is someone who would like to be invited to join your group with you. His name is Jesus, and He is your Big Brother if you have accepted His gift of eternal life which He paid for by shedding His blood on the cross for you. Will you let Him be a member of your group?

Jesus said if two believers get together and agree on something and pray to the Father about it, Jesus will be their advocate and see to it that it gets done. Other passages of Scripture explain that the requests must also be in God's will. He knows what is best for you, so sometimes He says no for your own good. If you knew the "inside information" He knows, you would want Him to say no under some circumstances. But, nevertheless, there is strength in numbers.

If two or three of you meet together as a group, Jesus says He is right there in your midst. He does this through the omnipresent Holy Spirit, who represents Him in the world. He wants to be invited to your groups. He loves you, and wants to be intimately involved. But Jesus is a gentleman. He won't come in where He isn't invited.

Meet regularly with other committed believers and be aware that Jesus is in your midst through the Holy Spirit if you invite Him.

And let us consider one another in order to stir up love and good works, not forsaking the assembling of ourselves together.
　　　　　　　　　　　　　　—HEB. 10:24

The apostle Paul wrote this passage and the majority of the other "one another" concepts in the New Testament. It is really amazing to me how God uses the foolish things of the world to confound the wise. Paul, though intellectually brilliant, had been an emotional and spiritual dwarf named Saul. He was a Pharisee who murdered Christians with a legalistic zeal. But God saved him, changed his name to "Paul" (which means little), and used him to have a great impact in the world.

Paul says do not forsake church attendance. They met on the first day of each week to give money and share personal struggles and study the Bible. But which day of the week is not as important as whether or not you are meeting weekly with true believers to do these things.

We don't know when Jesus will rapture the believers out of this world (see 1 Thess. 4:13–18), but the Bible says as that day draws closer, it becomes more and more important that we regularly attend a healthy local church where we can feel comfortable enough to exhort one another. God knows how tough it will be to do this in the end times.

As you plan lifetime maintenance, be sure to attend a healthy local church that believes in inerrancy of Scripture. Find one that also demonstrates love, rather than legalism.

He who walks with wise men will be wise,
But the companion of fools will be destroyed.
—PROV. 13:20

Peer influence is powerful, even among adults. We tend to become more and more like the adults we spend the most time with. That's why wise King Solomon said that a companion of wise men will become wise but "the companion of fools will be destroyed."

When selecting one or more lifelong support groups, you must be very careful which group you select. You never want to select a group that teaches any principles contrary to the Word of God, since only God's principles will bring you true growth and recovery. Most AA and ACA groups are excellent, for example, but each AA or ACA group stands alone to some extent, so a few have fallen under the influence of New Age personnel who will suggest that the power is "spirit guides" (which I feel are all satanic and encourage passivity). The Power is Jesus Christ and none other, so seek out only support groups that help you find the real Power.

God's Word is the only absolute authority for deciding principles of living and salvation itself. No denomination or religious leader is worth even listening to if he teaches anything that contradicts Scripture. Look at all groups and find true believers for your lifelong support. They can love you best because they have the love of Christ in their hearts.

I will choose support groups that Jesus will be happy to join with me. If there are none in my area, I'll start one myself.

Do not forsake your own friend or your father's friend, Nor go to your brother's house in the day of your calamity; For better is a neighbor nearby than a brother far away. —PROV. 27:10

These verses tell us that a brother is an important support in life, but that close friends are even more important. A true friend will love you at all times. You can go to him with normal, everyday problems.

Friends do not grow on trees. We have to spend lots of time together with an acquaintance, sharing good times and bad times, sharing feelings as well as facts. Friendships take planning and work. But they are a must. Intimate friends will stick even closer than a brother.

Proverbs 27:10 isn't saying you shouldn't get the support of your brother when you have a crisis, because that would contradict what Solomon said in Proverbs 17:17. What Solomon is saying is that when we do have calamities in our lives (and we will all *have some*), then your support group of friends nearby can help you out emotionally much better than a brother who lives away.

We all need to build a local support system wherever we go, and strong believers who are loyal to God's Word are preferable.

> *Then God blessed them, and God said to them, "Be fruitful and multiply; fill the earth and subdue it; have dominion over the fish of the sea, over the birds of the air, and over every living thing that moves on the earth."*
> —GEN. 1:28

God had a lot of options when He put Adam and Eve on planet earth. He could have just left them there and then come back to visit once every ten thousand years or so, leaving mankind totally independent of Him. But we would have destroyed ourselves long ago without His help. We have practically destroyed ourselves even with His help.

God could have also been totally controlling and made us like puppets. We would never have an original thought. We would have perfect behavior that way, and there would be no humans abusing other humans. But God does not want to fellowship with robots. He would not want to adopt us as sons and daughters if we were robots. He would quickly get bored with us, like a child with a toy robot.

So God made us independent in thought and interdependent (not codependent) with Him. He delegated His dominion and authority to us over the fish, birds, cattle and all the earth. He created us in His psychological and spiritual (not physical) image. He said to have children and subdue the earth. He told us to be the boss of our lives and the earth, but to live in subjection to His principles for our own best interest.

God trusted us with a great deal of autonomy and authority.

*"And these words which I command you today
shall be in your heart; you shall teach them
diligently to your children, and shall talk of them
when you sit in your house, when you walk by the
way, when you lie down, and when you rise up."*
—DEUT. 6:7

One area that God made us "boss" of is our own children while they are growing up. The New Testament says in the original Greek that *little* children should obey their parents, not grown-up children. Adult children are told to honor parents all their lives, but we are not told to obey them.

In our passage for today, Moses got pretty specific about what God expects of us when He makes us "boss" of our children. He wants us to teach His principles to our children diligently, talking about Bible passages when we sit down after work, when we go for walks with our kids, when we tuck them in bed at night, and when they wake up in the morning. Not teaching our children the wonderful principles of God is a form of spiritual abuse. However, we should not shove the Bible down their throats. I look for subtle ways to share a verse here, or a biblical principle there, or just to set a biblical example in certain situations. I give my children what they are ready to hear.

---

*God made us "boss" of our families and warned us to do the best job
we can. He wants us to break the multi-generational cycle of various
abuses, including spiritual abuse.*

> *Whoever has no rule over his own spirit Is like a
> city broken down, without walls.*
>
> —PROV. 25:28

Another area of personal responsibility that God delegates to us is the area of our emotions. He wants us to learn to be aware of them, express them, release them, and control them.

When God designed the human brain, he divided it into two main parts. The outer, convoluted gray matter is our thinking logical brain. It is called the cerebral cortex.

Underneath that brain, going from front to back, is a brain shaped like and about the same size as a hot dog. It's called our limbic brain and is the seat of our emotions. Some people impulsively follow this brain without using much logic, and some use logic without feelings.

These brains connect to each other, and God wants us to use both brains in our daily lives. Different personality types rely too much on one or the other, without balance.

In today's Scripture, God is not telling us to stuff our anger. He is merely telling us to control it, analyze it, own up to it, and handle our anger biblically. We should always forgive, whether the person asks for forgiveness or not.

---

*May God grant me the wisdom to take advantage of both brains He
gave me—both logic and emotions, and keep them in balance.*

Do you see a man who excels in his work? He will stand before kings; he will not stand before unknown men.
—PROV. 22:29

Dr. James Dobson has been our mentor and a major inspiration to us. He is an outstanding Christian psychologist, host of the "Focus on the Family" radio program, and author of scores of helpful psychological books. He loves God, his family, and America in that order, and strongly promotes the family.

He has consulted several presidents of the United States. One time I was with him for a medical meeting and he got interrupted by a phone call. The president of the United States wanted him to drop his plans and fly to Washington, D.C. for some consultation.

The first thing that came to my mind was today's passage, so I shared it with him: "Do you see a man who excels in his work? He will stand before kings."

God places our psychological and spiritual gifts under our authority and asks us to use them for Him. It does not mean we all need to end up in full-time Christian work, like Dr. Dobson. But we all have some gifts we can use for Him, maybe by teaching a Sunday school class, or helping widows and orphans, or a prison ministry, or singing in a church choir, or leading a growth group. Pray that God will show you your spiritual gifts.

Those who trust Christ and serve Him well on earth will not only stand before a King some day, but we will be kings in the messianic kingdom some day.

> So let *each one* give *as he purposes in his heart,
> not grudgingly or of necessity; for God loves a
> cheerful giver.*
> —2 COR. 9:7

Another area of responsibility God delegates to us is the area of donations. He places all money matters, including giving, under our command. There are no New Testament rules for giving, other than to give whatever you can give with a cheerful heart. He also promises us that it is better to give than to receive, that He will restore whatever we cheerfully give a hundred fold (but not necessarily financially).

Giving is the greatest investment we can make. The Old Testament Jews were told to give a tithe, but they actually gave much more than 10 percent because it was their income tax. The New Testament never mentions tithing unless it is the Pharisees doing it. I personally think a tithe (10 percent of take-home pay after taxes) is a good place to start. Giving is such an unbelievable investment (if you believe God) that I hope you choose to eventually give much more than that.

Be careful to whom you give. The Bible says your pastor is worthy of a wage for full-time pastoral work. A pastor should normally be paid the average annual income of the families in his church. Extra giving can go to quality, proven organizations that also stand for inerrancy of Scripture. God gave us the creative responsibility of designing our own giving plan. The rewards are great, not only for the recipient, but also for the donor.

Develop a giving plan starting right away, with a good local church.

> *Not that I speak in regard to need, for I have*
> *learned in whatever state I am, to be content: I*
> *know how to be abased, and I know how to*
> *abound.* —PHIL. 4:11

Another important area of responsibility God delegates to us is the responsibility to take care of our own basic needs and to be content with what we have. The apostle Paul was a tentmaker as well as a brilliant scholar. When he served God full time as an evangelist, there would have been nothing wrong with raising support for himself, like most missionaries do.

But Paul made or mended tents wherever he went. He decided to support himself, even though it took a lot of his time. He didn't want anyone to think he was serving God for the money.

Before his conversion, he had been a wealthy Pharisee. He knew what it was like to "abound" financially.

He knew also what poverty felt like. But he now enjoyed life whether abounding or being abased financially because he was investing in God, God's Word, and people—three things that will all last forever. Money was important only for survival and for continuing his ministry. His payoff will come in the kingdom.

If becoming Christ-like and serving Christ are my primary goals, then life's circumstances won't have as much power over how I feel.

For the eyes of the LORD run to and fro throughout the whole earth, to show Himself strong on behalf of those whose heart is loyal to Him."

—2 CHRON. 16:9

The apostle Paul, in Philippians 4:13, said that we can do all things that God delegates for us to do, but we have to do them in God's strength. Some believers see God as the big "sugar daddy" in the sky. They desire spiritual gifts for good conscious reasons, but subconsciously for their own emotional self-indulgence, or to impress more than to serve others.

Instead of waking up in the morning and asking God for a reasonable list of things to do that day for Him, they wake up and write out a list of things they want their "sugar daddy god" to do for them.

Because they are emotional, entitled, and super-spiritual, they become vulnerable to sexual addictions and thoughts. Yet they blame God by saying key phrases such as "I'm just waiting on the Lord," or "Let go and let God," phrases which can also have good meaning in the proper context.

Today's passage reassures us that God loves us so much that His eyes are searching all around the world for believers who are willing to be loyal to His kingdom, so He can exchange our weakness for His strength. He wants us to mature in Him.

To paraphrase former President Kennedy: "Ask not what the kingdom can do for you; ask what you can do for the kingdom."

The LORD is my light and my salvation; Whom shall I fear? The LORD is the strength of my life; Of whom shall I be afraid?
—PS. 27:1

If you brought home a brand new puppy and you were a loving owner, that dog would also love you, lick your hand, and follow you around wagging its tail. But if someone else in the home kept kicking it and abusing it, eventually that puppy would become paranoid and suspicious of everyone, including you.

The puppy would soon growl whenever anyone, including you, entered the room. He would fear further abuse.

Our passage for today shows us that the Lord is our source of salvation, by depending on what Jesus did for us on the cross. But God is also our "light." He gives us true perspectives and principles for living, including ways to protect ourselves from the abusers of this world. We will examine many of those passages in this devotional.

If we trust Him for salvation, and use His light for our self-protection and insight, then we can say with David, "Whom shall I fear? The Lord is the strength of my life; of whom shall I be afraid?"

The term, "wait on the Lord," means to *depend* on the Lord for His strength to replace your weakness, so you can do the work He wants you to do (see Ps. 27:14). There goes that teamwork again!

With God's strength enhancing my courage, I can use my insights from His light to protect myself from future abuse. To quote Franklin D. Roosevelt, "We have nothing to fear but fear itself."

> *To You, O my Strength, I will sing praises; For God
> is my defense, The God of my mercy.*
> —PS. 59:17

The adult child of abuse has had many days of trouble.
Not only have the days of abuse caused trouble, but
every day that the emotional pains from that abuse go
uncorrected is one more day of trouble. Many never
get the help they need, so they experience an entire
troubled life. That is so unnecessary. The effects of
abuse can be resolved.

If you can truly do all things through Christ, who
strengthens you (see Phil. 4:13), then you can surely
get over the pains from past abuse. No one said it
would be easy. It is very hard and painful and draining.
The pains are not your fault, but resolving them is your
responsibility, with the help of God. If you need a therapist, ask God to guide you to the best one for you.
When you finish, you will sing of God's power. You will
sing of His mercy toward you. You will see Him as your
defense and refuge from your troubled days. You will
sing songs of praise to your God, the "God of strength."
You will thank Him for your new-found personal
strength that you thought would never come. You will
sing praises to the God of your defense—to the God of
your mercy.

---

*If I am an adult child of abuse, I will see the best Christian psycholo-
gist or therapist I can find to get rid of my "bag of rocks" I am carry-
ing around.*

*The horse is prepared for the day of battle, but
deliverance is of the Lord.*   —PROV. 21:31

In most cases, God will not fight your battles for you.
God will only help you fight your own battle. The
"horse" has to be prepared for the day of battle, but
deliverance comes from the help of God.

A lady called me on the phone and was angry at
God. She had been an alcoholic for years and had
never gotten any treatment for it. She finally decided
to give it up. So she went to see a Christian therapist
(whom I didn't know) twice a week for two weeks. She
wondered why she wasn't "cured" yet. Surely God
could cure her in two weeks! Then she wanted a psychiatric evaluation but didn't want to pay anything,
even though she wasn't poor. She thought she was entitled to free treatment. When I refused to treat her for
free, she hung up on me.

What a raw deal! First, God refused to cure her without her doing the long, hard work of therapy followed
by lifetime maintenance, and then a Christian psychiatrist refused to treat her for free. In reality, I did feel
very sorry for her. She had probably learned to expect
these things from her parents.

Giving our children everything they want and doing
all their work for them *is* a form of child abuse. It may
be one of the worst. Entitlement is a painful curse; humility is a blessing.

---

*I hate hard work as much as the next guy, but I accept the reality that
I have to prepare this "horse" for the battles of life, while still depending on God's power for deliverance.*

> *But now, O LORD, You are our Father; We are the clay, and You our potter; And all we are the work of Your hand.*
> —ISA. 64:8

Try to imagine that you are a potter. Have you ever made pottery? It's lots of fun. We tried it in school when we were young. Imagine that you have magical clay in your hands. It is magical because it can talk back to you.

I guess that could either be a fun experience for you or a totally miserable experience, depending on the personality and attitude of the clay. If it complimented my gentleness and care and design and carried on an interesting conversation, it would be wonderful. But if the clay were negative and griped a lot and was over-bearing and overly controlling—telling me each step of the way what to do with it—then I think I would not appreciate that clay very much!

I guess it must be like that with God in some ways. He is the potter. We are the clay. We have no right to gripe about the way He made us. It was His right to decide.

Personally, I'm just extremely thankful that He not only used magical clay like myself that can think and talk, but that He decided to make me in His own image and allowed me to become His very own son. I certainly would not have expected that, just being a piece of clay in a potter's hand and all.

God resists the proud but gives grace to the humble pieces of clay that don't expect Him to do everything their way.

Then Jesus came and spoke to them, saying, "All authority has been given to Me in heaven and on earth. Go therefore and make disciples of all the nations, baptizing them in the name of the Father and of the Son and of the Holy Spirit."

—MATT. 28:18–19

I fear rejection. I absolutely fear talking about God with a neighbor that I don't know well. Maybe it comes from childhood insecurities.

I can talk live on the radio once or twice a week to two million people each time, even answering their phone calls, not knowing what they will ask. I don't even mind saying, "I really don't know," sometimes. I'm not scared to do that, but I'm scared to tell a neighbor how to put his faith in Christ. I do it anyway— but not as much as I should.

Jesus delegated to us the responsibility for telling loved ones how to trust Him. He also instructed us to tell them about baptism as a public symbol of the fact that they have trusted Christ. He also wants us to help them grow in Christ and teach them Christ's principles. Facing one on one rejection is frightening, but I'll do it anyway because Christ promises to be right there with me, encouraging me to go on, "even to the end of the age." In the millennial kingdom I'll have my new body with no depravity, so I won't be frightened at all. I look forward to that "age."

The kindest thing I can do is tell others how to trust what Jesus did on the cross to give them eternal life and forgiveness of sins.

April 6 – DEPENDENCE ON GOD

> *"Abide in Me, and I in you. As the branch cannot bear fruit of itself, unless it abides in the vine, neither can you, unless you abide in Me."*
> —JOHN 15:4

Now I would like you to imagine that you are a large branch of a grapevine, and you have many smaller branches and hundreds of grapes. You are resting in the seventy-five-degree California sun. Nourishment is continually oozing from the main vine, so you always feel satisfied. You are never hungry, and never too full. You enjoy it when people pick out your full grapes and eat them or make grape juice out of them, because you like making people happy.

Now imagine that you become arrogant and decide you don't like the attention people give to the huge vine you are a branch of, so you manage somehow to break yourself free. You are real proud, until you start getting hungry and thirsty, but have no nourishment. You get tired and weak. The sun seems hotter and hotter now because you are dehydrating. In fact, you turn into a real prune.

Jesus encourages us to stay dependent on the *vine* in heaven for our daily nourishment and power and vitality. He wants us to do our thing, but to realize we can do nothing without nourishment from the vine. So stay bonded.

It is good to be proud of our growth and usefulness as grapes, as long as we remember that everything we are made of and everything we are came from the Big Vine.

*But God has chosen the foolish things of the world
to put to shame the wise . . . that no flesh should
glory in His presence.* —1 COR. 1:27–29

When I was a graduate student, before medical school, I was doing scientific research on the cardiovascular effects of serotonin. I was trained in the scientific method and instructed not to think "teleologically"—which means they told me to quit asking questions about why God made these brain chemicals do these things.

The evidence for the existence of God is overwhelming. The human body itself is proof. Trillions of cells with thousands of enzymes. Many scientists think it all evolved from nothing. To me, that is like saying that Webster's Dictionary came about by accident, as the result of an explosion in a printing factory. And yet it is against the law in most states for a public school teacher to even discuss the possibility that a Higher Power may have actually designed and created the human body.

And yet the Bible is correct. The more educated people become, the more they refuse to even look at the obvious evidence. Maybe the most arrogant demand the most degrees to "intellectualize" their ignorance.

God wants us to depend on Him, not on arrogant pride.

———————

*May God grant us the humility to acknowledge our foolishness before
Him, so He can make us wise.*

> *Therefore let him who thinks he stands take heed*
> *lest he fall. No temptation has overtaken you except*
> *such as is common to man; but God is faithful,*
> *who will not allow you to be tempted beyond what*
> *you are able, but with the temptation will also*
> *make the way of escape, that you may be able to*
> *bear it.*
>   —1 COR. 10:12–13

We had better depend on God for power when it comes to temptations, because we need all the help we can get. If we think we can resist temptations by our own strength, then we will surely fall.

If we think we can resist them without being accountable to God, we will fall. If we think we can resist them without being accountable to a support group or at least one other human, we will fall.

If we think we can get in situations that harbor temptations but still resist them, we are deceiving ourselves, and we will fall. We are instructed to flee from temptations, and that takes God's power too.

If we think we can resist temptations without regular meditation on God's Word to continually modify our thinking, again, we will fall! If we blame God for our failure, we are foolish, because He always provides a way of escape from every single temptation. It's up to us to choose to escape or to choose to yield. It is never God's fault. When we do fall, hopefully, we learn to trust less in our strength and more on His power and guidelines.

_____

We need God's power to avoid moral failure.

*For God has not given us a spirit of fear, but of
power and of love and of a sound mind.*

—2 TIM. 1:7

Dr. Minirth and I treated an eighteen-year-old girl in
the hospital for severe suicidal depression. She was cut-
ting herself, leaving scars on her body. Lots of adult
children of abuse do that. They feel so much rage
toward their abusers that they redirect it on themselves. Pain reassures them that they really exist.

Her father is a political leader and to this day has
never suffered legal consequences for sexually abusing her for many years. Her mother held her down during the abuse. When she was seventeen years old, she
decided she would rather die than be abused again, so
she fought her mom and dad, and they broke her right
arm so severely that her nerve was severed and she
could never play the violin again. She had become a
concert violinist as an escape and source of self-worth.
Her parents were turned in, of course, but no one believed her over her politician-father. She escaped to
Dallas where we treated her. Six weeks later, she was
at peace with God and with herself. She had released
her vengeance to God. She had forgiven her abusers.
She had developed a deep faith in God, who removes
our spirit of fear, and replaces it with a sound mind.

God can heal any wound!

> *For this reason I also suffer these things;*
> *nevertheless I am not ashamed, for I know whom I*
> *have believed and am persuaded that He is able to*
> *keep what I have committed to Him until that Day.*
> —2 TIM. 1:12

The apostle Paul wrote this passage to his friend, Timothy. This was Paul's last epistle, and he wrote it from a Roman dungeon in A.D. 67, shortly before he was beheaded for being a believer.

Paul told Timothy to expect suffering if he continued to be an outspoken Christian. Paul had gone through quite a lot of abuse by the in-crowd of his day, including being stoned nearly to death, whipped, imprisoned and finally beheaded. He considered himself lucky to identify with the sufferings of Christ.

Paul was not a masochist looking for ways to get people to step on him. He was as innocent a victim of in-crowd abuse as a child is innocent of being abused.

Paul was not ashamed to be a prisoner for practicing freedom of speech about his views. He knew *what* he believed and *whom* he believed in. Paul was absolutely persuaded that God would keep good watch of the rewards he had earned until he got to heaven a short time later. I'm sure Paul's greatest reward, when he was beheaded, was to wake up half a second later in heaven with thousands of his converts waiting for him, applauding, and lining up to get Paul's new body used to all the hugs he would get for the rest of eternity.

We need to depend on God for the power to suffer for being convinced of what the world hates to believe—the Bible.

> *[You] are kept by the power of God. . . . In this you
> greatly rejoice though . . . you have been grieved by
> various trials, that the genuineness of your faith,
> being much more precious than gold that perishes,
> though it is tested by fire, may be found to praise,
> honor, and glory at the revelation of Jesus Christ.*
> —1 PETER 1:5–7

The difference between believing something in your
head and believing something in your soul is *faith*. The
more genuine faith you have that Jesus will keep His
promises to you, the easier it will be to develop Christ-
like attitudes and behavior.

Jesus promises to come back to earth, bringing deceased believers with Him, to rapture the believers
who have not died yet. After a seven-year banquet and
training time, we will rule the world for one thousand
years. Humans will finally understand how good we
can be to one another when Christ is on the throne.

Our future is guaranteed by Christ Himself. Jesus
says to remember this glorious future when you go
through unavoidable suffering now. Don't go looking
for suffering like a masochist, but when it is unavoidable, depend on Christ's power to accept the things
you cannot change and to endure it.

Jesus says to also look on the bright side of necessary suffering. Tribulations develop patience just like
gold becomes more pure when it is treated by fire.

*When I have some necessary pain, I ask God for His power to endure
it and grow Christ-like as a result of it.*

> *As a father pities his children, So the LORD pities those who fear Him. For He knows our frame; He remembers that we are dust.* —PS. 103:13–14

God hates abuse of any kind. All of us are abusers to some extent, because all sins abuse somebody and everyone has sinned. Lying abuses, cheating abuses, stealing abuses, gossiping abuses, and sins of the flesh abuse many. To some extent, then, we are all abused abusers in an abusive world.

Our behavior grieves God, and He has considered wiping out mankind on more than one occasion. But He promises He won't, because He is also full of compassion. He knows we are "dust." He knows we are weak. He knows we have to live with sinful motives that we ourselves often detest.

He pities us, like a loving earthly father would feel sorry for his own child who was suffering a severe injury or disease. We have a spiritual disease called human depravity, and God our heavenly Father pities us for having to struggle with it.

God also knows that from an eternal perspective our lives here on earth are brief like a single breath that passes away. He wants us to realize that, too. We will spend eternity without our depravity, and a very brief amount of time, relatively speaking, fighting against it as an attempt to love and serve one another.

When I feel sorry for myself for having to live with certain aspects of my personality, it is nice to know that my heavenly Father has compassion on me, too, for the same reasons.

> *As it is written; "There is none righteous, no, not one"; Who can say, "I have made my heart clean, I am pure from my sin"? Every way of a man is right in his own eyes, but the LORD weighs the hearts.*
> —ROM. 3:10, PROV. 20:9, 21:2

Becoming a psychiatrist required thirteen years of college *prior* to beginning seminary training. "Why did it take so long?" people often ask us. "What did you study for all those years?"

One of the main things we studied during all those years was defense mechanisms—the forty ways people lie to themselves every hour of every day: including projection, denial, displacement, and rationalization.

There are quite a few people who decide to quit lying to each other, but there is no human alive who can go one conscious day without lying to himself. Our control over our self-deceit can be improved with insight, but never totally conquered in this life.

There are no perfectly righteous people. No one can make his own heart clean or stop sinning altogether. We tend to think we are always correct, but the Lord looks right through us into our unconscious, like an X-ray machine. He doesn't have to bother "reading" our body language, like a psychiatrist does. God looks straight through into our hearts (our mind, emotions, and will).

I lie to myself many times in many ways every day of my life to protect myself from the pain of seeing the truth. The Bible tells me the truth.

> *All the labor of man is for his mouth, and yet the*
> *soul is not satisfied.*
> —ECCL. 6:7

Strip away all the defense mechanisms and facades and climb deep into any man or woman's soul and what you will see, apart form God in their lives, is a human rat race. The pain of nobodyness drives each of us to a life of quiet desperation.

We devote most of our energy to prove that we are *not* a nobody. We fill the bottomless "nobodyness hole" with food, with sexual fantasies or pornography or affairs, with money, with power or control, with cars and houses and jewelry and clothes, with philosophies, with anything!

Why doesn't it work? Why doesn't anything work?

When all else fails, trust Christ! But don't turn your whole life over to Him until you have sincerely given up on the rat race. Your depravity calls you from its bottomless pit. Your human nature keeps calling you to do it your way, even though your way has not brought you peace. The Holy Spirit also calls you. The Comforter wants to bring you His peace. He wants you to stop depending on yourself, trust Christ, and commit to living by His principles.

> *Just as I am Without one plea,*
> *But that Thy blood Was shed for me.*
> *And that Thou bidst Me come to Thee.*
> *O LAMB OF GOD, I come. I come.*

*"So I turned my mind to understand, to investigate
and to search out wisdom and the scheme of
things."*
                                        —ECCL. 7:25 (NIV)

Solomon wanted a doctorate in psychology and he sure got it! God gave Solomon more wisdom than any other man who ever lived except the God-man, Jesus Christ. God taught Solomon the truth about depravity, and about the unconscious. Solomon knew about defense mechanisms and described many of them.

And Solomon knew for sure all about the human race for significance. The whole book of Ecclesiastes is all about it. Solomon had tried in every major area of sin himself before becoming wise. He considered it all vain and meaningless.

Solomon filled that bottomless hole in his soul by trusting in the coming Messiah and devoting his life to serving God, which he called "the whole duty of man."

What did Solomon see when God shined His flashlight on the human soul? The more God showed him about human nature, the more Solomon wept and grieved (see Eccl. 1:18). Solomon said that what he saw was "the stupidity of wickedness and the madness of folly" (Eccl. 7:25 NIV). He understood the unconscious thoughts, feelings, and motives that pull us into the rat race. He also understood our utter dependence on the true Higher Power to escape it.

Sin doesn't really satisfy any of the holes in our souls. Christ is the answer.

> *"The heart is deceitful above all things, and desperately wicked; Who can know it?*
> —JER. 17:9

This passage is the key that unlocks the door of Christian psychology. It describes human depravity in a precise way. It talks about the human heart, referring to the mind, emotions and will.

Jeremiah said the heart is deceitful. He understood the concept of defense mechanisms and unconscious motives also. Somehow, all those inspired writers knew about the unconscious but the rest of the world didn't until modern-day research made it obvious.

Not only is the heart deceitful, it is more deceitful than anything else in God's universe. Not only is our heart more deceitful than anything else God created, it is desperately wicked.

And not only is our heart desperately wicked, but no one can possibly comprehend how wicked it really is. Who can know it?

But Christ came to save sinners. We can't surprise Him. He knows our heart inside out, and He's still madly in love with us. I don't know why God chose to be that way in His personality, but I can say this—I'm certainly grateful that He is.

I'm thankful that God—who knows me best—loves me more than anyone else could. He wants me to understand my failures so I can tap His power and gain victory over them.

———————

A fool thinks he is wise, and a wise man realizes that he is such a fool that God's wisdom is the only *thing he trusts.*

"There is no fear of God before his eyes. For in his own eyes he flatters himself too much to detect or hate his sin."

—PS. 36:1b–2(NIV)

David was not as wise as his son Solomon, but he was certainly no dummy! God gave David a share of His wisdom also. David gained wisdom from life's hard knocks, his own mistakes, and meditating day and night on God's Word.

In today's passage David clarifies how we think apart from God's insight into our souls. We think we are very wise; we really are not.

We think we are certainly a great deal smarter than our parents, so we must be smarter than all authority figures—including God, if there even is one. We flatter ourselves in our self-talk over and over in some ways, but criticize ourselves over and over again in others. Without insight from God, we don't hate our sin because we don't even realize we have any. Pragmatism rules.

With godly insight, we do detect our own depravity. We hate it, like Paul said he hated his in Romans 6 and 7. But we see ourselves as God sees us and accept the true dignity and self-respect that God gives us.

Genuine self-worth can only come after I have detected and hated my own depravity, then choose to forgive myself.

> *Woe to those who devise iniquity, And work out evil*
> *on their beds! At morning light they practice it,*
> *Because it is in the power of their hand.*
>
> —MIC. 2:1

Have you ever wondered why so many people have insomnia?

There are basically two types of insomnia: 1) trouble falling asleep, and 2) falling asleep OK, but waking up at 3 A.M. and taking an hour or more to fall back to sleep. Type one comes primarily from everyday worries or else anxiety (a fear of seeing your real motivations), and type two comes primarily from a serotonin depletion from harboring vengeful motives and bitterness in your unconscious. There are other less common medical causes as well.

At night, we are tired and our brains are tired. It is harder to keep lying to ourselves at night. Even our displaced unconscious is tired. We have glimpses into the truth, and it hurts. That's why so many people watch TV until they are so exhausted they fall asleep— to avoid those glimpses into their own painful depravity. That's why they drink themselves to sleep or take addicting prescription medications. That's why they stay up watching pornographic movies on cable TV. That's why they work on their business or bills or a novel until their brain finally shuts off like a wet noodle.

God wants us to focus on His truth and love for us.

Wouldn't you rather have a clear conscience, no grudges, great sleep, and sweet dreams? All drug-free? Try it sometime!

*O wretched man that I am! Who will deliver me
from this body of death? I thank God—through
Jesus Christ our Lord! So then, with the mind I
myself serve the law of God, but with the flesh the
law of sin.*   —ROM. 7:24–25

In 1890, Freud called all our unconscious self-deceit, drives and motives the "id." Freud called our will the "ego." He called our conscience the "superego." Freud said our ego is an unconscious slave to the id, and apart from God, I think Freud was absolutely right on this point.

In 1800, Johann Christian Heinroth, a German Christian psychiatrist, wrote textbooks and articles. He coined the word, "ego," for the will, not Freud. He called the conscience the *überuns*—similar to superego. He called the depraved unconscious drives the "flesh," just like Paul did two thousand years ago.

Heinroth would have been considered the father of psychiatry instead of Freud, except he recommended, like the apostle Paul, faith in Christ as the ultimate solution. Paul and Heinroth said as Christians we continue to live all our lives with the law of sin and the law of God battling it out in our minds. But we have victory with Christ in the sense that we, with God's power, can be in control with intermittent, less severe failures. And in Romans 8:1, Paul said we have no condemnation if we are choosing to walk in the Spirit.

I have no choice but to live with my "badness" while working all my life to gain more and more control over it with God's power.

> *For to will is present with me, but how to perform*
> *what is good I do not find. For the good that I will*
> *to do, I do not do; but the evil I will not to do, that*
> *I practice.*
> —ROM. 7:18–19

The apostle Paul continues to describe his own strug-gle with his own depraved nature. I'm very grateful to Paul for being vulnerable and doing that. It is very diffi-cult for me personally to accept my own evil motives that raise their ugly heads into my thoughts. I detest my depravity; and I feel so relieved to read that the apostle Paul, the greatest missionary who ever lived, also struggled with his depravity and detested it.

Paul also warns about addictions in today's passage. Our depraved, unconscious desires trick us into com-mitting little sins that we consider harmless until we become addicted. Then we move up a slight notch to the next level of sin, and so forth until we are addicted to major sins.

James also said that lust brings forth sin, which brings forth addictions that result in physical death. We have to fight even the little willful sins.

The apostle John told believers that we are practic-ing self-deceit if we claim we no longer sin. But John also said that committed Christians who walk daily with the Lord will not practice habitual, willful sin (1 John 3:6).

May God grant me spiritual insight, self-acceptance and more con-trol over the bad elements of my personality.

If we say that we have no sin, we deceive ourselves, and the truth is not in us. If we confess our sins, He is faithful and just to forgive us our sins and to cleanse us from all unrighteousness.

—1 JOHN 1:8–9

John was known as "the disciple Jesus loves." John must have been a pretty neat guy, because Jesus really loved John in a special way. They were close friends. And John was still a sinner—just a saved sinner.

In fact, it was the apostle John who was describing believers in today's passage, saying that if a believer claims he doesn't sin any more, he is lying to himself. Christians all do sin, and whenever we do, we are instructed to be accountable to God. Confess it to Him. He already knows about it anyway.

Looking at the original Greek words for this passage, we see that "confess" is *homologōmen*. It implies that we only have to confess the degree of sin we become aware of. But God forgives us of *tas hamartias*— all of the unconscious motives and drives associated with that sin, even though we are not aware of it at all. We don't need to worry about all the unconscious sins, just confess the ones the Holy Spirit points out to us.

The Holy Spirit convinces and convicts us of various sins, then we should confess them to God (admit them to Him) to restore fellowship.

> *Trust in the LORD with all your heart, And lean
> not on your own understanding; In all your ways
> acknowledge Him, And He shall direct your paths.*
> —PROV. 3:5–6

At age ten I went to a Christian camp in upper Michigan for one week. We didn't have a lot of money, so it was the only summer in my life that I got to go to camp. But at camp, I began having daily personal devotions because they got us into the habit of it.

At age sixteen, I wasn't openly rebelling, but I was struggling with a wide variety of sins and questions. Bob Schindler was an M.D. in our church. He invited me to his home, asked me to memorize our passage for today, and discussed medical school as an option for me to think about.

I went home and memorized that passage right away, and that night I dedicated my life to serving God. I felt certain God wanted me to serve Him somehow in a field of medicine. I "accidently" had Frank Minirth as my "cadaver-mate," we both chose Psychiatry to have an impact for Christ, and the rest fell into place.

I still reflect on that passage often, and on the special nights in my life that God used special saints to nudge me a little one way or another. I'm still a sinful man who struggles with the same selfish motives and temptations I had when I was sixteen. But God continues to direct my paths.

_____

Don't lean on your own understanding. Dedicate your life to serve Christ, day by day, and He will help you make "guided, nudged guesses" as to which directions to take.

> *I have taught you in the way of wisdom; I have led you in right paths. When you walk, your steps will not be hindered, And when you run, you will not stumble.*
>
> —PROV. 4:11–12

The last thing in the world that I would want to do is to give young Christians the false impression that if you dedicate your life to God, every little "step" or decision you make is obvious. There have been a number of things I thought God was calling me to do, but when I tried them, they failed.

When I look back at those failures, I can easily see in hindsight that the unconscious "ego" motives outweighed my conscious good intentions. Part of me is also lazy. I often want God to call me to the easiest possible lifestyle so I can blame my laziness on Him.

God clearly directs all our paths and all our steps morally. The Bible tells us hundreds of rights and wrongs. But decisions like who specifically to marry, our career, where to live, how many children to have—these are not moral decisions. God gives us a lot of authority in these decisions.

Our passage for today tells us that if we emphasize walking with His wise principles (moral decisions), God will keep us from stumbling too severely in our other decisions.

I will meditate on God's principles and try to base all of my decisions on them.

> *For we all stumble in many things. If anyone does not stumble in word, he is a perfect man, able also to bridle the whole body.*
> —JAMES 3:2

Whenever you see the word "perfect" in the Bible relative to believers, don't worry about it. Dig out your Bible knowledge commentary and look it up and see what it says in the original Greek or Hebrew. The word for "perfect" here is *teleios,* which actually means mature, or *fulfilled.* The original Hebrew and Greek are without error, but modern translators have all made a few poor decisions here and there.

There are no places in the entire original Bible where a believer is expected to be perfect—only mature or fulfilled or complete. James wrote in today's passage that we all sin in many ways regularly. But James encourages us to focus on the words we speak. He says a lot about the tongue in other passages as well. The tongue is like the relatively small rudder on a huge ocean cruiser. It controls the direction of the whole cruise ship. If we learn to control our communications fairly well, then we will be mature and feel fulfilled *(not perfect),* and we will be able to bridle our whole body like we would bridle a horse. We still won't be perfect. We will still stumble in many ways. But we will be more mature than we were and should take pride in ourselves for the progress (see Gal. 6:4).

Focusing on my communications is focusing on what comes out of my soul—who we are—which is better than focusing on perfect behavior.

Ponder the path of your feet, And let all your ways be established. Do not turn to the right or the left; Remove your foot from evil. —PROV. 4:27

Those who were abused as children are often more tempted to sin than those who had more fulfilling childhoods. It doesn't seem fair, but who ever said this life was going to be fair?

Solomon encourages all believers to watch both who you are and what you do in your daily behavior. He doesn't promise anywhere that we can be perfect, but we can keep improving and growing and becoming sanctified.

Solomon says to focus on your heart (mind, emotions, and will). And like James, Solomon advises working on your communications (deceitful mouth, perverse lips). Don't let your eyes seduce. Look straight ahead.

Watch where your feet go too. Make up your mind ahead of time which places would enhance sanctification and which places would cause regression. Since you are living in grace and liberty, the choice is yours. But what do you think would be best for your long-term happiness? You guessed right again! God says sin is not worth it; our flesh says it is. So when we choose sin, we are pretending to be smarter than God.

Sanctification is not automatic. It requires wise daily choices.

> *Behold the proud, His soul is not upright in him;*
> *But the just shall live by his faith. Indeed, because*
> *he transgresses by wine,* he is *a proud man, And he*
> *does not stay at home.*   —HAB. 2:4

Three percent of humans lose touch with reality at some time in their lives. We know now from recent research that it usually involves a dopamine problem in the brain. Dopamine is present in ample quantities, but it is blocked from getting into the correct cells and receptors. This can be due to any combination of excessive stress, severe inferiority feelings, drug reactions, and genetic predisposition.

Before 1950, over half of *all* hospital beds in America were taken by people who had become psychotic. But then God allowed psychiatric research scientists to discover major tranquilizers, which partially correct the dopamine problem. When a person becomes delusional and thinks he hears "voices," he will stay that way permanently in most cases unless he gets on a major tranquilizer soon.

Nebuchadnezzar was King of Babylon and about to take over the rest of the world. He got so arrogant that God made him psychotic for seven years. Then God cured Nebuchadnezzar, and he became a true believer because he had seen firsthand the power of God.

Some psychoses are related to the stresses of spiritual and emotional problems, but most are due to genetic factors. They are no one's fault, just like inheriting diabetes is no one's fault.

And Jesus answered and said to them, "Those who are well do not need a physician, but those who are sick."
—LUKE 5:31

There are a higher number of faithful Christians today than there were in the era of Dr. Luke, John and the apostle Paul. And yet, *genuine* miracles were very common then and more rare today.

God allowed special miracles and gifts to prevail then to prove Christ was the promised Messiah. But in 1 Corinthians 13:8–10, the apostle Paul said many of these special gifts and miracles would cease when "that which is perfect" is completed. Historically, these gifts ceased at the same time that the Scriptures were completed. Genuine miracles still occur today, but not as often.

Some people say you don't need a physician when you are physically sick, but Jesus said you do, *and* you need the Great Physician when you are spiritually sick. A friend of mine does laser surgery to restore sight to certain kinds of blind people and heal eye diseases. God uses his hands, eyes and instruments to heal blind believers and unbelievers. Without men like him, most of these patients would remain blind no matter how much faith they had.

God can easily heal anything supernaturally whenever He wants to. But progressive sanctification *of His saints* is *His bigger priority.*

> *"Sanctify them by Your truth. Your word is truth.*
> —JOHN 17:17

Carl and Heather had five teenagers. Carl maintained a full-time ministry.

An alcoholic ran into their son's motorcycle on the highway, killing their son. The family denied their anger and never grieved or wept, even at the funeral, because their friends said it was wrong. But they were grieving on the inside without knowing it.

Two months later, another of their sons died—this time by suicide. Again, no grief. Two months later, their teenage daughter committed suicide. Still no grief. Six weeks later, Heather became psychotic and finally her husband brought her to us.

With medications, she was brought back to sanity. Then we built her up with supportive therapy. *Then we told her the truth!* We told her she was filled with normal grief and rage from all her losses. We told Heather that her legalistic friends meant well, but were ignorant.

Finally, it all hit her like a ton of bricks and she wept for weeks. She forgave the alcoholic who killed her son, her two teenagers who committed suicide, and her friends. Her husband and surviving children received family therapy. All recovered, and have done well ever since.

May God sanctify us all with the truth.

When I was a child, I spoke as a child, I
understood as a child, I thought as a child; but
when I became a man, I put away childish things.
—1 COR. 13:11

Some parents don't allow their children to be children. They make their kids work and study nearly every day of their lives from the time they are five or six years old or even younger. I feel sorry for most "child prodigies."

I think it's wonderful that some children of all races are born with special genius. But they need to have fun, too. Academics should be down several notches on their priority lists. Knowing God, developing Christ-like character, and enjoying childhood should all be much higher. Pushing too much work and stealing a young one's childhood is a form of child abuse.

We also treat some adults who refuse to grow up. They refuse to be responsible, refuse to pay their bills, refuse to work, refuse to do the hard but enjoyable work of child-rearing, refuse to be faithful to their mates, and refuse to grow spiritually even though some of them claim they have trusted Christ.

May God grant us the ability to let children be children, but progressive sanctification requires that we, as adults, mature by learning to love.

> *Therefore, if anyone is in Christ, he is a new creation; old things have passed away; behold, all things have become new.* —2 COR. 5:17

This passage confuses a great many believers and requires another look at the original Greek for clarification.

The verse looks like it is saying that when a person with psychological and spiritual hangups (which includes *all* of us) becomes a Christian, everything is instantly changed. Everything is new. The hangups are gone.

If that were true, it would contradict hundreds of other Bible verses and the lives and failures of nearly every Bible hero. Even King David messed up pretty badly!

The original Greek says that when we become a believer, old attitudes and behaviors are passing away and all attitudes and behaviors are *becoming new*. It is *progressive sanctification* in the Bible that God wrote. Always go by the original.

Modern translators have a difficult task and do a great job most of the time. We are deeply grateful and indebted to them for making the original Greek and Hebrew so readable for lay people of all major languages today. The original Hebrew and Greek are absolutely perfect with no errors whatsoever.

Jesus, by trusting You as my Savior, You have made me a new creature. Please bring more and more godly behavior into my life.

*For the weapons of our warfare are not carnal
but mighty in God for pulling down strongholds.*
—2 COR. 10:4

Did you ever watch an athletic event (the Olympics included) where the referee made a deciding call that was so obviously bad that you were absolutely *certain* that he was paid off or else bet money himself on the outcome of that event? I have felt that way several times, but I have always restrained myself. I turned vengeance over to God, who will avenge every injustice eventually.

But sporting events are nothing compared to adults abusing children. I have to drastically limit the time I spend listening to the horrible but true stories of abuse many of our patients have suffered growing up.

I think we would be inhumane if we didn't feel like taking the law into our own hands and severely punishing the child abusers we know about. But that would be wrong. We *must* turn them in to the proper authorities as required by law. We can trust God to even it all out.

The apostle Paul said the weapons of our warfare are not carnal. That means we should obey the laws and use spiritual weapons. And you know what? We have confronted many abusers, using the Word of God, and some have genuinely repented, gotten long-term therapy, and matured into productive, Christ-like men and women.

"Progressive sanctification" means turning all vengeance over to God, obeying the laws of the land, and using spiritual weapons to do God's work. This one isn't always easy!

> *For this is the will of God, your sanctification: that
> you should abstain from sexual immorality; that
> each of you should know how to possess his own
> vessel in sanctification and honor.*
> —1 THESS. 4:3–4

Dr. Minirth and I have taught future pastors at several different seminaries over the years. When we teach them about "sexual sanctification," we like to ask them whether they are one-hour Christians, one-minute Christians, or one-second Christians.

Then we explain to them that when a nonbeliever gets a lustful thought, he dwells on it and develops it in his brain as long as he wants to—until he gets bored or figures out a way to actually carry the fantasy out in real life. But Christians have the Holy Spirit convicting us of sin.

All believers will also have lustful temptations. Some believers will get a lustful thought and rebel against the Holy Spirit by dwelling on it for a whole hour, then true guilt wins out and they stop and confess it to God. We call this person who does this a one-hour Christian. Fantasizing illicit sex will eventually weaken you until you practice it.

When the Christian becomes progressively sanctified, he fantasizes for one minute before stopping and confessing. And eventually, he or she can turn illicit sexual fantasies off within a second of the tempting thought. Now they are one-second Christians.

Help me strive to become a one-second Christian.

Faith by itself, if it does not have works, is dead.
—JAMES 2:17

If God's Word is inerrant, and it is, then every single verse has to gel with every other verse in the Bible, every single prophecy has to be fulfilled *perfectly,* and every historical fact will eventually be verified by archaeological research. I'm the world's greatest skeptic, so I have looked for mistakes. There's not a single "appropriate contradiction" that doesn't have a logical solution. I thank God for men like Norm Geisler and others who have painstakingly proven the Word of God to be true.

In Ephesians 2:8–9, Paul wrote that we are saved by grace through faith. Paul also said we cannot be saved by works. God knows we would boast if we could earn salvation and we can't be good enough to go to heaven anyway because the Father demands sinless perfection with not a single sin. That's why He accepts Jesus, who *was* and *is* sinless, in our place.

James said if anyone says he has trusted Christ, but has no good works, he is not really saved. James is correct, of course, because the very moment we trust Christ as Savior, the Holy Spirit produces good works in us. The good works become more and more frequent and better in quality throughout our lives as we become *progressively sanctified.*

Depending on Christ's death on the cross to save you is all it takes. Good works, as James declares, will automatically follow.

> *We know that whoever is born of God does not sin;*
> *but he who has been born of God keeps himself,*
> *and the wicked one does not touch him.*
> —1 JOHN 5:18

I picked out this passage for you today because it is another one that confuses Christians if you don't look at the original Greek and compare it to other passages of Scripture.

Remember that John himself wrote in 1 John 1, that *all believers sin*. John said that if we claim we don't sin any more, then we are liars and we are calling God a liar too, because He says believers do sin. Almost all the Bible heroes have their post-conversion sins exposed for the world to see. Paul talked about his sinning in Romans 6 and 7. Peter's impulsive sins were also recorded and he had quite a few.

What 1 John 5:18 is saying in the original Greek is that the true believer does *not* practice habitual, willful, conscious sins for very long. God said if someone does, he never trusted Christ in the first place and was never a believer. All believers commit willful sins once in a while. That's why we need to be progressively sanctified.

But Satan can't possess a believer or control a believer. He can't touch us unless we allow him to. If we resist him, he flees from us.

If you are committing conscious, willful, habitual sins, you are in grave danger. *Confess them to the Lord and repent.*

My iniquities have overtaken me, so that I am not
able to look up; They are more than the hairs of
my head; Therefore my heart fails me. Be pleased,
O LORD, to deliver me. —PS. 40:12–13

Nearly all addictions are *shame-driven*. Abused persons suffer from the shame of false guilt. They erroneously blame themselves for "deserving" to be abused. Then, on top of all that false guilt, all of us have sinned many times and experienced true guilt. If we could turn all vengeance over to God and trust Christ completely, we would not feel any guilt whatsoever.

You don't have to *feel* guilt-free to *be* guilt-free. The moment you trust Christ as Savior, you are permanently guilt-free positionally in God the Father's eyes, because you are clothed in the righteousness of Christ. But, of course, believers still sin and have to confess to restore fellowship with the Father.

King David was overwhelmed with shame and condemnation when Nathan confronted him about having committed adultery and murder. That was when David wrote today's passage. But David *felt* forgiven and felt relieved of his shame when he finally forgave himself much later.

————————

May God grant to each of us His tender mercies, His loving kindness,
His truth, and His forgiveness.

May 6 – SHAME AND CONDEMNATION

> There is *therefore now no condemnation to those*
> *who are in Christ Jesus.*
> —ROM. 8:1a

Many adult children of abuse refuse to accept the love that is offered to them. They are so down on themselves, and so ashamed for things that were not even their fault, that they feel falsely guilty if they accept love.

They push people away by sarcasm or isolation. In the hospital halls I know better than to walk up and give them a side-by-side hug. They will usually stiffen like a board and feel fear and panic. They will find a way to push me away. They might even check out of the hospital and not work on their emotional wounds. I go easy until they are ready for a hug.

Sometimes they have trouble accepting Christ's love, too. They say they don't deserve it. I tell them they are absolutely right! That's what makes Christ's love so special. He loved us while we were yet sinners, while we didn't deserve it.

And because He died in our place, if we accept His gift of grace, then there is no longer any condemnation, no more shame! Our sins are as far removed from us as the east is from the west. They are buried in the deepest sea. The Father says He will remember them no more, meaning He will never bring them up to us again (even though He does remember what we have done wrong).

We can learn to love and be loved again by accepting God's love.
Insight-oriented therapy with forgiveness also helps break down
those walls.

Having faith and a good conscience, which some having rejected, concerning the faith have suffered shipwreck.
—1 TIM. 1:19

Shame and condemnation are devastating enemies. They make it difficult to fall asleep at night. They lower self-esteem, which lowers our ability to live and feel loved by God, mate, children, and peers. They deplete our energy and motivation.

A clear conscience is worth more than being a billionaire and is something we should all strive for, but is difficult to attain.

There are several requirements for a clear conscience. The first is faith in Christ to wash away all of our past, present, and future sins positionally. Then we must have realistic expectations of what we can and cannot accomplish morally. We cannot accomplish sinless perfection. If that is our expectation, we will live with constant shame and self-condemnation.

Neither can we give up on morality and "live in sin that grace may abound." Our true guilt would eat us alive if we did that. Instead, we must grow in Christ as rapidly as possible and expect slow, steady progress. We should not compare ourselves to others but should compare ourselves morally now to how we used to be and pat ourselves on the back, with a clear conscience, for the progress we are making with God's help (see Gal. 6:4).

A clear conscience is a goal I should strive for, so I will write out a specific plan of attack in my own life for developing this valued prize.

> *By faith the harlot Rahab did not perish with those*
> *who did not believe, when she had received the*
> *spies with peace.* —HEB. 11:31

Adult children of abuse, especially sexual abuse, sometimes feel like they are "trash" to be used, abused and finally discarded. Probably the vast majority of prostitutes were sexually abused as children.

Rahab the harlot was a prostitute, but she made it to God's hall of fame in Hebrews 11. God loves to save prostitutes, too, if they will put their faith in Christ. Rahab trusted God and protected the Israeli spies when the Jews defeated Jericho. God made the walls of Jericho fall down because the Jews had faith in God and marched around the city for seven days. But God left standing the part of the wall attached to Rahab's house, with her relatives crowded in it.

We also see that God chose Rahab to be in the genealogy of Jesus. Does that tell you anything about whether Jesus accepts with open arms even prostitutes who repent? He said He came to save sinners.

Rather than being prejudiced against the sexually abused or sexually sinful, Jesus loves them and wants to adopt them.

Therefore it is also contained in the Scripture,
"Behold, I lay in Zion a chief cornerstone, elect,
precious, And he who believes on Him will by no
means be put to shame." —1 PETER 2:6

Shame can grow into negative addictions. Shame can also lead to obsessions (thoughts, that won't leave your mind even when you try to quit thinking about them) and/or compulsions (teeth-grinding, knuckle-cracking, excessive handwashing, spotless housecleaning, etc.).

These all serve two purposes: They are emotionally painful, so they are a way to consistently take vengeance on yourself; they keep your mind off your rage, shame and self-condemnation, so they are less painful than the alternative.

But obsessions, compulsions, rage, shame, and condemnation are all curable. Weekly outpatient therapy or intensive hospital therapy can help a person enjoy life shame-free. ACA groups really help too.

Most adult children of abuse have trouble trusting authority figures, so they have a tough time checking into a psychiatry unit. They are afraid of the pain of looking at truth. They are ashamed of betraying the abusers. They are afraid to give up their fantasy that the abuser will some day repent and love them.

Getting well from the effects of child abuse requires giving up all the bad habits, addictions, obsessions and compulsions.

May 10 – SHAME AND CONDEMNATION

> *For if our heart condemns us, God is greater than our heart, and knows all things.*
>
> —1 JOHN 3:20

When I was thirty years old, I was a workaholic and a masochist to a large extent, ignoring my wife and infant children. My family got squeezed out by "service to God."

When I repented and obeyed God by meeting the needs of my family and my own spiritual health *before* ministering to others, I struggled with lingering false guilt for about three years. I was doing exactly what I thought God wanted me to do. He said if I didn't take care of needs of my family, I am worse in His eyes than an infidel.

Basically, this passage is saying that if your heart condemns you for something God clearly does *not* condemn you for, then assume God is correct.

For the next seven days, try this experiment: Every time you hear yourself or your mate use the word "should" or the word "shouldn't," interrupt the conversation to ask, "Where is that should (or shouldn't) coming from?" Is it from God's Word? If so, where? Is it from parental injunctions? If so, do I choose to keep living by this non-biblical injunction? Why? If one mate is using lots of "shoulds" and "shouldn'ts" on the other, he or she is trying to be a substitute parent. That is codependent. Put a stop to it right away. You have a right to your own feelings, but not to control the other person's behavior as a parent-child relationship.

This single seven-day experiment could revolutionize your life.

Now to Him who is able to keep you from stumbling, And to present you faultless Before the presence of His glory with exceeding joy, To God our Savior, Who alone is wise, Be glory and majesty, Dominion and power, Both now and forever. Amen.
—JUDE 1:24–25

I wish I could take a little trip to heaven to have a chat with Jesus. I'm sure it would quadruple my courage and He would give me insights as to how I could be more effective for Him on earth. But if God granted that wish, I would be afraid of first meeting Him. I would be ashamed for all my countless sins of thought and action since trusting Christ at age six. I know they are forgiven, but no one is perfect at self-forgiveness.

But as soon as Christ would lift up my head to face His eyes, and I would see a smile on His face, and He would give me an accepting hug, I would feel fine. I would confidently start rattling off a thousand questions I have for Him.

From the moment I trusted Christ I have been and always will be *positionally faultless,* because the Father sees me clothed in the righteousness of my Substitute. When it comes to our everyday behavior and thoughts as believers, we are not faultless.

It sure feels good to know that when I do face Jesus in person for the first time, I am already positionally faultless. There is no valid reason for shame or condemnation, since He bore my shame.

> *Behold, You desire truth in the inward parts, and*
> *in the hidden* part *you will make me to know*
> *wisdom. Purge me with hyssop, and I shall be*
> *clean; Wash me, and I shall be whiter than snow.*
> —PS. 51:6–7

Some believers are so heavenly minded they are no earthly good. They live in the future so much they don't help people in the present. God obviously wants us to know about the Rapture, the one thousand year messianic kingdom, the eternal state, the New Jerusalem, and the new earth. He wouldn't have given us half the Bible as prophetic books if He didn't want us to study it and hope for the future.

But if I study my future during all my waking moments, and don't help others in pain, then my talents are wasted.

Other extremists live in the past. They keep dwelling on past failures and harboring bitterness toward themselves for past sins. As a result, they are partially serotonin-depleted and without enough energy and motivation to serve Christ. They will still go to heaven, but will also lose much of their reward. What a waste of good talent.

King David wrote today's passage. In it he strongly encourages us to seek truth in our inward parts. Sure we have sinned a lot. Welcome to the human race! So what? God forgave us and washed us positionally whiter than snow the day we first trusted Christ to save us. My sins are blotted out—I know! Jesus said so!

Ask God to create in you a clean heart and a clear conscience. Put the past behind you.

And He came and preached peace to you who were afar off and to those who were near. For through Him we both have access by one Spirit to the Father.
—EPH. 2:17–18

If someone grew up in a good home, Christian or non-Christian, where they felt loved by both parents and their parents were trustworthy, then most of this group will trust Christ easily. All they need are the facts and some objective evidence that Christ really is who He claims to be—God in the flesh. They are near to knowing Christ before you ever share the facts with them.

Adult children of abuse have more difficult psychological blocks in making the correct spiritual decision. Their abusers were con men so they suspect that whoever is sharing Christ with them is having primarily ulterior motives as well. They couldn't trust their earthly father in some cases, so why should they trust a supernatural Father? That kind would be especially fearful to be around. They are *far off* from trusting Christ. The Holy Spirit has to work overtime to help empower them over the hump of personal faith.

When making spiritual decisions of any kind, we won't be objective if we prejudice our decisions by past abuses. We have to put the past behind us, whether we are near, or far off, because "through Him we both have access by one Spirit to the Father."

Quit looking prejudicially at God through sunglasses colored the shade of your past abusers. Be objective.

> _Brethren, I do not count myself to have_
> _apprehended; but one thing I do, forgetting those_
> _things which are behind and reaching forward to_
> _those things which are ahead, I press toward_
> _the goal._
> —PHIL. 3:13

If you put grasshoppers in a jar, they can easily jump out. But if you put a lid on it (with small breathing holes), they will try to jump out for a day or two, bump their heads on the lid, and give up. You can then remove the lid, and they will never jump out, because they have negative self-talk: "Don't try; you'll only bump your head."

Some adult children of abuse think like that. Now the abusers are gone or they can choose to not be abused any longer, but they won't put the past behind them and serve Christ with all their heart.

Other adults have had some great successes in their Christian walk. They could easily dwell on past successes and "retire" from Christian service. They could rest on past laurels. We need to also put past successes behind us and keep serving Christ, not as masochistic workaholics, but as happy servants.

When my friends ask me what specific age I plan to retire, I tell them it will be when I am either brain dead or in heaven and not a day sooner. I will always do whatever I can to live a balanced life and serve Christ as efficiently as possible.

Lord, help me not to be so ashamed of past failures or so proud of past successes that I fail to press on in my service to You.

It is *better to dwell in a corner of a housetop, Than in a house shared with a contentious woman.*
—PROV. 25:24

Adult children of abuse are prone to masochism. Some of them tend to go through life continuing to get stepped on or to be taken advantage of by all the selfish people they subconsciously surround themselves with.

There are several reasons why some are masochistic. Because of false guilt, they feel as though they deserve continued abuse *unconsciously.* They keep punishing themselves.

It's a way to stay depressed and pass the unconscious vengeance they have toward the abusive parent to a mate. This is a way to "punish" that abusive parent.

They use masochistic suffering as a way to get attention at church groups and with other groups.

From our two passages for today from Proverbs, we see that we are not supposed to be masochistic. We should not put false hopes on an unfaithful person or we will end up with a psychological "toothache" or "foot out of joint."

If we are married to a critical, contentious mate, we should learn coping and communication skills to protect ourselves. If we let it affect us, that is our own fault once we learn a self-protecting system.

God expects me to protect myself from the insults of my abusers.

> *Whoever slaps you on your right cheek, turn the other to him also.*
> —MATT. 5:39

Many people misinterpret this passage to be a call to general masochism. I have seen believers let others take advantage of them, use them, abuse them, rip them off financially, lie about them, etc. When I ask them why, they tell me they are trying to be like Jesus and bring up this passage as an example.

That's what can happen if you misapply one verse out of context. You have to interpret Scripture in light of other Scripture.

What did Jesus do when he saw religious leaders ripping people off in the temple? Did he correct them politely, then lie down and ask them to please step on Him? No! He took a whip and beat the hot air out of their sails.

Many verses tell us to protect ourselves from abusers. In this passage, Jesus is saying only that if you are slapped on the cheek for being a committed believer, then turn the cheek and give them permission to slap the other one. If they have any conscience at all, this will "heap coals of fire on their heads" (Prov. 25:21–22).

You will also notice that Jesus doesn't say what to do if the abuser *does* slap you on the other cheek. He leaves that up to your good judgment. I would leave all my biblically acceptable options open.

Pray for godly wisdom and be prepared to "turn the other cheek."

*The wicked borrows and does not repay, But the
righteous shows mercy and gives.* —PS. 37:21

For the next couple of weeks, we will be carefully ex-
amining the psychological and spiritual traits of abusers. Sociopathic personalities are people who are
extremely self-centered and see other humans as ob-
jects to be used, abused, manipulated, ripped off and
discarded. They have almost *no* conscience, but pre-
tend to be sorry when caught in a manipulative device.

Every sin that you or I commit is a sociopathic trait,
since every sin hurts somebody. But if you feel guilty
when you sin, that is great. True guilt is *good*. It motivates you and me to change—to grow Christ-like.

Today's passage tells us the difference between a sociopath and a good person when it comes to money.
The *sociopath* will rent an apartment from you, pay a
deposit and one or two months rent, then stay there for
free, making excuses about why he can't pay the rent.

The Bible says to boot him out. If you let him get
away with it you are promoting his sin. If you love him,
you will face his hostility and rejection. It is best for
you and him (or her).

_____

*Most severe sociopaths will never change no matter what you do.
And they almost certainly won't change if you are foolishly paying
them to be that way.*

He devises evil continually, He sows discord.
Therefore his calamity shall come suddenly;
Suddenly he shall be broken without remedy.
—PROV. 6:14—15

Sociopaths (abusers) are lost unless they turn to Christ. They must either turn or burn. They have perverse mouths, spouting out curse words, sexual innuendoes, and arrogant boasts. If a person talks this way, you can be certain he or she has no conscience.

He flirts with someone who belongs to someone else, or lets his sociopathic friends know he is conning someone. Don't listen to his words. His actions speak louder than his words. A trained person watches the body language. Sociopaths tend to dramatically draw attention to themselves by excessive gestures, squinting, tears, and or trying to look extra "holy."

The sociopath is perverse, always thinking secretly about sins he can commit. He loves to sow discord; it relieves his boredom. He especially loves to set people against each other at work, at church, or in his own home.

Sociopaths suffer sudden calamity because God wants it that way. God does this supernaturally at times, and through His natural laws as well.

Avoid being manipulated by people who exhibit sociopathic traits. God gave us passages like this one to protect us.

*These six things the L*ORD* hates, Yes, seven are an*
abomination to Him: A proud look, A lying tongue,
Hands that shed innocent blood, A heart that
devises wicked plans, Feet that are swift in running
to evil, A false witness who speaks lies, And one
who sows discord among brethren.
—PROV. 6:16–19

If we took a poll of about a million people in each nation and asked them to list the seven worst sins, probably no two nations would come up with the same list in the same order.

Surprisingly, when we study God's list we see that we have probably all exhibited some of these behaviors at some time. We must search for sociopathic traits and "weed" them out of our behavioral "garden."

Number one on God's list is a proud look, probably because pride is a root cause of nearly every sin. A lying tongue is listed second. Many Old and New Testament passages tell us that if we could control our tongue, we could control our whole bodies. The third sin listed (not necessarily the third worst) is murder. The fourth listed is the mind, emotions, and will that keep thinking about sinful fantasies or plans. The fifth is a tendency to "run" into sinful habits when the opportunity presents itself. The sixth is telling lies about anyone. The seventh is sowing discord among fellow believers in particular. This can even refer to telling the truth about a fellow believer to a person who is not part of the problem or part of the solution.

As we grieve and forsake our own sociopathy our sense of self-worth grows and grows.

> *To do evil is like sport to a fool, But a man*
> *of understanding has wisdom.* —PROV. 10:23

If sociopaths have no conscience, why put them in prison? Do they really learn anything from the prison experience? Actually, prisons are good for two reasons. They keep sociopathic people off the streets. And sociopaths do fear punishment even though they generally have no sorrow for the pain they have caused others.

God loves to save sociopaths if they do repent. There are many passages in the Bible about reaching out to help prisoners, many of whom are sociopathic. We owe a debt of gratitude to people like Chuck Colson who devote their lives to helping men and women in prisons. Most sociopaths never go to prison, though, and all of us humans have sociopathic tendencies.

Our passage for today tells us that sinning is like competing in a sport to a sociopathic fool. His fear of consequences will come true, because God says to be certain that all of our sins will be found out and consequences suffered unless we genuinely repent. Then we will be forgiven, but still may suffer natural and legal consequences for years to come. Remember that as fast as a whirlwind passes, the unrepentant sociopath will be dead and in hell, but the righteous (who have put their faith in Christ) will live in heaven forever.

Don't worry about a sociopath except to lovingly minister to him in a non-codependent way, while protecting yourself from him.

He who is *slow to wrath has great understanding,*
But he who is *impulsive exalts folly.*
—PROV. 14:29

Impulsiveness is one of the most classic sociopathic tendencies. The sociopath wants *what* he wants, *when* he wants it. He is the victim of his own emotional impulsiveness, without enough logic to control his impulses, and without enough wisdom to comprehend the eventual consequences of his sin.

When a mature man or woman has normal, God-given, hormonal sexual urges, he thinks about his or her mate and makes plans for delayed gratification at the convenience of the spouse. Their pleasure makes God happy (see Prov. 5).

When a sociopath has a similar hormonal sexual urge, he is ruled by it, seeking *immediate* gratification. He will resort to adultery, homosexuality, bestiality, or whatever is available to fulfill his urge right away.

He also feels a sense of entitlement. He feels the arrogant right to use whomever or whatever he wants to fulfill sexual or any other urges, regardless of consequences to others or even to himself. He doesn't care about the person he uses either, although he pretends to. In fact, he thinks illicit fulfillment is preferable to fulfilling his urges in moral ways because fear of getting caught and the challenge of sin causes a pleasurable adrenaline release, which is what he is after anyway.

Logically thinking out the truth takes all the fun out of sin, which is what it is intended to do.

> *The rod and reproof give wisdom, but a child left*
> to himself *brings shame to his mother.*
>
> —PROV. 29:15

Every one of us was born with a sociopathic personality, impulsiveness, and entitlement. The love, discipline, and example of our parents are *major* influences that move us away from those tendencies.

The Minnesota Crime Commission released the following statement a number of years ago: "Every baby starts life as a little savage. He is completely selfish and self-centered. He wants what he wants when he wants it—his bottle, his mother's attention, his playmate's toy, his uncle's watch. Deny him these once, and he seethes with rage and aggressiveness, which would be murderous were he not so helpless. He has no morals, no knowledge, no skill. All are born delinquent. If permitted to continue in the self-centered world of his infancy, every child would grow up a criminal—a thief, a killer, or a rapist." (From Charles R. Swindoll's book, *Growing Deep in the Christian Life*, 214–215: Multnomah Press, 1986)

In a large poll of businessmen and businesswomen a few years ago, 75 percent admitted that they would lie and cheat in business to get money if they thought that they wouldn't get caught.

Most sociopaths received too little discipline growing up, but about a third were physically abused. They became angry at authority figures in their lives and, as adults, they transferred their anger to decent authority figures.

It takes love and discipline to change our children or ourselves.

Do not remove the ancient landmark
Which your fathers have set. —PROV. 22:28

Today's passage tells us to honor literal, legal, and physical land boundaries. But by implication, and from many other passages throughout the Bible, we can easily see that God expects us to honor many kinds of boundaries: sexual, social, moral, financial, psychological, legal, etc.

Boundaries are a vital issue in our development.

The sociopath was usually spoiled as a child. As a three-year-old sitting in a grocery cart, his mother tends to buy whatever he grabs rather than teaching him limits and slapping the back of his hand for open rebellion. As an adult, he still feels *entitlement* to everyone and everything.

Beautiful children have a real disadvantage in life. They grow up getting away with too much. Even peers want their approval, so they give them power and things they are not really entitled to. It's hard to find a very beautiful or handsome adult who doesn't struggle with more sociopathy than he or she would have if he or she had not been handicapped with great beauty. If you have a beautiful child, mention it *rarely*. Praise him or her instead for developing godly character traits.

———————

The rights of others end where my nose begins. I will affirm and defend my God-given boundaries.

> *A lying tongue hates* those who are *crushed by it,*
> And a flattering mouth works ruin.
> —PROV. 26:28

Don't believe it when a sociopath tells you he didn't mean to hurt anyone with his (or her) lies. The hatred may be conscious, unconscious (out of awareness), or subconscious (just below the surface). If they loved you, they wouldn't lie about you.

Don't believe them when they flatter you, either. They master flattery at a very early age to manipulate and get what they want. For all practical purposes, they hate you if they manipulatively flatter you also.

Remember that most sociopaths were spoiled so they feel entitled. Whenever the *real* world hits them (school teachers, bosses, scout leaders, etc.), they hear loving authorities tell them "No!" This makes them angry, so they hate authority. They lie about authorities and manipulate them via flattery.

Remember also that about a third of sociopaths were the victims of child abuse, especially excessive physical abuse. Their hearts are filled with hatred toward the abusive parents. But this hatred gets *displaced* to authority figures in general, even good authority figures. They call all policemen and policewomen "pigs." They will use a few "bad cops" as examples to justify hating them all.

Lord, protect me from flattering lies.

Those who forsake the law praise the wicked, But such as keep the law contend with them.
—PROV. 28:4

Misery loves company. Sociopaths do too. Most pick a "religion" that will justify their behavior.

Remember that the biggest sociopaths in Jesus' days on earth were the Pharisees—religious leaders whom the culture of that day would have considered very *moral* outwardly.

Many believers who have a lot of unconscious sociopathy honestly think they are "called" by the Holy Spirit to raise support for ministries that don't really require much work out of them. Plus, there are out-and-out conscious sociopaths who use trusting people to support "ministries" that don't exist and promise to send Bibles but really don't.

In their own little group of sociopathic friends, they laugh at you for being stupid enough to send them money. They praise their wicked friends for being "takers" like they are, rather than "givers" and "do-gooders" like those who support them. If you are a moral person who loves the law of Christ and obeys the laws of the land, Solomon said you will *contend* with them. Be careful to whom you donate money. If they go broke without your support, there's an excellent chance God wanted it that way.

Sociopaths tend to pick friends and a religious system that they can manipulate. Don't put up with it. Contend with them, but be careful how you do it.

> "There is *no peace*," says the LORD, "for the
> *wicked*."
> —ISA. 48:22

Sociopaths may have lots of money. They may have lots of momentary pleasure and adrenaline release. They may even have lots of excitement. But they have a high anxiety level and very low genuine self-esteem. They come across very prideful and with great arrogance, but that phony mask covers up loads of unconscious pain, insecurity and inferiority feelings.

After all, their entire lives are a rat race, dedicated to proving they are not really nobodies via lusts of the flesh, lusts of the eyes (materialism) and the pride of life (power struggles and prestige). If they felt significant on the inside, they wouldn't have to devote so much time, energy, and money, at such great risks of danger to themselves, to the human rat race to disprove their fear of nobodyness. They would rather be dead than to be a "nobody."

They have both traditional anxiety (worry) and true anxiety (a psychiatric condition). They worry frequently about getting caught and suffering consequences. They also have true anxiety, which comes from a *fear* of seeing the truth about the extreme extent of their own sociopathic thoughts, feelings and motives.

Sociopaths have no peace because they fear the consequences of their risk-taking and because they unconsciously fear seeing the truth.

Sow for yourselves righteousness; Reap in mercy;
Break up your fallow ground, For it is time to seek
*the L*ORD*, Till He comes and rains righteousness on*
you.
                                        —HOS. 10:12

I read my Bible almost daily. But this passage never "stood out and hit me between the eyes" until a time of personal rededication in my life.

Remember that *all* of us, Christian or non-Christian, have some sociopathy (sinful behavioral tendencies). I detest it in myself. I wish it wasn't true, but it is. Once we trust Christ, we are positionally perfect forever in the Father's eyes. We begin a progressive sanctification process immediately that lasts a lifetime whereby we grow toward Christ-likeness gradually. We have occasional spiritual regressions, but we have growth spurts too!

We have special times in our lives when the Holy Spirit breaks through our sociopathic defenses and we "see the light" shining on our subtle, sociopathic motives. During those special times, we should break up our "fallow ground"—like a farmer does before he plants his crop. *Now* is the time to seek the Lord. He promises that if we open the "fallow ground" in our hearts to Him, He will excitedly come into our hearts in a special way to "rain righteousness" on us. What a glorious promise. What a merciful God.

_____

I will allow today to be one of those special days in my life when I gain insight into my own depravity (sociopathy); I will detest it, expose it to the light of God's Word, repent of it, and make re-decisions about my level of morality.

> *But exhort one another daily, while it is called*
> *"Today," lest any of you be hardened through the*
> *deceitfulness of sin.*
> —HEB. 3:13

You may have noticed that all of the passages we have examined on sociopathy so far have come from the Old Testament, especially Proverbs. Solomon was the wisest human, other than Christ, to ever live, and he specialized in human behavior. We will examine Solomon's teachings off and on throughout this book.

We thought it would be good to also get a perspective on sociopathy from the apostle Paul, a former Pharisee. He used to murder Christians and fool himself into thinking he was serving God by doing so.

In Hebrews 3:13, Paul encourages all of us who are true believers to exhort each other daily, as the opportunities present themselves. Exhorting means not only positive encouragement, but constructive criticism as well—speaking the truth in love with a humble attitude.

We need loving exhortation on a regular basis to become aware of the subtle sociopathic weeds growing in our spiritual garden. Those weeds are easier to face when we are exhorted by a loving, humble friend who has our best interest at heart.

I will love my friends enough to humbly exhort them when I see obvious sociopathic "weeds" in their lives. I will ask them to do the same for me.

> *Now the works of the flesh are evident, which are:*
> *adultery, fornication, uncleanness, licentiousness,*
> *idolatry, sorcery, hatred, contentions, jealousies,*
> *outbursts of wrath, selfish ambitions, dissensions,*
> *heresies, envy, murders, drunkenness, revelries, and*
> *the like; of which I tell you beforehand, just as I*
> *also told you in time past, that those who practice*
> *such things will not inherit the kingdom of God.*
> —GAL. 5:19–21

In today's passage, the apostle Paul writes his own list of sociopathic (sinful) behaviors to avoid. He calls them "works of the flesh."

Paul's list includes: extramarital affairs, premarital sex, sociopathic thoughts, words or deeds, shameless, open, conscious display of sociopathic behaviors, worshipping anything other than God, witchcraft, satan worship, astrology, or the use of "spirit guides," hatred between groups of people, contentions, jealousies, temper tantrums, competing to prove your significance compared to others, dissensions, doctrinal factions that disagree with Scripture, wanting another person's possessions, murders, drunkenness, drunken orgies.

Paul said that those who habitually practice such things prove they never trusted Christ in the first place.

———

I will examine myself today to see if I have tendencies in any of these areas, so I can depend on Christ to help me weed them out.

You shall not hate your brother in your heart . . .
but you shall love your neighbor as yourself: I am
the Lord.
—LEV. 19:17–18

Many Christians have been poorly trained in the correct handling of anger. They have been taught: Anger is always a sin, sharing it is rude, you are a bad person if you experience it. Some have also been erroneously taught that you should only forgive if the offender apologizes and that it is OK to get even (vengeance) if he doesn't apologize.

In our passage for today, as well as in Ephesians 4:26 and many other places, we see clearly the opposite. We should not hate a brother who offends us, but when we do feel angry toward him, we should rebuke him *without sinning.* Never "get-even." Turn all vengeance over to God (see Rom. 12). That's His department, not ours. Don't hold any grudges, because God designed human physiology so that prolonged, severe grudges toward God, others, or ourselves cause insomnia, sadness, trouble in concentrating, tiredness, and suicidal thoughts. Most of the depression psychiatrists treat are caused by violating the principles God put in today's passage. God wants us to love our neighbor by being honest with him about our anger, speaking the truth in love. He wants us to forgive and bear no grudges or vengeful motives. Leave the rest up to God.

Lord, help me avoid depression in my life by handling my anger biblically.

Do not reprove a scoffer, lest he hate you; Rebuke a wise man, and he will love you. —PROV. 9:8

There have been some people who offended me, and when I tactfully shared my feelings with them, they thanked me. Their behaviors that offended me had offended many of their other friends for years, but none of their friends had the courage to confront the behaviors. We all fear rejection.

My confrontations also helped me. I choose to forgive my offenders no matter what. But I find it much easier to forgive if I have verbalized my anger to my offenders, and easier yet if they apologize, although my forgiving doesn't depend on an apology.

I have also had very negative confrontations. I remember one, for example, a spoiled, beautiful, multi-millionaire woman who was so selfish that she got into frequent conflicts with her loved ones. I was afraid to tell her the truth, even though she was my patient. I had her take a psychological test so the "test" could tell her the truth.

Just as I suspected, she came out higher than 99 percent of respondents on being sociopathic (self-centered). I told her the test results. She stormed out and never came back.

Proverbs says to reprove wise friends, but not to waste your time reproving arrogant scoffers. We have to decide who is mature enough to handle the truth and who isn't. But we must forgive all.

May God grant me humility to accept loving confrontation and courage to speak the truth to my loved ones.

A word fitly spoken is like *apples of gold in settings of silver.*
Open rebuke is *better than love carefully concealed.*
Faithful are *the wounds of a friend.*
　　　　　　　　　　　　　　　　—PROV. 25:11, 27:5–6a

Some people are physically clumsy. I am six feet, five inches tall, but never made a basketball team in high school or college even though I kept trying. I simply cannot walk and chew gum at the same time!

Other people are verbally clumsy. When they confront a friend it comes across as though they are throwing rotten tomatoes at their friend. Solomon said a confrontation should be like golden apples in a silver setting.

The words should be thought out, loving, honest, nonjudgmental, spoken with humility, and primarily a sharing of how you feel about what your friend did. Don't tell your friend what he should or shouldn't do. He needs a friend who loves him enough to tell him what it is that he does that results in anger in others.

Open, loving rebuke is better than secret love. Sociopathic friends seldom confront tactfully. They are phony. They either don't confront at all or they intimidate. Their goals are selfish—to be able to manipulate you and their other friends. But the "wounds" of a loving friend are faithful and helpful. The "kisses" of an enemy are deceitful.

A wise, loving confrontation is a gift—a work of art.

As iron sharpens iron, So a man sharpens the countenance of his friend. He who rebukes a man will find more favor afterward Than he who flatters with the tongue.   —PROV. 27:17, 28:23

When iron rubs against iron, sparks fly. But both iron instruments get sharper. Their value goes up. Their usefulness improves.

Sociopathic "friends" will seldom lovingly confront you. They will either flatter you or intimidate you to manipulate and use you. A true, loving friend will rebuke you tactfully. It may hurt at first, like iron sharpening iron. In fact, sparks may even fly at first. But if both you and your friend are reasonably mature, the friendship will grow deeper and you will both become more valuable and useful to God.

God wants to change you. He wants you to keep your same basic personality, but he wants you to modify yourself, with His help, to become more like His Son, Jesus Christ.

Following are some confrontations God's Word says God uses to sanctify you: from the Holy Spirit, from life's circumstances, from God's powerful Word, the Bible, from your mate who knows the real you, from your children, who don't yet see their own faults but are experts on yours, from your true friends, from sociopaths.

Confrontation is a painful necessity, just like going to the dentist.

The righteous considers the cause of the poor, But the wicked does not understand such knowledge.
—PROV. 29:7

Another "one another" concept God is very intent on teaching us is to help one another financially. There are more verses in the Bible on finances than on heaven and hell. Our financial behavior patterns probably say more about our personality and morality than almost any other area of behavior. We will address these financial patterns extensively later on in this devotional.

Helping the poor is one of the most rewarding experiences in life. It truly is more fun to give than to receive. But there are some important guidelines to follow to avoid sin or codependency.

Don't brag about it. Don't give to the poor so others can see you do it. Jesus said to not even let your left hand know what your right hand is giving to the poor.

Honor the dignity of the poor person. He or she will be a king or queen some day in God's kingdom, so don't be patronizing.

Don't ever make a poor person dependent on you. Only do for him what he cannot do for himself. If he won't work, he should not eat. But if he is having legitimate problems, help him with his overburdens. Get his input on how you can help. Give him some control and dignity.

———————

When it comes to helping the poor, do unto others as you would have them do unto you.

*"Judge not, that you be not judged. And why do
you look at the speck in your brother's eye, but do
not consider the plank in your own eye? Hypocrite!
First remove the plank from your own eye, and
then you will see clearly to remove the speck out of
your brother's eye."*
                                        —MATT. 7:1, 3–5

The "one another" concepts of the Bible include things
to do for each other and also things to avoid. The defense mechanism of "projection" is one of those self-
deceiving mechanisms we are to avoid.

Eighty percent of our thoughts, feelings, and motives are out of our awareness, so we call them unconscious faults or "secret sins." We feel anxious when the
truth about them threatens to emerge. This happens
when we are around someone who has a fault that we
hate in ourselves but don't yet know we have.

When we are around this person, we hate our own
fault but it would hurt to look at it, so we project our
self-hatred onto a person with the mild but similar
fault. It saves face.

Instead of humble insight, we sit up on our self-
righteous high horse and judge and rebuke tactlessly
or in a condescending manner. God says to first remove the plank out of your own eye before you help
your friend remove a "toothpick" or "speck" of saw-
dust in his.

———————

*Looking at all our innermost faults and accepting our own "bad-
ness," subjecting it to God's progressive sanctification process, enables us to love others as we love ourselves.*

> *Therefore if you bring your gift to the altar, and*
> *there remember that your brother has something*
> *against you, leave your gift there before the altar,*
> *and go your way. First be reconciled to your*
> *brother, and then come and offer your gift.*
> —MATT. 5:23–24

This passage really shows us how important our relationships are to God. They are so vital to Him that Jesus said that if we find ourselves sitting in a church some Sunday morning and getting ready to put our donation in the offering plate, then remember somebody who is feeling angry toward us, we should get up and leave and give our offering later.

We should go straight to the person who is feeling angry toward us, even if we aren't mad at him at all. Get him to verbalize his anger toward us with our improved friendship as the goal. Listen to his criticisms and evaluate if they may be true or partially true.

Apologize for whatever you do agree about, but speak the truth in love about the rest. Encourage him to forgive you whether you agree with him or not. Agree to disagree if you must, then drive back to church and put your money in the offering plate. Giving is important, too, just not nearly as important as being reconciled to a brother or sister in Christ.

Lord, show me if there is someone I've offended and give me the courage to go to that friend in a spirit of love and reconciliation.

*Moreover if your brother sins against you, go and
tell him his fault between you and him alone. If he
hears you, you have gained your brother. But if he
will not hear you, take with you one or two more,
that* 'by the mouth of two or three witnesses every
word may be established.' *And if he refuses to hear
them, tell* it *to the church. But if he refuses even to
hear the church, let him be to you like a heathen
and a tax collector.*   —MATT. 18:15–17

There is a "one another" concept in the Bible that a lot
of believers choose to ignore, since we tend to fear rejection. It is to "discipline one another" in the local
church setting.

If a fellow member of your local church clearly sins
against you by lying about you, stealing, not paying
back a loan, making a dishonest business deal, or
whatever, God gives us clear instructions. First, we
should get together with him one-on-one, so as not to
embarrass him publicly if there could be a misunder-
standing.

If he refuses to apologize and repay financial losses,
go to the person with one or two other members of the
local church and confront him again. If he still refuses,
the elders are to confront him, and if he refuses to obey
the church elders, he must be forced to leave the
church. The brother offended should not take him to
the courts until all these procedures are completed
first.

---

*God wants to protect His own reputation, so he wants believers' dis-
putes with each other to stay out of the courts, except as a last resort.*

> *Brethren, if a man is overtaken in any trespass, you*
> *who are spiritual restore such a one in a spirit of*
> *gentleness, considering yourself lest you also be*
> *tempted.*
> —GAL. 6:1

Another "one another" concept Christians are scared of is the command to confront each other when we see a believer sin. God tells us not to "judge" each other in Matthew 7:1–5, then turns around and commands us to confront each other when we think a brother is sinning. It seems like a contradiction, but it isn't.

The confronting person in the Matthew 7:1–5 passage was being hypocritical and condemning. The confronting person in Galatians 6:1 is telling a brother the truth, in a loving manner and a spirit of gentleness, genuine humility, and vulnerability—saying something like, "I am a sinner too; I make mistakes, too. But because I love you as a brother, I am afraid this particular truth is going to hurt you."

The goal of the first confronter was one-up-manship and displacement of projected self-hatred—at least subconsciously. The goal of the second confronter is restoration, in love. Sometimes, because we deceive ourselves so much, we will think we are the second kind when we are being the first. That's why we should examine *ourselves* before confronting sin in a brother, but we should not use the "judging" passage to pass off on our responsibility to confront a sinning brother.

We are commanded, for the sake of all believers, to humbly confront sins we think we see in a fellow believer, but not to self-righteously judge our fellow believers.

> Be *hospitable to one another without grumbling.*
> *As each one has received a gift, minister it to*
> *one another.*   1 PETER 4:9–10

This "one another" concept is more fun to practice. It could be phrased: Use your spiritual gifts and natural talents to benefit one another.

When we become believers by putting our faith in Christ, the Holy Spirit immediately and permanently indwells us and seals us (see Eph. 1) until we get to heaven. The Holy Spirit also gives us spiritual gifts.

Christian scholars sometimes disagree on the extent that special spiritual gifts are a factor today. Opinions range from all of them being currently extinct, to some of them being extinct (1 Cor. 13:8–10 appears to indicate that some would cease when the Bible was completed), to all of them still being present. We need to avoid being dogmatic, and let God decide which gifts to use in which ages.

The phrase "spiritual gift" means that God enables you supernaturally to do something you would not be able to do using your natural talents alone. For example, when I am doing therapy, sometimes a verse will pop into my head that I have never memorized and it can be a significant help to that patient.

Is remembering that verse word for word a mental talent? Is it a spiritual gift? Is it some of both? I suspect it is both, but my self-concept does not *depend* on having supernatural gifts.

I want to use every spiritual and natural gift God has given me.

> *And be kind to one another, tenderhearted,*
> *forgiving one another, just as God in Christ*
> *also forgave you.*   —EPH. 4:31–32

Obeying this one concept would eliminate many of the depressions and anxiety disorders that we treat in Minirth-Meier Clinics around the country. However, forgiving is one of those concepts that is easy to agree with, but difficult to do.

It is impossible to forgive when you don't even know how angry you feel deep in your soul. Even when you become aware of those grudges forgiving is still difficult.

For example, a man finds out his wife had an affair. He is shocked and feels betrayed. But she confesses and repents. After many tears and long discussions of what they should do, together they come for therapy to restore their bonds. With faith they can try to forgive each other and work on the problems that caused the affair. They both accept responsibility for their actions and pursue a new peace together.

This is obviously an optimistic scenario, but even here it will take about a year of therapy for that husband to forgive in his gut what he forgave in his head on the day she repented. Our God has commanded us to live in peace with one another and to practice forgiveness. It isn't easy, but His grace will support us.

To have joy and peace, we must forgive everyone who has hurt us. It will take hard work and God's help.

> *Therefore, as the elect of God, holy and beloved,*
> *put on tender mercies, kindness, humbleness of*
> *mind, meekness, longsuffering; bearing with one*
> *another, and forgiving one another.*
>
> —COL. 3:12

*B*earing with one another is another of those concepts we don't really like to think about, but need to. The Greek words for *bearing with one another* means to "put up with each other."

A local church is not like some exclusive country club where you only accept members who are executives with stable families and able to pay a $100,000 membership fee. A local church is like Jesus wants it to be—open to all personality types, all maturity levels, all socioeconomic levels, all colors and nationalities.

Nonbelievers are encouraged to attend churches, but may not become members. But willfully disobedient believers are forbidden to attend.

Even though we all choose to love one another, there are still certain personalities that don't enjoy frequent company with other personalities. Our best friends are people we enjoy being with. But in local church settings, some people have to "put up" with me and I have to "put up" with some of them.

That's all God asks us to do. "Put up" with certain people, choose to love them and hope for the Lord's blessings on their lives, but don't feel obligated to be best friends with them.

A local church is a fellowship of all kinds of people who humbly admit that we are sinners in need of insight, and love.

> *Pray without ceasing, in everything give thanks; for*
> *this is the will of God in Christ Jesus for you.*
> 1 THESS. 5:17–18

Praying for one another is fun to do the more we learn to love, but a real chore when we regress into our more selfish moods. It feels good to know people you love are praying for you too.

In today's passage, Paul encourages us to pray without ceasing with a thankful attitude. Paul does *not* mean to get on your knees and pray every waking moment and never tell God your gripes. He means to be in an *attitude* of prayer all your waking hours, with an *attitude* of thankfulness, praying briefly and often.

What is the very best thing you can ask for when praying for someone you love? The absolutely best prayer request is for that person's personal righteousness if he is a believer or his salvation if he is an unbeliever. If he becomes truly righteous, then he will be happy and at peace, regardless of the circumstances.

I was praying for a friend of mine last week who was regressing to some extent in his spiritual walk. Then a minor crisis and setback occurred in his life a day or two later, which I was thankful for, because I was praying for his righteousness, not his financial status. It woke him up and he has been more humble and committed to Christ since his "setback" which was really a "set forward." I hope my friends pray for my personal righteousness as well—it's what I desire the most.

Stay in an attitude or prayer all day with thankfulness in all circumstances.

Pure and undefiled religion before God and the Father is this: to visit orphans and widows in their trouble, and *to keep oneself unspotted from the world.*
—JAMES 1:27

The local church is to be a *family*, not a building. It is a place where all of us can be loved, cared for, and confronted and supported with special needs. It is a wonderful institution—affection for the lonely, a home for the homeless, a place of rest for the weary.

An "orphan" is not just a child whose parents have died. Any abused child is an orphan. Any child of an alcoholic is an orphan. Any child of divorce is an orphan. Many children live at home with both parents, but are still psychological orphans because one parent or the other ignores them for a variety of reasons.

Wherever we have lived, my wife and I have "fathered" and "mothered" scores of children in our neighborhoods either through family functions or through helpful groups like Young Life.

Churches should help single parents to spend as much time as possible with their children and even provide some financial support while avoiding codependency. Honor her (or his) dignity by avoiding her total dependence on the church. Provide male and female Sunday school teachers and adult friends for her children, to fill their "vacuums" so they won't develop promiscuity or homosexual conflicts later in life.

It's easier to help people you want to impress. God wants you to impress those in pain with significance to Him and to you.

> *Since you have purified your souls in obeying the truth through the Spirit in sincere love of the brethren, love one another fervently with a pure heart.*
> —1 PETER 1:22

Forgiving one another is vital, but the most important "one another" concept by far is to love one another. That love is to be sincere, without hypocrisy, not phony. That love is also to be fervent, "at full stretch," or "with an intense strain." It is also to be a deep, from the heart, kind of love—a *pure* love.

When you spend lots of time in local church socials and mini-churches and church meetings, you will literally fall in love in a pure way with lots of people. Because we have "parent vacuums" and often family dysfunctions, we will naturally develop sinful temptations with these fellow believers.

We will have sexual temptations. We will also develop subconscious desires to demand too much attention, dependence, or control. We will tend to see them as "business opportunities" instead of brothers and sisters and may even want to take advantage of them.

A *pure* love means that when one of these motives crops up, and some certainly will in all of us, we are to use our willpower—with God's help—to remove and keep our motives as pure as possible.

Sincere, fervent, pure love means you enthusiastically desire what is best for someone you love, expecting nothing in return.

Finally, all of you be of one mind, having compassion for one another; love as brothers, be tenderhearted, be courteous; not returning evil for evil or reviling for reviling, but on the contrary blessing, knowing that you were called to this, that you may inherit a blessing. —1 PETER 3:8–9

Our passage for today lists two more "one another" concepts that we would like to cover for this devotional section: *having compassion for one another* and *blessing one another.*

The original Greek word for compassion is a tender, emotional term that implies that you care so much about someone that the organs in your gut actually move. When you have deep compassion for someone and empathize with their pain, your heart speeds up, your stomach and intestines actually churn and move enough to feel them. You may even get stomach cramps, or "heartburn."

We are also told by Peter to bless one another. The Greek word for bless is *eulogountes* from which we get the English word "eulogize." It means to speak well of one another. My wife has developed a wonderful habit. Whenever she hears someone criticize a fellow believer, rather than bluntly correct the critic, she "blesses" the person being criticized by saying something nice about him or her. It brings the criticism to an abrupt halt.

―――――――――

Who are the people you love so much they make your gut churn or heart speed up? Go bless them today!

> *He who gets wisdom loves his own soul;*
> *He who keeps understanding will find good.*
> —PROV. 19:8

We can serve God best if we are emotionally and spiritually healthy. But mental and spiritual health depends on our ability to bond in love to God and to others—believers in particular. However, we can only love others as much as we love ourselves. If our "love tank" is empty and we have low self-esteem, we have no love to give, so we become arrogant, "prideful," and vain as our evil brains deceive ourselves and compensate for the pain of low self-esteem. Arrogant self-love is actually a sign of severe inferiority feelings and results in legalism. Some legalists even think self-worth is a sin. They take great pride in their self-hatred. Loving ourselves biblically produces true humility and results in grace.

In our passage today, we are told to be "wise" (the Hebrew word is *leb,* implying *good common sense*), by loving our own soul (our personality, our will, the nonbody part of us that goes to heaven in a new body when we die). If we have enough common sense to love ourselves, we will cherish, keep, guard or preserve our godly, biblical understanding of things, which will in turn result in our good (implying spiritual, psychological wealth). Worldly wealth could be one blessing God may choose for you if it won't spoil you by leading to the sinful type of selfish self-love.

Be your own best friend. Guard your biblical convictions. Don't believe the legalists who tell you self-hatred is a virtue.

"Teacher, which is the great commandment in the law?" Jesus said to him, "'You shall love the LORD your God with all your heart, with all your soul, and with all your mind.' This is the first and great commandment. And the second is like it: 'You shall love your neighbor as yourself.' On these two commandments hang all the Law and the Prophets."

—MATT. 22:36–40

The Pharisees of Christ's day were very proud of their humility. They were proud of the fact that they were so "spiritual" and obeyed all the "rules." But Christ called them the most sinful people of His day—a "generation of snakes and vipers."

They tried to trick Christ by asking which of the Ten Commandments was most important. Jesus replied quickly and without hesitation. He said if people would obey the one, greatest law, they would automatically obey *all* the laws in the whole Bible.

This passage is not a call to selfish, vain self-love. It is a call to love your neighbor with the assumption that you already have enough common sense to love yourself in a biblical sense—as Solomon called for in Proverbs 19:8.

We know from psychiatric research that you can only love your neighbor as much as you love yourself in a healthy self-concept way. If our own love tank is full—and love for and from God can help fill it—then we have enough love to give some of it to others.

The more we love God, others, and ourselves in a godly way, the less we will sin.

*And the LORD God said, "It is not good that man
should be alone; I will make him a helper
comparable to him."*
—GEN. 2:18

We don't know how many billions of years ago God
created our universe, or whether he did it all at once
with a "big bang" or in stages. He could have created
the world with apparent age. More likely there is a
great gap of time between Genesis 1:1 and 1:2.

New species of dogs, cats, roses, tulips, etc., are still
being "evolved" in a micro-evolutionary sense, but no
new *kinds* of animals have ever evolved from other
kinds of animals. On the sixth day of creation, God created man from the elements in the dust and in His own
psychological and spiritual image (God didn't have a
body).

God knew man would be lonely and needed hori-
zontal bonding, so He created Eve from the elements
in Adam's rib. He made Eve a helper, comparable in
importance to Adam. He uses the same Hebrew word
for helper to describe Himself (see Ps. 33:20, 70:5, and
115:9).

God delegated to *both* of them (see Gen. 1:28) the
authority to subdue and rule the world. After each day
of creation, God looked at what He had created and
called it good. When He created Adam and Eve on the
sixth day, however, and looked them over, He called
them "very good" (see Gen. 1:31).

---

*God Himself created man and woman so they could bond emotion-
ally to each other.*

Do not be unequally yoked together with unbelievers. For what fellowship has righteousness with lawlessness? And what communion has light with darkness? —PS. 119:63, 2 COR. 6:14

King David said his best friends were those who were committed believers who lived by God's wise precepts. The apostle Paul told us (in 1 Cor. 5:9–11) to live in the real world and have acquaintances among nonbelievers, even though they may be sexually immoral and commit other habitual sins as well, but *not* to have fellowship with brothers in Christ who are currently living rebellious lives.

In 2 Corinthians 6:14, Paul warns us not to be unequally yoked to unbelievers but never specifies exactly what "yoked" means. We know it refers to much more than casual friendships because otherwise it would contradict Paul's earlier advice in 1 Corinthians 5:9–11. Logically it must mean binding, intimate relationships. Believers have to guess prayerfully how far to carry it in their career relationships.

I made up my mind at age sixteen that I would only date committed believers because I wanted to eventually marry a believer. I also decided then that I would have only business partners who were committed believers. I have non-Christian friends, but my close friends are all committed believers. You need at least one other human to bond with for good mental health.

Plan your human bonding and work at it each week.

> *Behold, how good and how pleasant* it is *for
> brethren to dwell together in unity!* It is *like the
> dew of Hermon, Descending upon the mountains of
> Zion; for there the* LORD *commanded the blessing—
> Life forevermore.*
>
> —PS. 133:1, 3

If your goal in life is to further the kingdom of Christ
and you decide to build intimate bonds over the years
that will support you in that commitment, then a
healthy local church is a great place to build those relationships. It takes about two years of weekly fellowship to build a deep, intimate friendship. Mini-churches
are a great place to do that.

When my wife and I moved our family to California
in 1989, we joined a mini-church within two weeks to
begin building a local support system. No matter
where we have lived, we have found really neat believers to bond to. We find a sense of unity among true
believers all over the world.

You could go to Eastern Europe, Asia, Africa, South
America, Australia—*anywhere,* and Bible-believing
Christians welcome you with open arms. This world-
wide unity of believers is really exciting. It is a glimpse
of what heaven and the kingdom will be like. We
should strive to maintain that unity. It's like the dew
that nurtures the grass. Jesus said people will know we
are Christians by our love, and that has certainly
proven to be true.

---

*There is nothing this old world has to offer that compares to loving
and being loved by like-minded believers.*

*Let your fountain be blessed, And rejoice with the
wife of your youth. As a loving deer and a graceful
doe, Let her breasts satisfy you at all times; And
always be enraptured with her love.*
—PROV. 5:18–19

There is a sexual aspect to bonding. That is why it is
safer to have only one, deeply intimate friendship with
a member of the opposite sex—your own mate. Other
intimate friends need to be of the same sex. There is
always a danger that any other close friendship with a
member of the opposite sex could end up becoming a
sexual affair.

If you saw the hundreds of cases of "accidental" affairs we have seen among our patients, you would understand better why we take such a strong stand on
this issue. Spending time together is not wrong in itself,
but the intimacy that results from long-standing friendships with other members of the opposite sex can be
deadly to a marriage.

People risk it, thinking it could never happen to
them. They are shocked by their own impulsive failure.
Families are often ruined.

Solomon said to enjoy an emotional and physical relationship with your mate. The Bible says God designed marital sex for your mutual pleasure and for
procreation. We have written an entire book on this:
Sex in the Christian Marriage (Baker Book House).

---

*It makes God happy if you enjoy only your mate with both emotional
and sexual bonding.*

He who *finds a wife finds a good thing, And obtains favor from the Lord.* —PROV. 18:22

Many believers suffer from the illusion that God will send the perfect mate for you up to your front door, and when you open the door, will say, "Here I am. God sent me!" God probably won't send you a mate at all, but He will help you find one.

When you do find a fellow-believer for a mate, it pleases God. If you want a friend (or a mate) you have to get one the old fashioned way—earn one! You must show yourself friendly. You have to work at it.

About 85 percent of us end up marrying someone very similar in personality dynamics to our parent of the opposite sex. A son of a domineering, critical mother will usually marry a domineering, critical substitute mother. A daughter of an alcoholic will usually marry a future alcoholic. If he gets therapy and gives up his alcoholism, there's more than a 50 percent chance she will divorce him and marry another alcoholic. We continue what we got used to in childhood.

If your father was an abusive alcoholic, you will have "crushes" on alcoholics. You will find committed Christian men boring unless your father was one. Just be aware of that when you are hunting and praying for a mate.

If you are single and desire marriage, pray and search for a stable Christian mate—with your eyes open to codependency issues.

"Are *You not our God*, who *drove out the inhabitants of this land before Your people Israel, and gave it to the descendants of Abraham Your friend forever?*"
— 2 CHRON. 20:7

It isn't easy to develop an intimate friendship with someone you cannot see, hear, or touch who writes one, very long love letter for you to share with billions of other people.

The Holy Spirit really helps. When we pray to the Father, the Holy Spirit interprets our intent to the Father. When we read the Father's Word the Holy Spirit touches our hearts with key passages that the Father wants to communicate to us.

Sometimes the Holy Spirit passes along thoughts or convictions while we are walking the beaches, or standing on a mountain, or sleeping. The Bible tells us to "try the spirits" to see which messages are actually from God. When a seminary student tells me God suddenly "told him" to marry a certain woman he hardly knows, I ask him, "How do you know it isn't lust or transference, or even gas pain? Just think it out, pray about it, and seek counsel from mature believers."

One thing gives me much hope. For eternity we will communicate face-to-face with our Triune God. Like Abraham, we will be God's intimate friend forever.

Intimacy with God is built by trusting Him, by prayer, meditation on Scripture, and "listening" to His Spirit.

> *I will bless the LORD who has given me counsel; My heart also instructs me in the night seasons. I have set the LORD always before me; Because He is at my right hand I shall not be moved. You will show me the path of life; In Your presence is fullness of joy; At Your right hand are pleasures forevermore.*
> —PS. 16:7–8, 11

Another way to *bond* to God is to "think God." Think about His nature. Think about His teachings. Think about His exciting plans for you. Bless the Lord—compliment Him and thank Him.

Like King David, listen to the Holy Spirit's convictions and insights while you lie in bed at night reflecting. Set the Lord always before you. He is your right hand and will keep your life at peace and will keep it stable—so you won't be emotionally "moved."

If we trust the Lord's guidance and apply His principles to our lives, He will show us the path to a meaningful life. When we have an intimate walk with Him, chatting with Him throughout the day, we experience fullness of joy.

But the fullness of joy we experience here is only a glimpse of the *continual* joy we will experience in eternity. Our joy here on earth is often interrupted by the realities of necessary pain. But some day, at His right hand, we will experience continual pleasures forevermore.

Bonding in intimacy with God can and should become a positive daily practice—one we thrive on for fullness of joy.

> *As the deer pants for the water brooks, So pants my soul for You, O God. My soul thirsts for God, for the living God. When shall I come and appear before God?*
> —PS. 42:1–2

We start off life with a God-shaped vacuum that no one but God can fill. On top of that, a boy will have a father-vacuum if dad is emotionally distant. He will have a mother-vacuum if mom is either distant or treats the boy like a substitute husband and gives him too much attention. This is especially true if mom and dad don't have much to offer each other emotionally.

The same would be true of a girl with either a mom who is emotionally distant and/or a dad who is either distant or treats her like a substitute wife. But whether your God-vacuum is the one you were born with, or one that stems from a dysfunctional family, or both, God wants to fill it up!

David "panted" for intimacy with God like a running, thirsty deer pants for some cool, fresh water he sees in the distance. David thirsted for heaven too, when he could appear before God in person.

David said we should thank God for being so good to us—for all the wonderful things He does for us. We should thank Him for filling up the vacuum of a longing soul, and also filling up the hungry holes in our souls with goodness, including good friends.

The primary source of satisfaction for what feels like "loneliness" or "abandonment" is a personal relationship with God—the Holy Trinity!

> *"If you love me, keep My commandments. He who has My commandments and keeps them, it is he who loves Me."*
> —JOHN 14:15

How can we know if our intimacy with God is adequate? How can we tell if we really love Him? We think we love God, but how can we tell if our hearts are so deceitful?

Our passages for today tell us how. Our love for God is directly proportional to how well we obey Him. If we think that we love God but really don't, and are just being "religious" to manipulate Him, then we will be living with areas of willful, continued disobedience of one or more of His guidelines.

Humans all fail periodically and we all have sinful thoughts daily, but if we have some genuine love for God, we will commit ourselves daily to obey Him. We will keep coming back to that commitment when we do fail.

God's love for us is *unconditional*, even though it doesn't feel that way sometimes because of His blessings and discipline being *conditional*. Even though His love for us is unconditional, His sense of fellowship with us and our feelings of fellowship and intimacy with Him *are conditional* on our obedience to His principles. When we sin we must confess it to Him and restore fellowship.

_____

God wants to manifest Himself to me in many different ways. He wants to come to me and make His home with me.

For I am persuaded that neither death nor life, nor angels nor principalities nor powers, nor things present nor things to come, nor height nor depth, nor any other created thing, shall be able to separate us from the love of God which is in Christ Jesus our Lord. —ROM. 8:37–39

Once we decide to depend on what Christ did on the cross to pay for our sins, God bonds to us like super glue. We can't shake Him loose from then on.

Our sense of intimacy with Him will wax and wane depending on a multitude of factors, including our obedience to Him, how we feel about ourselves, our brain amine and hormone levels that day, our state of physical health, and how much sleep we got the night before. But His love for us is fixed.

Not only does the Holy Spirit permanently *seal* us until the day of redemption—the day we get to heaven (see Eph. 1), but Jesus and the Father wrap their hands around us and will not let us out (see John 10:27–31). All three permanently, unconditionally bond to us when we depend on Christ's atonement.

Tribulation, distress, persecution, famine, nakedness, peril, the sword, death, life, angels, principalities, evil powers (demons), things present, things to come, height, depth and any other created thing *cannot separate us from God's super glue bond of love.* In other words, absolutely nothing can cause God to give up His love for you.

God knows we are human. He expects our love for Him to wax and wane. But His love toward us is full strength all the time.

*In my distress I called upon the LORD, And
cried out to my God; He heard my voice from
His temple, And my cry came before Him, even to
His ears.*
                                    —PS. 18:6–7

When you were a child, you probably said some
"goodnight prayers" before you went to sleep. It may
have been a memorized prayer, such as "Now I lay me
down to sleep, I pray the Lord my soul to keep." It may
have been a spontaneous prayer. I love to hear and
analyze the spontaneous prayers of children.

When you were three years old and prayed the
words, "Dear Heavenly Father . . . ," you were actually
thinking in the depths of your brain, "Dear Heavenly
version of my earthly father."

You see God through sunglasses that are colored by
the personalities of your father (primarily) and mother
(usually to a somewhat lesser extent). We see it in research, and we see it over and over again empirically
in our own thousands of patients.

In today's passages, we see that the real God always
listens to our hurts, gets angry whenever we are
abused, supernaturally shakes things up in rage, draws
us out of our emotionally painful waters, delivers us
from our strong abusers. Our abusers hate us and the
ties of codependency are too strong for us, but God will
provide deliverance if we will also do our part.

*How do your father and mother contrast to the real God of this pas-
sage? Ask yourself that question daily as we examine the differences
for the next three weeks of devotions together.*

*Are they not all ministering spirits sent forth to
minister for those who will inherit salvation?*
—HEB. 1:14

I have seen how my own family of origin system operated. My wife and I have also examined and reexamined our current family system over the years.

Have you examined your own family of origin with a fine tooth comb, using a detailed inventory of all significant relationships? Every human should do this to set himself free from patterns of codependency. The truth sets us free. Do this with a Christian therapist for personal growth for half a dozen sessions or so. If you were abused as a child, you may need to do this for a year or more to truly be set free.

Have you examined your current family system with a fine tooth comb? Do you see yourself repeating some of the same negative patterns you grew up in? Are you incorporating some of your parent's good patterns?

I have another suggestion as well. Study God's family system. Pattern yours after His in practical ways. God loves you intimately. He lets *you* decide whether to love Him back. Even after you trust Him, He gives you a lot of rope. He lets you make many daily choices for yourself.

And yet, He "hires" a huge staff of gifted "helpers" to watch your every move and protect you from some accidents and allow you to suffer through others. God steps in whenever it would be in your best interest.

We have a God who loves us enough to send guardian angels to serve and protect us.

> *For unto us a Child is born, Unto us a Son is given;*
> *And the government will be upon His shoulder.*
> *And His name will be called Wonderful, Counselor,*
> *Mighty God, Everlasting Father, Prince of Peace.*
> —ISA. 9:6

Sometimes I compare myself to my own earthly father. He's in his eighties and I highly respect him. I compare him and myself to God the Father and I do see a few differences—quite a few, in fact!

My father and I have had the government of our respective families on our shoulders and have done a respectable job. Our heavenly Father governs the universe and makes no mistakes.

My father and I are occasionally wonderful. God always is. We have usually been good counselors to our children. God's counsel is perfect. We have a few areas of personal strengths. He is all-powerful.

My father and I both had a beginning in this century. The Father, Son and Holy Spirit had no beginning and have no end. They are eternal spirits.

My father and I both have pushed for peace in our respective families, but I had a few conflicts with him growing up and my six teenagers certainly have with me. Jesus Christ, is the Prince of Peace. He will rule one thousand years on earth in the near future for His messianic kingdom.

Our Triune God will reign over the new earth, the New Jerusalem, and all of heaven and the universe forever. God is Omnipotent and will keep His promises.

Reexamine our passage for today. Then sit back, relax, and thank God for being such a wonderful, everlasting Father.

He was oppressed and He was afflicted, Yet He opened not His mouth; He was led as a lamb to the slaughter, And as a sheep before its shearers is silent, So He opened not his mouth.

—ISA. 53:7

In yesterday's passage, we saw Jesus as a future messianic Ruler. We saw His omniscient and omnipotent attributes.

In today's passage, however, we see Jesus the Lamb of God whose first coming to earth was to take away the sins of the world. Isaiah wrote this hundreds of years before Christ. A copy of Isaiah was in the Dead Sea Scrolls and radiocarbon dated, so we know it was before Christ came.

Isaiah said the Messiah would come down from heaven in human form and be despised, rejected, a man of sorrows, a grieving Messiah, afflicted, wounded, bruised, whipped, abused, and as silent as a lamb about to be slaughtered as He went to His own death for our sins.

Because of our pride and insecurities, we demand a Messiah who will take over the earth and make us rulers and end injustices. That Messiah had to come a first time, to satisfy the heavenly Father's insistence on having perfect sons and daughters. Now the Father sees Jesus' robe of righteousness around you if you have accepted His gift and says to you, "You are my perfect child. Welcome to an eternal relationship."

The one real God includes two aspects of the Messiah: the Lamb of God who took our place on the cross, and Messiah the Lion who will roar His rage at the abusers in this world when He returns.

> *"It shall come to pass That before they call, I will answer; And while they are still speaking, I will hear.*
> —ISA. 65:24

I am a very imperfect father. I have often promised my sons or daughters I would pray for them when they took important tests at school, then forgot. But I have a "neat out."

Before the children get home, but *after* they have already taken their exams, I go ahead and pray that God will help them remember what they have studied, anyway, and I know God answers that request just as well as if I had prayed it when the test started. Let me explain.

We operate life on finite time. God sees the past, present and future on one continuum. Isaiah said that before he even calls out his requests to the Father, the Father has already heard it and often even answered it.

My wife sometimes prays that God will help her to have chosen a better husband twenty-five years ago, but once you have gotten your "test scores," it is too late to pray this kind of request!

God knows what we need before we ask it, but He frequently won't give it to us unless we do ask, because He wants us to have a healthy interdependence on Him. He depends on us for intimate fellowship. He longs for us, as unbelievable as it may seem.

Thank You, Lord, for loving me so much that before I even call for You, You hear me.

Thus says the LORD: "Heaven is My throne, And earth is My footstool. Where is the house that you will build Me? And where is the place of My rest?
—ISA. 66:1

Three thousand years ago, King Solomon built a temple for God—a very beautiful and expensive temple. Prophecy demands that it be rebuilt someday, but I am guessing (and hoping) about the "our lifetime" part.

My wife and I have traveled Europe and enjoyed visiting the beautiful cathedrals that have been built in the past two thousand years. There are some beautiful churches still being built today. Sometimes I think the money could better be spent helping the poor and the missionaries, but who am I to judge? God *wanted* Solomon to build the expensive temple in Jerusalem and even gave him very specific directions.

Our passage for today, however, lets us know that heaven is God's throne and earth is His footstool. He doesn't really live in a little house called a temple or a cathedral. He will never die (other than Christ's death and resurrection), so don't bury Him symbolically. He has no "place of rest." He told us where He really wants to live in hundreds of passages of sacred Scripture: *in your heart!*

I'm sure God dwells in a beautiful heaven, since He designed and created it. And He will enjoy the millennial Temple one day (Ezek. 40–42). But He is a God of relationships who delights more to rest in your heart.

Thank You, Lord, that You consider my heart a great place to stay.

> *"But let him who glories glory in this, that he understands and knows Me, that I am the LORD, exercising lovingkindness, judgment, and righteousness in the earth. For in these I delight," says the LORD.*
> —JER. 9:24

My earthly parents had to make thousands of decisions during my growing up years. My wife and I have to make thousands of judgments now.

We try very hard to be fair, and our six teenagers usually agree that we are. You do the best you can to be a reasonable "judge" and let the chips fall wherever they fall.

You have to be able to face occasional rejections if you want to be a good parent. You also need to admit it when you have made a mistake.

In our passage for today, the prophet Jeremiah tells us we have a perfect judge in our heavenly Father. He is loving. He is kind. He is righteous—all decisions are moral and correct.

Perfectionists hate to make decisions because they are afraid they may make a mistake. God knows that all His judgments are what is best in the eternal perspective. He doesn't like our rejections of Him when we accuse Him of not being fair, but He can never be surprised or have His self-esteem threatened.

God is a perfectly righteous, loving, and kind judge. In that regard, He differs from me or my father.

Through *the Lord's mercies we are not consumed,*
Because His compassions fail not.
—LAM. 3:22

In my attempt to be a good earthly father, I attend nearly all of the performing events of six children, including musical, dramatic, academic and athletic events. Sometimes my wife goes to one, I go to another, and we both miss a third one going on at the same time. We take turns and try to be fair.

When our children make mistakes in these performances we try to be gracious, merciful, and compassionate, but we are far from perfect. Part of us wants them to perform well *for us,* to impress our neighbors (I'm ashamed to say). That's an example of conditional acceptance, and all parents have at least a little of it.

One of my boys fell during a soccer game and hurt his thumb. He wanted compassion and an X-ray. But being a macho M.D., I quickly examined it, declared it to be fine, and sent him back onto the field. No son of mine was going to be a "wimp." After the game his thumb still hurt and was starting to swell, so I reluctantly took him to the hospital and had it X-rayed. It was broken. Talk about being embarrassed!

Jeremiah said we have a heavenly Father who is merciful. His compassions never fail. He feels compassion for our past and present abuses and hurts every morning. He is always faithful.

The heavenly Father sees through us like an X-ray and still remains loving, compassionate, merciful and faithful.

> *God* is *jealous, and the* LORD *avenges . . . And He*
> *reserves* wrath for His enemies; The LORD is *slow*
> *to anger and great in power, And will not at all*
> *acquit* the wicked.
> —NAH. 1:2–3

As an earthly father I have occasionally lost my temper and said things I later regretted on those occasions. I nearly always apologized to my children later.

The prophet Nahum informs us that our heavenly Father also gets very angry at times. But God can't "lose" His temper. His rage is just. His rage is controlled. His vengeance is fair. He makes no mistakes.

God is jealous when we worship greed or sexual fantasies or food or power or prestige instead of Him. He disciplines His children with love and perfect fairness. His goal is to help us grow to prevent a lot of future emotional pain by going through a little bit of discipline now. He doesn't take revenge on believers; He disciplines us.

However, God does take revenge on the ungodly, and He avenges fairly. He is furious with unrepentant abusers. He'll forgive them with open arms if they do trust Him. Most never do. They are too proud.

God is slow to anger, but great in power. He will avenge every abuse and every sin. We can either suffer for our own sins or depend on Christ's *atonement* which results in "at-one-ment" with the Father.

The real *God is not only loving, merciful, compassionate and kind, but He is also angry at all sins and abuses.*

And he will turn the hearts of the fathers to the children, and the hearts of the children to their fathers, lest I come and strike the earth with a curse.
—MAL. 4:6

Fathers and mothers all feel inferior to some extent or another. We all go through life trying to prove we are *not* a nobody even though we think we are. The truth would set us free because in reality, God says we *are* a *somebody* if we trust Him and become His sons and daughters.

As parents, we frequently sacrifice time spent with children—time that they need with us to fill their voids and fill their love tanks and parent vacuums. God the Father wants to restore the hearts of human fathers and mothers to their children and vice versa.

But children don't appreciate us as parents very often—at least not until they get older. They embarrass us in public at times. They rebel at times.

We get much greater "strokes" for our significance from select groups of peers. We can find groups of people who accept us and even praise us. We spend lots of time with them and very little with our children.

Or, we can be loners but strive to be rich and famous or powerful workaholics, to "stroke" ourselves and avoid rejection by peers and children. Or, we can be lonely alcoholics and stay "buzzed" to kill the pain of rejection, rage, and inferiority.

God's plan for us as fathers and mothers is to choose to bond to our children, expecting very few strokes from them until they mature, although they do surprise us often with hugs and loving acts.

> *Know therefore and understand, that from the*
> *going forth of the command to restore and build*
> *Jerusalem until Messiah the Prince, there shall be*
> *seven weeks and sixty-two weeks . . . And after the*
> *sixty-two weeks Messiah shall be cut off, but not for*
> *Himself; and the people of the prince who is to*
> *come shall destroy the city and the sanctuary.*
> —DAN. 9:25–26

In our clinic, we try to have "today plans," to serve God effectively today and let tomorrow worry about itself. We obviously have to make some long-term plans, but never engraved in cement.

God operates on a "trillion-year plan" and each one thousand years is like a day to him. More than half of the Bible drops hints, telling us His plan in small pieces.

Daniel foretold a decree to rebuild Jerusalem. Daniel said that 173,880 days after the decree, the Messiah would enter Jerusalem and then be "cut off." Then, Jerusalem would again be totally destroyed. Many years later, the Antichrist would terrorize Jews again. Then the Messiah would return to set up His kingdom.

Jesus fulfilled the first part of this prophecy when he rode into Jerusalem, was crucified and resurrected. In A.D. 70, Titus and the Roman legions destroyed Jerusalem. Christ will rapture true believers soon, and the "prince" (the Anti-Christ) will be made known.

The real God is different from many earthly fathers. He operates on a precise, loving plan for us that stretches into eternity.

Rejoice greatly, O daughter of Zion! Shout,
O daughter of Jerusalem! Behold, your King is
coming to you; He is just and having salvation,
Lowly and riding on a donkey, A colt, the foal
of a donkey.   —ZECH. 9:9

Israel didn't want a passive Messiah. Believers in Jahweh have been victims of abuse since Cain killed Abel. Why more abuse? We don't want a Lamb, we want a *King* of the world—*now,* to put us on thrones beside Him and to protect us from further danger.

Scores of Old Testament prophecies like today's predicted a Lamb Messiah to be bruised for our iniquities (see Isa. 53) and "cut off" (see Dan. 9:25–26). Scores of details were given. But even Christ's own twelve disciples totally overlooked these signs.

Instead, they argued with each other over who would be the greatest when Jesus took over the world. No wonder He was rejected and despised of men. Who wants a Lamb-Messiah? The Lamb of God was a disappointment to humans, but He satisfied our heavenly Father.

Half of the messianic prophecies are "Lamb prophecies" and half are "end times-messianic kingdom" prophecies. People ignored or laughed at the "Lamb-half" until Jesus came. Now many of their descendants are ignoring and scoffing the "end times-messianic kingdom" prophecies. When will we learn? *Soon!*

Jesus, thank You for Your self-sacrificing love.

> *Behold, your King is coming to you, Lowly, and*
> *sitting on a donkey, a colt, the foal of a donkey.*
> —MATT. 21:5

Jesus is the Alpha and Omega. He always has existed and always will. He is equal in importance to the Father and the Holy Spirit.

And yet Jesus chose to take on a human body; be born of a virgin in a manger in the poor village of Bethlehem. He entered Jerusalem on a *donkey*, on schedule—exactly 173,880 days after Antaxerxes Longimanus recorded the decree to rebuild Jerusalem on March 5, 444 B.C., a century after Daniel predicted he would (see Dan. 9:25–26).

Christ was beaten, spit at, bruised, whipped, scoffed, and crucified without protest. After all, it was His plan. He rose again and was seen by over five hundred witnesses on numerous occasions before ascending from the Mount of Olives forty days after His resurrection. The Rapture, the Antichrist, and the Battle of Armageddon are yet to come. The Antichrist will desecrate the new temple in Jerusalem and try to annihilate the Jews. Christ will descend with all deceased and raptured saints on the Mount of Olives and set up the messianic kingdom (see Dan. 12:11–3).

The Lamb on a donkey will become a Lion on a throne, to the surprise of many.

*"O Jerusalem, Jerusalem, the one who kills the
prophets and stones those who are sent to her! How
often I wanted to gather your children together, as
a hen gathers her chicks under her wings, but you
were not willing!"* —MATT. 23:37–38

Loving mothers are protective of the safety of their
children. My wife screamed in pain and ran to grab our
two-year-old son many years ago as he was running
into a busy street. I also remember falling down on
some broken glass in a field when I was about eight. I
almost cut off my thumb. My mother heard my cries
before I even made it near the house. She rushed me to
the hospital. They were able to save my thumb.

During a sudden hailstorm, a mother hen will hold
out her wings for her chicks to run under. She will
stand her ground and die from the hail landing on her
head. Here, love and loyalty override her survival instincts.

Jesus loves His Jewish brothers and sisters. He also
loves Arabs, Orientals, Germans, Africans, Indians, *all*
people are precious in His sight.

Jesus told His beloved friends and relatives in Jerusalem that He was the Lamb-Messiah. They rejected
Him, as we would have. He went out of the city and
wept about how much He wished He could tuck them
safely under His wings like a hen protects her chicks.

---

*Whether Jewish or Gentile, the Messiah, like a loving, protective
mother, holds out His wings to cover us.*

> *"My sheep hear My voice, and I know them, and*
> *they follow Me "And I give them eternal life, and*
> *they shall never perish; neither shall anyone snatch*
> *them out of My hand."*   —JOHN 10:27–28

There are times in life that I feel all alone even in the middle of a crowd of relatives and friends. There are times when I feel insecure. There are times that I detest my own depraved thoughts and motives. Being an insight-oriented psychiatrist enables me to see things about myself that are painful until I deal with them biblically for a sufficient length of time.

During those painful, insecure times that occasionally come, I go to a quiet place and meditate on this very passage. I visualize climbing physically into Jesus' outstretched hand and He wraps it warmly around me.

He tells me no one, not even myself, can pluck me out of His hand. The Father puts His hand around Jesus' hand and tells me the same thing, and Jesus says He and the Father function as one, as a husband and wife should function as "one" authority in the family.

Ten minutes or so of meditating on this passage gives me peace, courage, strength, hope and security. It also tells me a lot about the nature of God. The God who created the entire universe also wants to hold us in His hand. The Father and Son agree on that, and together They secure our eternal destiny.

_____

Father and Son, thank You for securing me eternally in Your hands
and comforting me with Your Spirit.

> *"Oh, the depth of the riches both of the wisdom
> and knowledge of God! How unsearchable are His
> judgments and His ways past finding out!"*
> —ROM. 11:33

One of the hardest things about being a father is being so ignorant. It seems that at least half of the questions that my teenagers ask me I have to answer, "I don't know."

Then, when my wife and I have to make everyday decisions about how to handle our six teenagers, we don't know. We throw our hands up, guess what to do, tell them we are guessing (which doesn't increase their confidence level a whole lot), and go with it. We often get their input and go with that. We have a democratic family with parental veto power.

I am glad that I am God's child and not my own, even though I think I'm a pretty decent dad. Our heavenly Father is omniscient, which means He knows everything there is to know about everything and everybody. The apostle Paul said His judgments (decision-making processes) are *unsearchable*. His ways of doing things are past finding out in this life. Who understands the mind of the Father? How foolish are we when we frequently try to be His counselors by telling Him what to do and what gifts to give who? His works are great. His thoughts are deeper than the depths of the ocean. His I.Q. is so much above ours there is no comparison. We can trust Him with our decisions, with our lifestyle, and with our future.

Earthly fathers make good and bad guesses. Our heavenly Father is omniscient and has the benefits of hindsight, foresight, and insight.

*Let this mind be in you which was also in Christ
Jesus, who, being in the form of God, did not
consider it robbery to be equal with God, but made
Himself of no reputation, taking the form of a
servant, and coming in the likeness of men. And
being found in appearance as a man, He humbled
Himself and became obedient to the point of death,
even the death of the cross.*   —PHIL. 2:5–8

Every morning when I wake up I pray the same three
quick requests before I even get out of bed: help me
Father to become more like Christ today (see Rom.
8:29); help me to serve Christ today, doing His light,
easy yoke without masochism (see Matt. 6:33); help me
to handle the troubles of the day (see Matt. 6:34).

But when I think about what it really means to be
like Christ, I often don't really want to do it. It goes
against the grain of who I am. After all, who wants to
be a servant? I'd rather get attention. I'd rather be
pampered. Christ came to seek, save, and serve.

But I made a commitment to Christ when I was sixteen years old, so I repeat it daily even though it goes
against my nature. He died voluntarily on the cross. I
certainly wouldn't want to be a full-time servant or die
on a cross. I'm too proud and arrogant. But if He called
me to do it, He would help me.

---

*Before you decide to dedicate your life to Christ, decide if you are
willing to become a reluctant servant.*

For in that He Himself has suffered, being tempted,
He is able to aid those who are tempted.
—HEB. 2:18

When you explained your trials and failures to your earthly father, how often did He wrap His big arms around you in love and empathy and sincerely say, "I understand." How often have we responded in that way to the setbacks of our children?

. God became flesh and dwelt among us. Christ was an eternal Spirit with no body, but He limited Himself for all of eternity future so He could not only die for our sins, but through experience *understand* our sins and setbacks.

He was tempted just like we are, except He chose in *every* situation not to sin. Now when we tell our heavenly Father about our trials, tribulations, sins, disobedience, and failures, Jesus is there in heaven as our High Priest.

He explains to the Father what it is like to be a suffering human. And the Holy Spirit passes our prayer along to Jesus and the Father with godly groanings that cannot be uttered. The Father then makes a fully informed decision about how to lovingly answer our requests in times of need.

Our earthly father sometimes understands us with complete empathy. Our heavenly Father always does, because Jesus and the Holy Spirit help Him understand us.

Thank You, God, for Your divine teamwork in loving me and caring for my needs.

*And there is no creature hidden from His sight, but
all things are naked and open to the eyes of Him to
whom we must give account.* —HEB. 4:13

One trait our heavenly Father has that no earthly
father on earth has is "X-ray vision" of the soul. He
sees right through us and sees our every thought, feeling, motive, fear, emotion, drive, desire, and intent.

I have often wondered what it would be like to have
special psychiatry hats that had a screen on top that
showed everyone all our true conscious and unconscious thoughts. Some would go psychotic by finding
out the truth about themselves too quickly. Some
would get depressed. Some would commit suicide. All
would be surprised by the extent of our rage, selfishness, etc. But it would speed emotional healing a great
deal.

Curing people's depression and anxiety would be
really easy, if we could all look at the truth about ourselves and deal with it biblically. God offers us that;
except He sees all our reality and loves us and knows
how to cure our souls. He gently and lovingly shows us
the truth a little at a time and sanctifies us a little at a
time. Maybe that's why He hasn't allowed us to invent
an X-ray for the soul yet. He knows that overzealous
psychiatrists would try to show the truth too quickly.

*We have a heavenly Father who has X-ray vision, loves us anyway,
and cures us patiently and gently.*

Jesus Christ is *the same yesterday, today, and forever.*
—HEB. 13:8

According to extensive psychiatric research, one of the most important factors for a "functional family"is parental consistency. Not only should each parent be consistent, but the two parents must also be consistent with each other.

Some fathers, for example, will discipline one child severely for a certain behavior, then turn around and laugh when another child does the same thing. Or he may punish severely and laugh the next time the same child does the same offense, depending on what mood he is in.

One parent is often very strict while the other is very lenient. Children pick this up quickly and learn to become good manipulators by pitting one parent against the other. When parents disagree on discipline, they should meet privately and compromise so they can provide a united front. Most of the time, the compromise is what would be best for the child anyway.

One way to promote consistency is to sit down with your children and get their input into rules, chores, and consequences they will live with. Then all of you sign and date the contract and modify it every few months as the children mature. As they mature, they can handle more chores and fewer rules.

Jesus Christ is unlike our earthly parents. He was perfectly consistent and will be forever.

To be like Christ means to strive for personal consistency.

> *Blessed be the God and Father of our LORD Jesus Christ, who according to His abundant mercy has begotten us again to a living hope through the resurrection of Jesus Christ from the dead, to an inheritance incorruptible and undefiled and that does not fade away, reserved in heaven for you.*
> —1 PETER 1:3–4

When you receive an inheritance here on earth, you divide it up—you pay taxes, you tithe, you pay your lawyer, you catch up on bills, share a little with your kids, and hope something may be left.

The death and resurrection of Jesus Christ earned a far better inheritance than our earthly father will leave us. Our heavenly Father has begotten us again in His own royal family. His inheritance is a *permanent* one. It never runs out.

Our inheritance is secure. God Himself keeps watch on it in heaven. Since our inheritance of eternal life does not depend on works—it is a gift—the Bible tells us in scores of places that we *cannot* lose it. Our earthly fathers get angry and rewrite their will, but our heavenly Father promises to never rewrite the will. Our good or bad works only make a difference in what rewards we get—that part of our inheritance—not whether or not we make it to heaven.

We have a heavenly Father who has already written an unchangeable, unending inheritance for all who are born again.

The LORD is not slack concerning His promise, as some count slackness, but is longsuffering toward us, not willing that any should perish but that all should come to repentance. —2 PETER 3:9

Sometimes our earthly fathers make promises that they fail to keep. Sometimes they change their minds, not giving us what they promised. We need to develop realistic expectations of our father (and others) to protect ourselves from severe disappointments and depression.

However, our triune God is not slack. God will not *hesitate*. He will not *linger*. He will not *delay*.

He wants to come back to rapture us soon. After the rapture He wants to start His millennial reign. One thousand years after that the earth and heavens, as today's passage says, will pass away. This time He will recreate it pollution-free to make up for all the garbage man has put in it.

The reason Jesus has not raptured His saints yet is because of His compassion for your friends and mine who have not been saved. He is not "willing" for me or anyone else to perish and go to hell. This phrase means he *wishes* everyone would go to heaven but does not decree it. He only wants people there who have not refused His gift on the cross.

We don't have a codependent God who rescues people who refuse to be rescued. We have a perfect God who rescues any who say "Help!"

> *In this the love of God was manifested toward us,*
> *that God has sent His only begotten Son into the*
> *world, that we might live through Him. In this is*
> *love, not that we loved God, but that He loved us*
> *and sent His Son* to be *the propitiation for our sins.*
> —1 JOHN 4:9–10

One major way that God the Father is different from our earthly fathers is in the quantity and quality of His love. Your dad may love you quite a bit, but your Father loves you infinitely more. As a father, I know I love and enjoy our six teenagers a great deal. I love their hugs. I love their friendship. I love comforting them during their crises. And yet I am certain their heavenly Father loves them even more than I could ever hope to.

The Father sent His only Child. We are the Father's sons and daughters, too, when we trust Christ, but we are adopted "chosen ones." Jesus is and always was God. He loved us before we ever learned to love Him.

We have a very perfectionistic Father, but His Son became the "propitiation" for our sins. The Greek word for "propitiation" means "the placating of God's wrath against sin." When the Father looks at us now, He loves us unconditionally, and He accepts us because we trust Christ.

God didn't send Christ to die just for good, moral people. Christ died for all of us while we were sinners.

When I get angry at God I will acknowledge that He loves my children infinitely more than I do. Eternal joy is really important to God—enough to send His only Son for sinners like me and my children.

"For God so loved the world that He gave His only begotten Son, that whoever believes in Him should not perish but have everlasting life."
—JOHN 3:16

When Dr. Minirth and I were medical students, we started a weekly Bible study for other medical students. One of the students who attended regularly decided to invite the wildest, most devout atheist in our class to attend, but he just ridiculed us for wasting our time. Our friend dared the atheist to read just the book of John from the New Testament and to see if he still felt that way.

The class atheist didn't want his friends to think he was chicken, so he accepted the challenge. In the privacy of his room that night he started reading the book of John. When he finished reading John 3:16, he closed the Bible, wept, and trusted Christ as His Savior. Not only that, but the very next morning he started to share the gospel with his bar-hopping buddies.

John 3:16 is the gospel in a nutshell. It is the most quoted and most powerful verse in the Bible.

John 3:16 says simply that God the Father loved the people of the world so much He sent His only Son so that the people of the world who depend on *Christ* will have eternal life.

In John 6:37, Jesus says He won't cast *anyone* out who comes to Him for salvation.

Lovingly challenge someone you care about to read John 3:16, even if it annoys him or her a little.

> *For by grace you have been saved through faith,*
> *and that not of yourselves; it is the gift of God, not*
> *of works, lest anyone should boast.*
>
> —EPH. 2:8

If the Bible had to be destroyed except for one passage, I would choose Ephesians 2 for the world to keep—not for myself, but for unbelievers to know how to trust Christ.

Satan uses the religions of the world to fool the people of the world. Some teach that heaven and hell are only here on earth in this life. Others say there is only a heaven. Others believe part of the Bible—that there is a literal heaven and a literal hell—but teach that people who are "good" go to heaven and people who are "bad" go to hell.

The Bible says that we are *only* saved by trusting Christ, not of works. Salvation is a gift—a free gift—by God's unmerited favor.

You are probably sitting down right now as you are reading. You are trusting your chair or couch to hold your body up off the floor. It may break, but you are taking that chance by faith.

That's how you get to heaven. You take a chance on Christ. You trust Christ. He shed His blood and died on the cross to pay for your sins and rose again. Merely depend on what He did for you to save you from hell. *Choose* to do that right now and ask Jesus to save you and dwell in your heart forever.

Dear Jesus, I want to become Your masterpiece—Your special work of art—today, without any good works to offer You.

"In the sweat of your face you shall eat bread Till you return to the ground, For out of it you were taken; For dust you are, And to dust you shall return."
—GEN. 3:16–19

When Adam and Eve were in the Garden of Eden, they were perfect. They had intimacy with God in a person-to-person friendship, intimacy with each other, authority to rule the perfect earth, and even perfect bodies. But even for them, it wasn't quite good enough. Satan appealed to their human need to feel even *more* significant—and it worked—even before the Fall. How powerful that human drive must be.

As a result of the Fall, all of nature became corrupted. Animals began eating other animals, for example. In the Millennium, lions will lie down beside lambs and rest together in peace. God told Eve she would experience pain in future childbirths. Adam would work the soil with sweat, hard work, thorns, mosquitoes. etc. The Hebrew word for "toil" is the same for Adam ("painful toil") as the word for Eve's labor pain ("painful toil").

Now Adam and Eve would experience the aging process, die, and go to heaven. But their bodies would return to the ground that Adam was made out of and named after. *Necessary suffering* for mankind thereafter had begun.

When Adam sinned, he represented you and me. We would have done the same thing. He sinned in our place. Christ, the "second Adam," died in our place. Some human suffering will be necessary for those still confined to this earth.

> *Then He said to Abram: "Know certainly that your*
> *descendants will be strangers in a land that is not*
> *theirs, and will serve them, and they will afflict*
> *them four hundred years. And also the nation*
> *whom they serve I will judge; afterward they shall*
> *come out with great possessions."*
>
> —GEN. 15:13–14

All of us must suffer in this life, some more than others. Suffering is necessary in the sense that it is unavoidable. But about half of our suffering *is avoidable*. Clinical depressions can be avoided, but grief reactions can't. Anxiety disorders can be avoided, but we will all experience some "worry."

Some suffering is unavoidable, however, and some limited suffering is also necessary—meaning absolutely needed, for our own growth, maturity, and perspective.

God made a covenant with Abraham thousands of years ago, and God will still keep it in the future. Abraham is in heaven right now. The triune God is chatting with God's "friend forever"—Abraham. God will bring the messianic kingdom to fulfill His covenant with Abraham, just like He delivered Abraham's descendants from Egypt in 1446 B.C. as He promised He would. God also desires to be faithful to you and keep His many promises to help you in your time of suffering and need. Like Abraham, God also desires for you to be His friend forever.

All suffering is but for a moment compared to eternity in heaven, if you are depending on Christ to pay for your sins in your place.

> *"The secret* things belong *to the* LORD *our God, but those* things which are *revealed* belong *to us and to our children forever, that we may do all the words of this law."*
> —DEUT. 29:29

I was driving home from Pomona, California, two weeks ago when, as I was driving south on Highway 5, I saw the victim of a car wreck that had occurred just a minute or two before. A young man about twenty years old had burned to death from the spilled gasoline and his body was hanging out of his car window, where he had tried to escape. It was still flaming. I sickened and wept. The ambulance was too late. I have wept many times the past two weeks as that memory flashes back.

When we grieve, part of us nearly always gets angry at God for allowing the loss to occur. Some people simply don't admit it to themselves. I was angry and sad. I asked God repeatedly, "Why did you allow that suffering to occur?

I really don't understand why God allows so much suffering. But I trust God. I trust His Word. When I get to heaven, I will enroll immediately in the University of Heaven for a Ph.D. in "God's Answers to the Secret Things."

There are many things in life that I won't fully know the answers to until I ask Jesus in person. In the meantime, I live patiently with not knowing the secret things. In the meantime, I will use and teach the things of God that are not secret.

> . . . *Shall we indeed accept good from God, and
> shall we not accept adversity?* . . . *For I know* that
> *my Redeemer lives, And He shall stand at last on
> the earth; And after my skin is destroyed, this* I
> know, *That in my flesh I shall see God.*
> —JOB 2:10b, 19:25–26

God tells us in over a hundred places in the Bible to expect suffering, even as a committed believer, but somehow we choose to overlook those passages. We simply don't expect to suffer when we are living right, but we should, because expecting it would at least decrease the unnecessary suffering of being shocked and enraged and disappointed when it does come—and it will.

Job is our model. He was a committed believer in the coming Messiah.

Job was the richest and godliest man on earth. But God allowed Satan to kill Job's children, take away his wealth, and give Job a painful skin disease with boils all over his body. Our passages for today show Job's response.

Job expected adversity. He was even more of a positive thinker than my friend and inspirational speaker Zig Zigler.

Job said to himself, Some day the Redeemer-Messiah will come and I'll spend eternity with Him face-to-face. I can hardly wait.

Expect necessary suffering. Bear necessary suffering. Realize all suffering is temporary.

*But He knows the way that I take; When He has
tested me, I shall come forth as gold. My foot has
held fast to His steps; I have kept His way and
not turned aside.*   —JOB 23:10–12

As we saw from yesterday's passage, we should
model our attitude after Job's and expect necessary
suffering, bear necessary suffering, and realize that all
suffering is brief and temporary relative to eternity.
But Job's positive thinking carried him even further.

God certainly allowed Satan to throw a whole bushel
of lemons at Job. He lost his children, his life savings,
and his own skin to a chronic, painful skin disease.

Job's attitude and positive thinking led him to wonder how much better a person he would become as a
result of this painful period in his life. He realized that
necessary suffering produces maturity *if* we let it—*if*
we don't allow bitterness and chronic depression to
take root.

Job said God would bring him out of this suffering
eventually, and his personality and spiritual maturity
would become more like polished gold. He kept obeying God's Word. In fact, even in sickness and grief, Job
craved God's Word more than even the food necessary
to sustain him. Daily meditation on God's eternal
promises is a big part of what kept Job going in spite of
the pain.

_____

When you are going through a tough period of necessary *suffering in
your life, ask yourself how you can learn and grow from it?*

You laid affliction on our backs. You have caused men to ride over our heads; We went through fire and through water; But You brought us out to rich fulfillment.
—PS. 66:11–12

I mentioned earlier a car accident that I had on November 15, 1989. It was a necessary suffering in my life that improved my perspective.

I had just been to our hospital units in Dallas, Texas. I was driving home to visit my parents, with whom I stay when I go to Dallas. I was listening to the Psalms on cassette tape, using the New King James Version.

As I made a left turn at a crowded intersection, a car appeared from nowhere and hit my car so hard that my car flipped up into the air and landed on the roof. Water and steam came pouring out of my upside-down car and I thought it would burst into flames. I had just filled the gas tank. The other car was also totaled, but fortunately no one was hurt.

That night, I put the same cassette tape into a player because I wanted to remember what verses were playing during the minutes prior to the accident. I wanted to be sure I didn't miss whatever message God wanted to teach me. I didn't want another accident like that. Today's passage played about two minutes before the accident and it ministered to me.

God laid me on my back but He brought me out. It doesn't guarantee that I won't die in a car wreck or some other way today, or tomorrow. But He wasn't finished with me yet. He wanted me to count my days and help people.

*In You, O LORD, I put my trust; Let me never be put
to shame. Deliver me in Your righteousness, and
cause me to escape; Incline Your ear to me, and
save me.* —PS. 71:1–2

Meditating on Scripture has a soothing effect. It gets
you out of your depraved thinking and into God's perspective of things.

In yesterday's devotional, I told you of my car accident. When the car landed upside down, the cassette
player stopped on today's passage.

If I hadn't been listening to the Bible on cassette that
moment, I'm sure I would have screamed and been
scared half to death like the next guy.

But instead I was perfectly calm as my car was in the
air, flipping. I honestly thought to myself while flipping, so this is what God has in store for me right now. I
wonder what He wants me to learn from this? *BAM!*

Not only was no one hurt (no guarantees for next
time), but my car landed right in front of a van (and
partially on top of a third car). When I crawled out of
my upside-down driver's window, the driver of the van
recognized me from our cable TV psychiatric program, even though she had never met me. She and her
mother and her two children drove me to my parents'
home nearby. They were "angels" sent by the Lord to
help me in that momentary crisis.

---

*God is my deliverer. I trust Him to decide when I should die or be
raptured. He is my rock and my fortress.*

This is my comfort in my affliction, For Your word has given me life. It is good for me that I have been afflicted, That I may learn Your statutes.
—PS. 119:50

If anyone understood the concept of necessary pain, King David would have to be at the top of the list. He suffered necessary pain when he was innocent. When he had killed Goliath and was working for King Saul, Saul tried to kill David on more than one occasion.

David also suffered other pain in his life. Some was necessary, but much would have been avoidable had David not made some sinful choices. He chose to watch from his roof when Bathsheba took her backyard bath. He chose to commit adultery. He chose to have her husband killed. He chose to spoil his son Absolom for some unknown reason.

As a result of these and other poor choices, David suffered the death of his first baby with Bathsheba. Absolom tried to kill David and take David's throne and died himself in the process. David suffered depression as a result of his severe guilt and initial unwillingness to forgive himself.

But David was a man of faith who trusted in the coming Messiah. Good and bad deeds have nothing to do with David's salvation or your own.

I look forward to meeting David, who will be my king during the messianic kingdom. I also look forward to meeting my King, Jesus Chr·st, who came to save those who trust in Him.

*Though He causes grief, Yet He will show
compassion According to the multitude of His
mercies.*
—LAM. 3:32

Another person who had a great deal of first-hand
experience with suffering was Jeremiah. He was
known as the "weeping prophet." Unlike David, most
of Jeremiah's suffering was national grief for his fellow
Jews rather than personal suffering, but he knew both
kinds.

Jeremiah even wrote a book about suffering. He
called it *Lamentations,* a less-often read book of the
Bible. In today's passage, Jeremiah teaches us two important things about grief and suffering.

God sometimes causes grief. We hate to admit that.
We want a God who only gives us pleasure, makes us
rich and popular, and gives us whatever we want. But
God loves us, so he wants us to become mature. He
sends us grief and necessary pain at times to help us in
the long run.

In spite of causing grief, God *shows compassion.* He
is filled with pity for us. He is actually *sad* when He has
to allow suffering.

What a puzzle—the God who loves us is the same
God who also sends us some of our necessary afflic-
tions or allows them from time to time.

---

*Young children need loving discipline to grow up responsible and
considerate. It is worth their pain and a parent's own grief.*

> *For You cast me into the deep, Into the heart of the seas, And the floods surrounded me; All Your billows and Your waves passed over me.*
> —JONAH 2:3

Jonah was what we call a passive-aggressive personality. He pouted. He procrastinated. He was purposefully inefficient. He was stubborn. He blamed others. He was selfish. He was lazy. He was rebellious. He was passive in the sense that he stuffed his anger and ran away from problems. He was the type of guy who would walk away and pout if his wife wanted to resolve a conflict. He also set himself up for repeated failures. He was probably always late and didn't even know why.

But Jonah was a believer, and God takes great pride in choosing the foolish, immature people of the world to confound the wise. He loves Jonahs like you and me.

God has to send some necessary pain at times to help us grow up. He had to throw Jonah into the ocean and get him swallowed whole by a huge fish who vomited him up close to shore. But it all worked together for good. God loved the thousands of innocent little children in Ninevah, even though their parents were brutal murderers. Ninevah repented, the children were eventually led to believe in the real God, and passive-aggressive Jonah was used by God in spite of himself.

I am personally very grateful that God uses imperfect people.

> *Concerning this thing I pleaded with the Lord three*
> *times that it might depart from me. And He said to*
> *me, "My grace is sufficient for you, for My strength*
> *is made perfect in weakness." Therefore most*
> *gladly I will rather boast in my infirmities, that the*
> *power of Christ may rest upon me.*
>
> 2 COR. 12:8–10

The New Testament Saul was a Pharisee, a workaholic, a brilliant scholar, and very religious. He was what we call an obsessive-compulsive personality. He was insecure on the inside but came across very much in total control. He caused a great deal of suffering.

He was convinced in his own mind that Christianity was an anti-Semitic, bad disease. He killed many and threw many others into prison.

But God loves sinners. He appeared to Saul on the road to Damascus. Jesus converted Saul, changed his name to Paul (which means "little"), and gave Paul an incurable disease, probably an eye disease that made Paul look ugly. Paul had to write with big letters. He told some believers he knew they loved him enough to exchange eyes with him.

God gave Paul this necessary suffering to keep the "pride of Saul" from cropping back up in Paul. Three times God refused to heal Paul, so Paul accepted his lifelong disorder and made the best of a bad situation. God's grace was sufficient.

Paul looked forward to necessary suffering. I often pray that God will keep mine to a minimum.

> *You therefore must endure hardship as a good*
> *soldier of Jesus Christ. No one engaged in warfare*
> *entangles himself with the affairs of this life, that*
> *he may please him who enlisted him as a soldier.*
> —2 TIM. 2:3–4

Pastor Ray Stedman wrote a book many years ago called *Body Life*. In it, he told believers how we can get rid of superficial, phony Christianity by small group interaction, loving confrontation, honesty and support.

I have often jokingly threatened to write a sequel to *Body Life* and call it *Body Odor*. In it I would write about all the "armpits" of Christianity—the phony religious leaders who make false promises to nonbelievers and believers alike. Send them your money and God "promises" to send you one hundred times as much cash back, answer all your prayers affirmatively, and straighten out your mate.

In today's passage, Paul promised committed believers quite the opposite. He told us we should expect to endure hardship. He told us to become self-disciplined soldiers with mental toughness. He also warned us to play by the right rules.

Some religious leaders are not going by God's game plan. They make their own rules and as a result, some people don't get what they were promised and fall away from active Christian living.

Nonbelievers see all the disappointment and phoniness, make fun of it, and never trust Christ because of all this.

Invest your time and donations to body life, *not* body odor.

"For whom the LORD loves He chastens, and scourges every son whom He receives." If you endure chastening, God deals with you as with sons; for what son is there whom a father does not chasten? But if you are without chastening, of which all have become partakers, then you are illegitimate and not sons.
—HEB. 12:6–8

Divine discipline implies divine love (see Prov. 3:11–12). God the Father loves us infinitely more than we could ever even hope to love someone. That's why He disciplines us when we become His children.

God encourages us to expect discipline from Him periodically and to "endure chastening"—to persevere. He wants us to become truly holy like He is. This requires that we become *partakers* in His holiness by being *partakers* in His discipline.

Solomon said if you don't discipline your child promptly for open rebellion, you are hating him, because you will spoil him. God won't spoil us because He loves us. If you never experience His discipline—His necessary suffering—then be sure you have not genuinely trusted Christ. You may be an illegitimate child.

The Greek word for discipline in our Hebrews 12:6–8 passage, by the way, is *paideia,* which literally means "childtraining." If we endure it and learn from it, we will also become partakers in special rewards from our Father in the messianic kingdom and in eternity.

Have you had enough necessary suffering to prove to yourself that you are God's legitimate child?

Now no chastening seems to be joyful for the present, but grievous; nevertheless, afterward it yields the peaceable fruit of righteousness to those who have been trained by it. —HEB. 12:11

When I was a young boy and openly rebelled from time to time, my father applied the "board of education" to my "seat of knowledge." I found out pretty quick which boundaries I had better not cross.

When we are born, we don't think there are or ever should be any boundaries. We are born sociopathic. But my parents both loved me, which made me want to obey, and they both disciplined me for open rebellion, which made me afraid to disobey. I will always struggle in this life with sinful temptations and tendencies because I am human. I will even occasionally rebel against my heavenly Father, because my IQ is extremely low relative to His. But my heavenly Father will discipline me like my earthly father did—in love.

I respect and even am now grateful for the discipline I have received from both my earthly and my heavenly Father. As a psychiatrist, I have often seen the misery that befalls a full-blown, undisciplined sociopath. I don't want that.

I didn't like discipline whatsoever when I was five, but I understand its value now that I am forty-five. I think I'll share this passage with my children today.

Thank you, Lord, for the peace and clear conscience that come from learning and valuing Your boundaries. Forgive me whenever I step over the line—and discipline me as needed.

> *My brethren, count it all joy when you fall into*
> *various trials, knowing that the testing of your faith*
> *produces patience. But let patience have its perfect*
> *work, that you may be perfect and complete,*
> *lacking nothing.*
> —JAMES 1:2–4

In our passage for today, James is not saying that whenever suffering comes your way you should deny your anger and grief. He is not saying that you should say to yourself, Oh great! I get to suffer today! James is not asking us to be stupid, just mature.

In the original Greek, it is clear that James is asking us to be joyful *in* our trials, not *for* our trials. Be proud of what you and God together can do about each trial. Take each trial as a challenge to apply biblical principles.

The Greek word here for "trials," *peirasmois,* means both external and internal tests of stamina. "Knowing" is *dokimion,* implying the approval of your faith, not proving that it is there. "Patience" is *hypomonēn,* or "steadfastness in the face of difficulties."

God never expects a believer to be perfect before heaven. The Greek word here for perfect is actually *teleioi* and means mature not perfect. The Greek word for "complete" is *holoklēroi,* implying whole or mature in every area spiritually.

I don't long for trials, but when they come, I will accept them as a challenge to put into practice, with God's power, the biblical principles I have learned by experience to depend upon.

> *For this* is *commendable, if because of conscience*
> *toward God one endures grief, suffering wrongfully.*
> *For what credit* is it *if, when you are beaten for*
> *your faults, you take it patiently? But when you do*
> *good and suffer for it,* if *you take it patiently, this is*
> *commendable before God.*
>
> —1 PETER 2:19–20

We have talked about the suffering of Job, who was innocent, the probable eye disease of Paul, to keep him humble; the unnecessary suffering of David from his sins, and others, but there is one more type of necessary suffering that God says we will go through: *persecution.*

It's sad to say in a country like America, but if you do a great job rearing your children and they become Bible-believing, law-abiding citizens, they will probably be discriminated against in many circles. They will be made fun of for reserving sex until marriage or for not getting drunk and killing their brain cells.

I know of an admissions committee member at a major medical school who warned a Christian pre-med student to "leave all that Christian stuff off your application or most medical schools won't admit you." I personally sat in on a meeting where an A-average medical school graduate from Harvard was turned down for a psychiatry residency because they found out he believed the Bible. The committee said, "How could anyone naive enough to believe the Bible ever become a good psychiatrist?"

Keep praying for freedom of religion, not freedom from religion, in America.

*But even if you should suffer for righteousness'
sake,* you are *blessed.*   —1 PETER 3:14

Today's passage continues the theme of necessary suffering we all should expect, even in America, from religious persecution. Last week I talked to a psychiatry resident at a, top-ranked university. He is keeping his faith in Christ a secret until he passes the board exams. He told me his university takes great pride in their open-mindedness and tolerance. They promote and tolerate everything from the ultra-right to the ultra-left. Except they have profound prejudice and discrimination against evangelicals—those of us who believe in the inerrancy of Scripture and, therefore, salvation by grace through faith in Jesus Christ.

I have counseled businessmen who lost their jobs because they refused to supply prostitutes to visiting salesmen from other companies. I counseled a nurse who got in trouble because she refused to dehydrate to death an elderly patient.

High schools that allow and even teach New Age or Eastern religions like transcendental meditation won't even allow Christian groups to meet by themselves on campus for a Bible study.

Our passage for today says if you suffer religious discrimination or persecution you are blessed even though you probably won't feel delighted at the time.

Expect persecution. Look what "society" did to Christ, and He was perfect. Remember that religious leaders persecuted Christ the most.

> *For it is better, if it is the will of God, to suffer for*
> *doing good than for doing evil. For Christ also*
> *suffered once for sins, the just for the unjust, that*
> *He might bring us to God.*
>   —1 PETER 3:17–18

In today's passage, Peter continues the "necessary suffering in the form of persecution" theme. He says it is God's will, not that people persecute you, but that you be brave enough to face it at appropriate times.

Christ suffered persecution *for our sins*. He witnessed to non-repentant nonbelievers who were facing death and hell. They were lost "spirits in prison" but didn't know it. Then Peter reflected on Noah.

Noah, his wife, and their three sons and three daughters-in-law obeyed God even when they were the only ones left. It took one hundred twenty years for Noah to build the ark and during that time Noah kept warning the people of a coming judgment of God by a world-wide flood, but he was ridiculed by all.

Matthew 24 says that it will be just like the days of Noah at the end of the Great Tribulation when Christ comes with His saints to set up the messianic kingdom. Religious persecution will be at an all-time peak, making the persecution we feel now seem about as irritating as a fly on a bull's horn.

Religious persecution has been around since Cain killed Abel for obtaining God's favor by obeying God in his religious practices. It will eventually get worse. In the meantime, expect persecution and take advantage of the freedom we still have around the world.

*Beloved, do not think it strange concerning the
fiery trial which is to try you, as though some
strange thing happened to you; but rejoice to the
extent that you partake of Christ's sufferings, that
when His glory is revealed, you may also be glad
with exceeding joy.* —1 PETER 4:12–13

Today, the apostle Peter tells us the good news—there
is a great payoff for any necessary suffering we go
through, especially if it is for religious persecution like
Christ experienced. Let's take a look at what Peter has
to say about it.

The first thing is that we should not think it is
strange that people would persecute or discriminate
against us. If the Bible is *true*, then there is a real eternal hell and people go there when they die. We are all
accountable to a Holy God. Many things sinners love to
do are forbidden, such as sex outside of marriage (even
fantasizing it), getting drunk, etc.

Peter says there is a payoff, though. When Christ's
glory is revealed then we will be specially blessed.

We know there are different kinds of rewards but we
don't know specifically what they will be. When Christmas comes around each year, would you rather know
what your presents are a month ahead of time or be
surprised on Christmas day? Well Christmas II is coming.

---

*If we really knew what the payoff will be some day for being per-
secuted, we would probably be out there begging people to persecute us instead of feeling sorry for ourselves.*

> *But may the God of all grace, who called us to*
> *His eternal glory by Christ Jesus, after you have*
> *suffered a while, perfect, establish, strengthen,*
> *and settle you.*
> —1 PETER 5:10

Many depressed patients have come up to me in our hospital units and asked, "I've been working on my depression a whole week now—why don't I feel any better yet? Why won't God just make it go away?"

I tell them that at the end of the first week in our hospital unit, most people feel *worse* than they did when they came in because they are finding out so many things about themselves that they don't really want to know. By the end of the second week they feel like when they came in. At the end of the third week they usually feel better. The fourth week is usually a week of solidification.

On an outpatient basis, seeing a therapist once a week for forty-five minutes will usually take nine months to accomplish what we can accomplish in one month in the hospital.

I wish God would wave a magic wand and make people's pain go away, but instead He makes them work through a process: insight, grieving, forgiving, giving up expectations, stopping codependency, etc.

God won't wave a magic wand, but "after you have suffered a while," He will make you stronger than you ever were before.

Pain relief takes hard work, lots of tears, lots of forgiving, and often a Christian, insight-oriented therapist.

Then Elkanah her husband said to her, "Hannah, why do you weep? Why do you not eat? And why is your heart grieved? Am I not better to you than ten sons?" So Hannah arose after they had finished eating and drinking in Shiloh. Now Eli the priest was sitting on the seat by the doorpost of the tabernacle of the LORD. And she was in bitterness of soul, and prayed to the LORD and wept in anguish.
—1 SAM. 1:8–10

Unnecessary suffering is all the emotional, physical or spiritual pain that we could improve or even eliminate by knowing the truth and taking steps to recovery.

Hannah was a committed believer a few thousand years ago. But she was bitter of soul, depressed, weepy, couldn't eat, and grieving. She was barren and wanted a child very badly.

Hannah's suffering was totally unnecessary. If she had committed her life to God to such a great extent that she wanted whatever God wanted for her, then she would have requested but not demanded a child. Plus, if she could have seen into the future, she would have realized that God was planning on giving her several children. One of them, Samuel, would be an extraordinary man of God, chosen to write part of the Bible.

―――――――

When I set my personal goals, I won't do what Hannah did and demand that God fall in line. I will ask God what He wants for my life and be grateful for whatever it may be. I will grieve the dreams I gave up on to avoid clinical depression from bitterness of soul.

> *Be angry, and do not sin. Meditate within your*
> *heart on your bed, and be still. Offer the sacrifices*
> *of righteousness, and put your trust in the* LORD.
> —PS. 4:4–5

We all feel depressed from time to time. That's normal. But fifty percent of Americans get *so* depressed at some time in their lives that they develop a biochemical depression.

If we obey our passages for today by going ahead and getting angry, which we naturally do, without handling the anger sinfully, and if we meditate on the anger-producing situation and forgive (Eph. 4:26), and trust God to take care of vengeful motives (Rom. 12:19), then we will have peace.

However, if we disobey today's passages, then our *bitterness* will cause a chemical depletion in our brains, resulting in a clinical, biochemical depression induced by the sin of holding grudges. We typically develop insomnia, sadness, trouble concentrating, tiredness, appetite changes, irritability, and eventually we become suicidal.

Forgiving is the only cure for a sin-induced clinical depression. That's why every passage in this book is designed directly or indirectly to enable you to be *free to forgive*, whether you were ever abused or not.

Lord, please help me to eliminate clinical depression from my life by obeying You in regards to anger.

*When I kept silent, my bones grew old through my
groaning all the day long. For day and night Your
hand was heavy upon me; my vitality was turned
into the drought of summer. I acknowledged my sin
to You, and my iniquity I have not hidden. I said, "I
will confess my transgressions to the LORD," and
You forgave the iniquity of my sin.*

—PS. 32:3–5

God actually gave each one of us two brains to operate life on: the cerebral cortex and the limbic brain.
You use your cerebral cortex to make logical choices,
to think, to move, etc.

But God also gave you an equally important brain
underneath the cerebral cortex called the limbic brain.
You need it to be in touch with your feelings, to express
your emotions. You must *use* it to maintain mental
health. There are millions of neurons connecting it to
the cerebral cortex. God wants you to use them both.

King David didn't use his limbic brain after his sins
with Bathsheba and Uriah. He "kept silent"—he
stuffed his guilt feelings. He stuffed his self-hatred. He
stuffed his vengeful motives toward himself. Therefore, he became clinically depressed. Eventually he
got over it with help from God using an indirective
counselor by the name of Nathan, who got David in
touch with what his limbic brain was feeling by using a
story rather than confronting David directly.

---

*God gave me two brains to think and feel with—I will use them both.
I will thus prevent a lot of unnecessary pain.*

> The righteous *cry out, and the Lord hears, And
> delivers them out of all their troubles. The Lord
> is near to those who have a broken heart, And
> saves such as have a contrite spirit.*
> —PS. 34:17–18

One of the primary causes of unnecessary pain in our
lives is an attitude of sinful pride and arrogance.

The Bible tells us not to cast away our self-confi-
dence (see Gal. 6:4).

But God hates the kind of false pride that says, I'm
better than you; I deserve to use you or abuse you.
That kind of arrogance raises its ugly head in all of us
from time to time.

What are the worst sins you have ever committed?
You were somehow prideful when you committed
them. What are the worst sins others have committed
against you? They were arrogant too.

Do you have an attitude of humility? A contrite
heart? If you truly do, you will *forgive yourself* for your
sins. Not forgiving yourself is also arrogant. It is wanting to play God and get vengeance on yourself. The
Father already accepted Christ's atonement. Accept
that gift. Don't be too proud. And tell the Lord
"thanks."

Have you forgiven your arrogant abusers? If not,
you are trying to play God again. Vengeance is none of
your business. God is great at it. Trust Him (Rom.
12:19).

---

*If I can develop a humble spirit that is apologetic to God and forgiv-
ing of myself and others, then God will deliver me.*

I am troubled, I am bowed down greatly; I go mourning all the day long. For my loins are full of inflammation, And there is *no soundness in my flesh.*
—PS. 38:6–7

According to some national polls, our three greatest fears, in order, are: fear of failure; fear of abandonment; fear of death.

When David sinned with Bathsheba, he repressed his feelings of guilt and self-hatred and temporarily allowed his arrogance to dominate him. Then when Nathan confronted him, David asked God to forgive him, but he refused to forgive himself.

As a result, he developed a biochemical depression. He also developed a lot of unnecessary *physical* discomfort. When we are stressed out like David was, our brains put out ACTH. Our adrenal glands put out stress hormones. Our white blood cells are affected. We have fewer antibodies to fight flu, bronchitis, yeast infections, and sometimes even cancers. Stress can also cause arthritis, migraine headaches, ulcers, and other psychophysiologic disorders.

David felt abandoned. He felt like a failure morally. But his feelings of abandonment were amplified and exaggerated by the fact that he had abandoned himself. We should always remain our own best friend, next to God, of course. David eventually forgave himself and recovered.

We can save ourselves a great deal of physical, unnecessary pain by dealing with our emotions biblically—forgiving ourselves and others after confessing our part to God.

> *I was mute with silence, I held my peace even from*
> *good; And my sorrow was stirred up. My heart was*
> *hot within me; While I was musing, the fire burned.*
> *Then I spoke with my tongue.* —PS. 39:2–3

We have already shown you how stuffed feelings of anger and vengeance cause a whole chain of biochemical reactions in your brain and entire body. The result is not only depression but also lowered resistance to illnesses.

In today's passage, David explains how this process took place in his own life. "Holding his peace" kept him from obtaining peace. His sorrow got "stirred up." In psychiatry, we call this unresolved grief. His heart was "hot" within him and the more he chided himself for his sins, the more the fire burned within him.

David was probably describing both "heartburn" and anguish of heart. Heartburn occurs from stress. It can burn a hole in your stomach and kill you if it gets severe enough (a bleeding ulcer). But David finally verbalized his feelings to God and friends. I'm sure Nathan the prophet also helped David to forgive himself—to realize that no sin is too great for God to forgive.

Don't cause yourself unnecessary pain. Verbalize your sad and angry feelings as they appear.

Lord, help me to verbalize my feelings and to forgive when my emotional "fires" are burning.

"Be angry, and do not sin": *do not let the sun go down on your wrath.* —EPH. 4:26

As we have already stated, over ninety percent of biochemical depressions are caused by holding on to our anger in the form of grudges and vengeful motives. If people learned to be in touch with their anger, verbalize it, and forgive the abusers of this world then over half of our psychiatric practice would be eliminated. But it would be worth it. That's why we are writing this devotional.

In Proverbs 16:20, Solomon said to heed (ponder) the Word (Hebrew word *dābār* refers to the instructions of God). If we do this wisely (properly), then we will find good (prosperity in a general sense). God will relieve our depression and make us happy.

In Ephesians 4:26, the words "be angry" are in the passive imperative tense in the original Greek. This means that as we begin to feel the emotion of anger, we should go ahead and allow it to come to our conscious awareness so we can deal with it biblically rather than sinfully. We are able to verbalize it, speaking the truth about it in a loving manner and choose to forgive by bedtime even though it may take a lot of reforgiving before your "gut" also forgives.

When my anger comes, I will allow it to be verbalized lovingly; I will choose to forgive my abusers in my head by bedtime, even though it may take a while for my gut to catch up to my head.

> *Do not say, "I will recompense evil"; Wait for the
> LORD, and He will save you. Repay no one evil for
> evil.*
> —PROV. 20:22

Christians have their own "hit man." His name is God.
You don't need to call the mafia. And you don't need to
take vengeance into your own hands.

Vengeance is God's business. He is omniscient (all-
knowing), omnipresent (present everywhere), and omnipotent (all-powerful). He is the one who created hell
for abusers. He is the one who designed our bodies to
deplete serotonin when we demand to take over His
job and harbor personal grudges.

Don't do it! Don't get vengeance on *anyone*. But
don't get stepped on, either. Protect yourself. But when
you protect yourself, and the abusers of this world get
to you anyway, then tell it to God. Don't tell God how to
"fix" it, either. Let God be God. Let Him decide, because He is also perfect love.

God the Father's ultimate "hit" was on His own Son,
Jesus Christ. Christ willingly took our "hit" for us on
the cross. The Father, who demands perfection, created eternal hell to punish us for our abuses of ourselves and others. But if we accept Jesus as our
substitute, the Father accepts us.

Lord, please convict my abusers of their sins. I release them to you.

Do not rejoice when your enemy falls, And do not let your heart be glad when he stumbles; Lest the LORD see it, and it displease Him, And He turn away His wrath from him. —PROV. 24:17–18

We must remember that every human life is significant to God, from the day of conception to the day of death. We all have sinned and all sins abuse somebody. We must realize that God loves abusers but absolutely detests their abuses. He created hell for those who won't repent. But He is fair. The only people who go to hell are people who reject the conviction and call of the Holy Spirit to realize Christ is God and thus refuse to depend on Christ's shed blood to save them. If anyone seeks after true righteousness, God will show him how to be saved.

So when you see an abuser suffer consequences from God, be humble. Don't rejoice or gloat over it. That is an attitude of superiority and God hates that. God will quietly punish your abuser and also discipline you if you do that.

Don't get even with your abusers either. If you dig a pit to get even with your abusers, God will see to it that you fall into your own pit. Let God get even.

Our criminal justice system sometimes works and sometimes fails. But God never fails. If you knew what God's plans are for your abusers, you would probably feel sorry for them.

> *Who can understand his errors? Cleanse me from*
> *secret faults. Keep back Your servant also from*
> *presumptuous sins; Let them not have dominion*
> *over me.*
> —PS. 19:12

Anxiety is much more complex than depression. If someone is depressed, psychiatrists know now to look for vengeful motives most of the time, while also searching for medical or genetic factors as well. When a patient comes to us with the primary complaint of anxiety, however, there are potentially many different repressed emotions that could be causing it, as well as medical factors again.

Anxiety is "fear of the unknown." It is a fear of finding out the truth about our own unconscious thoughts, feelings, and motives. About eighty percent of our thoughts, feelings, motives, and drives are unconscious—out of our awareness.

In our passage for today, David (three thousand years ago) said we cannot understand our unconscious errors without God's help. Therefore, David prayed for insight and cleansing from his unconscious sins. He had already confessed and been forgiven for his conscious sins—the ones he knew about. But David wanted a blameless conscience. He wanted even his innermost unconscious thoughts to be pleasing to the Lord.

Pray for insights today into your own depravity. Don't be shocked when you find some. Depravity is a disease none of us are immune to.

Rest in the LORD, and wait patiently for Him; Do not fret because of him who prospers in his way, Because of the man who brings wicked schemes to pass.   —PS. 37:7

There are several forms of anxiety. True anxiety, from a psychiatrist's point of view, is when you feel uptight, fearful and anxious but you don't know why. Whenever that happens, barring some rare medical cause, you are close to having some emotion or motive emerge from your unconscious to your conscious awareness. We call that *true* anxiety.

But we have two other kinds of anxiety. One is a healthy concern. Your teenager is late coming home from a trip and you are concerned, out of love, about his or her safety. That's a good form of anxiety.

A third kind of anxiety is everyday *worry*. We worry about what to wear, what to eat, whether we will be liked. We worry whether our abuser got punished yet, or whether our abusers are still getting away with their sins.

David says not to fret over whether your abusers temporarily prosper. Quit stirring up your anger over and over again. Call on God and let Him take care of it in His own way and in His own time.

Just think, some day you will inherit the earth—both in the Millennium and then in the new earth. Your abusers are not your concern.

> *In God (I will praise His word), In God I have put*
> *my trust; I will not fear. What can flesh do to me?*
> *You number my wanderings; Put my tears into*
> *Your bottle; Are they not in Your book?*
> —PS. 56:4, 8

Being an innocent victim of abuse can create a great deal of anxiety in various forms. The victim fears further abuse. That is only logical.

Then there is the rage. The abused is afraid to be in touch with all the rage. He feels he may lose control if he sees it. He may even kill someone and end up in prison.

Then there is the false guilt, the foolish assumption that getting abused was somehow your fault.

Then there is the fear of rejection. If your abuser was a parent, and if you erroneously base your self-worth on what your parents happen to think of you instead of what God thinks of you, then you will deny their abuse. You will put your abuser on a pedestal, protect the family secret, and have panic attacks because of the fear of betraying a parent.

Then there is the fear of losing control—of being out of control of your own life.

If you are mourning under oppression or abuse, then hope in the God who helps you. You are so significant to God that He has numbered every tear you have ever cried and put them in the "bottle" of His compassionate, loving memories of you.

Unless the LORD had been my help, My soul would soon have settled in silence. If I say, "My foot slips," Your mercy, O LORD, will hold me up. In the multitude of my anxieties within me, Your comforts delight my soul.　　—PS. 94:17–19

The greatest anxiety that people acknowledge in opinion polls is the worry that they will fail in life. We fear failure in our careers. We fear failure in our ability to rear our own children. And perhaps our greatest fear is the fear of losing control morally.

Part of us is evil and contaminated and desires to use and abuse people to feel significant. Parts of each of us, especially if we are believers, want to be moral, to be kind to others, to be loving and loved. But we all fail, and each time we fail morally, the fear of future failure grows.

Without God, this would be a never-ending cycle leading to greater and greater anxiety. But God paid for the penalty of our sins by total *grace*, through *faith* alone. We live by grace. Total freedom. But since the Holy Spirit is now in you permanently, you will want more than ever to be good. God knows you will still fail, but you will get better and better over the years in a gradual sanctification process.

When our foot slips, God lifts us back up. God's grace gives us comfort—and the freedom to fail and learn.

> *Search me, O God, and know my heart; Try me,*
> *and know my anxieties; And see if there is any*
> *wicked way in me, And lead me in the way*
> *everlasting.* —PS. 139:23–24

We have mentioned that real anxiety is the fear of becoming aware of the *truth* about our own contaminated thoughts, feelings, motives, or drives. As Christians, the Holy Spirit's goal is to help us mature gradually toward more and more Christ-likeness and more and more freedom.

The more we see the truth, scrape out the old emotional wounds, forgive and heal, the more our conscious mind will be in control, overruling our sinful drives.

The Holy Spirit is deep inside us, *pushing up* a hidden area of sin from our unconscious to our conscious. Our depraved brain, meanwhile, is pushing that hidden area of sin back down so we won't see it. That tension between the Holy Spirit pushing the truth up and our depraved brains pushing the sin down is anxiety!

The Holy Spirit is not weak, but He will only work with willing, cooperative saints. We have to let go of our fear of the truth and let God guide us in the healing process when we see the truth. Then we must take control of that area of our lives by making *redecisions*—new decisions about how to live with that new insight.

David wanted to get rid of his wicked ways. Let's pray, like David did, for insights into our unconscious anxieties.

> *You will keep* him *in perfect peace,* Whose *mind* is
> *stayed* on You, *Because he trusts in You.* "Blessed
> is *the man who trusts in the* LORD, *And whose hope
> is the* LORD."
>   —ISA. 26:3

In our Minirth-Meier Clinics throughout the country, we treat many thousands of believers and nonbelievers for anxiety disorders ranging from mild anxiety to panic attacks, obsessive-compulsive disorders, phobias, and agoraphobia (the fear of many things including crowds, leaving your own house, etc.).

By doing insight-oriented therapy, Gestalt and other psychiatric techniques research has taught us; a thorough medical evaluation; and the application of biblical principles, we are able to help believers and nonbelievers. But the "cure" doesn't last very long in nonbelievers.

No human can stay on a steady, low level of anxiety without God's help. The nonbeliever does not have the Holy Spirit in him, pushing the truth up, except to convince him of his sinfulness. And even then, the Bible says the Spirit will convict to a certain point, then give up on that person when his heart has become irreversibly hardened to the Holy Spirit's conviction.

Our passages for today remind us to trust God to relieve our anxieties. He will give us perfect peace, "genuine, complete" *peace both now and also in the Millennium.*

Lord, I will trust You and focus on becoming like You and serving You. Thank you for the genuine peace I experience as a result.

> *Therefore, having been justified by faith, we have*
> *peace with God through our Lord Jesus Christ,*
> *and the peace of God, which surpasses all*
> *understanding, will guard your hearts and*
> *minds through Christ Jesus.*
>
> —ROM. 5:1, PHIL. 4:7

There are several kinds of anxiety and many ways anxiety shows its ugly head. Anxiety may cause a headache or heartburn in me, but panic attacks or phobia in someone else.

There are also different kinds of peace. Paul told us in Romans 12:18 to strive to be at peace with all men. We need to be at peace with ourselves and develop a clear conscience to prevent insomnia. We need to be at peace with the abusive jerks in our past by turning vengeance over to God, forgiving them, and protecting ourselves from further abuse.

We also need peace with God. We all have a vacuum only He can fill. We must trust Christ to save us, then grow into an intimate fellowship with Him. We can do this over the years with prayer, obedience, circumstances, and daily meditation on God's Word.

In Romans 5:1 Paul used the Greek word *echomen* to tell us to "keep on having and enjoying peace with God." And in Philippians 4:7, he told us about the inner tranquility (the peace of God) of a believer who has a close walk with God. It guards our hearts and minds from anxiety.

―――――――

Lord, thank you for helping me to be at peace with You, with a clear conscience. It is truly a peace that passes understanding.

Rejoice in the Lord always. Again I will say, rejoice!
—PHIL. 4:4

The opposite of anxiety is *peace,* and peace is a "fruit of the Spirit." It is not automatic. When an anxious person becomes a true Christian, he becomes an anxious Christian. He has peace with God as far as his salvation is concerned, but there is lots of work to do to obtain greater degrees of peace.

The apostle Paul recommends that we grieve our losses, but even in the middle of a grieving period we can always rejoice in the Lord, delight in Him, and accept His loving help during our grief.

Paul also encourages us to strive for gentleness. The Greek word for gentleness here implies a forebearing, nonretaliatory spirit.

The phrase, "The Lord is at hand" here refers to the Rapture (see 1 Thess. 4:13–18). Thinking about the Rapture, the messianic kingdom, and the new heavens and new earth should excite us and make our everyday worries of less significance. What difference will our worries make a hundred years from now?

If we concentrate on our self-talk and our attitude throughout the day, we will be able to determine if we are generating peace or anxiety. By developing Christlike attitudes, our level of peace will progressively improve.

Lord, help me to have Your attitude of gentleness and rejoicing and to only say to myself things that You would agree with.

> *Be anxious for nothing, but in everything by prayer and supplication, with thanksgiving, let your requests be made known to God; and the peace of God, which surpasses all understanding, will guard your hearts and minds through Christ Jesus.*
>
> —PHIL. 4:6

Would God have told us to "be anxious for nothing" if anxiety were not something we could control? I don't think so. He told us that because He knows any of us, with His help, can overcome anxiety.

There are spiritual as well as psychological tools we can use to overcome anxiety. *Prayer* is one of them. It not only reminds us of our dependence on God for power, but prayer makes a difference in what God will do for us. He demands it. He will withhold some of His help without it.

Thanksgiving is another great tool. Thanking God for His blessings and for the psychological and spiritual "tools" He has given you to make life's lemons into lemonade.

Let God know your requests (*aitēmata*—specific, definite requests). God is the one who will guard (*phrourēsei*—a military term implying "to protect with a garrison") your hearts and minds.

Anxiety is a choice. Freedom from anxiety is also a choice and a process.

Lord, with a thankful attitude I will verbalize to you my innermost worries and anxieties. When you show me what to do about them, I will do it. In the meantime, I will focus primarily on positive, dignified thoughts.

But above all these things put on love, which is the bond of perfection. And let the peace of God rule in your hearts, to which also you were called in one body; and be thankful. —COL. 3:14–15

In yesterday's passage (see Phil. 4:6–9), the apostle Paul told us to choose worry-free living and gave us some good tools for doing so. In today's passage he gives us more tools we can use to gradually get to worry-free living.

Love is a major tool. One of our greatest worries is the worry that we will be lonely, isolated, rejected, or abandoned. Learning to love God and experience His love for us on a gut level helps. Choosing to love ourselves and see ourselves as God sees us helps. Deciding to be our own best friend is vital. Getting active in small growth groups or mini-churches in a healthy local church is vital. We need to love and be loved by people with common goals and interests. That requires spending time with them in honest relationships.

Paul also tells us to let the peace of God *rule* (*brabeuetō*—to decide every debate in our hearts. This is the only time this Greek word is used in the whole New Testament.).

Daily devotions is also a must, so God's principles can become part of our daily routine.

Go to your local Christian bookstore soon and purchase some good, biblical Christian music tapes and also a copy of the New King James Version of the Bible on tape, narrated by Cliff Barrows.

*If I have made gold my hope, Or said to fine gold,
"You are my confidence"; If I have rejoiced because
my wealth was great, This also would be an
iniquity worthy of judgment, For I would have
denied God who is above.*   —JOB 31:24–28

There are more verses in the Bible on money and
finance-related topics than all the verses on heaven
and hell put together. Why would God do that? We will
spend a whole month finding out.

About 70 percent of the marital conflicts we treat
involve money. Show me a person's financial habits
and nothing else about him and I'll know a great deal
about his childhood, his control issues, his entitlement
issues, his passive-aggressive tendencies, his drives,
his source of pain, and his most likely future sources of
unnecessary suffering.

Job was the wealthiest man on earth about four
thousand years ago, but Job had his great wealth in
perspective. He said gold was not his hope. His confidence was not based on gold (money). Rejoicing in the
sense of arrogant pride over his ability to accumulate
wealth would be sinful. It would be denying God, the
true source of all good things.

---

*It is a sin to live to be rich, but it's not a sin for God to choose, in some
cases, to give wealth to those who put Him first. God blesses others
with a wealth of children, or a wealth of friends, or a wealth of
talents.*

For the love of money is a root of all kinds of evil,
for which some have strayed from the faith in their
greediness, and pierced themselves through with
many sorrows. —1 TIM. 6:10

All humans feel inferior. We never completely conquer these feelings in this life. It even drove Adam and
Eve to sin, wanting to be like God. It eats away at us. It
motivates us to make poor choices.

The three main "ways of the world" that we use to
compensate for our inferiority feelings are: lusts of the
flesh (illicit sex, excessive food, drugs); lusts of the eyes
(materialism); pride of life (power, prestige).

These are discussed by Solomon in Proverbs and Ecclesiastes and also by the apostle John in 1 John 2:15–
17, as well as by others.

You can see how money can be the root of all kinds
of evil. Money is good when used according to God's
principles. It is *not* the root of all evil, as some mis-
quote. It is the root of all kinds of evils. Greed is one of
the big three (lust of the eyes) and it takes money for
illicit sex, excessive food, drugs, alcohol, power and
prestige.

Those believers who foolishly (like Demus in the
Bible) give up living for the kingdom for living for
greed pierce their lives and their family's lives through
with many sorrows (literal pains).

Money from and for God is good. I hope God sends me as much as I
can handle spiritually and not one penny more.

> *Honor the LORD with your possessions, And with*
> *the firstfruits of all your increase; So your barns*
> *will be filled with plenty, And your vats will*
> *overflow with new wine.*   —PROV. 3:9–10

Becoming a believer and inheriting eternal life doesn't take any good works whatsoever (see Eph. 2:8–9). We don't have any that would satisfy our heavenly Father as far as salvation is concerned. We owe the Father a great debt—eternity in hell. But Jesus paid our debt. His payment is only accepted by the Father if we accept it.

If you commit your life to Christ, then psychologically you will eventually give Him all your things including your mate, kids, career, possessions and money. You will do this by realizing that they all *belong to·Christ* already. You are just borrowing them. He wants you to use them to advance His kingdom and also to enjoy the abundant life spiritually.

When we get our paycheck, the Bible says we should give the "firstfruits" of it to our local church if it is one that holds to inerrancy of Scripture. If it doesn't, then we should get out of it and in one that does and put our "firstfruits" there where we can see what is happening to it. Then we can give extra money to honest, dependable Christian ministries.

Lord, help me to mean business about my commitment to You by giving You the firstfruits of my financial increase.

*Do not withhold good from those to whom it is
due, When it is in the power of your hand to do so.*
—PROV. 3:27

I read a quote in *Reader's Digest* many years ago when I was a teenager and it stuck with me over the years. I have thought about it many times. I don't remember who said it. It stated: "Before borrowing money from a friend, decide which you need most."

It is a slight exaggeration, but there's a lot of truth to it. I know of many friendships that have ended because one friend borrowed money from another friend and never paid it back. I know of friends I have loaned money to and they never paid it back even though they could have and loving hints were dropped that they should. I refuse to be friends with open sociopaths, and anyone who borrows and doesn't repay when they can are openly sociopathic.

There are times when I have loaned a friend money and was blessed by doing so, and times I have borrowed money from a friend and been blessed. In these cases, the loans were promptly repaid.

If we borrow money from our friends and don't promptly pay them back, we will have their money and no friends—a very unwise trade. We need to love and be loved by good friends to have joy, peace, and basic mental health. Money is overrated as a source of these things.

Lord, keep reminding me that relationships with my mate, children, and friends are worth infinitely more than money.

> *My son, if you become surety for your friend, If you*
> *have shaken hands in pledge for a stranger, You*
> *are snared by the words of your own mouth.*
> —PROV. 6:1

It is very aggravating to get a great business idea that would be profitable, then go to a bank to borrow the money, only to have the banker turn down your loan. He says he will only loan you as much as you have in your savings account. You think to yourself, If I had that much in my account, I wouldn't be here trying to borrow it from your bank.

Then you go to a wealthier friend and ask him to cosign the loan. He has plenty of money in the bank. Should he do it?

No! He will be sinning against God if he does it. When I was young, I overlooked this verse somehow. It's probably the most overlooked verse in the Bible, and it cost me years of earnings. I can understand why God made this rule. I have seen the violation of it destroy friendships, marriages and lives.

The banker was correct in the first place. There is no hurry to get rich. God only wants you to give Him some of your money for *your benefit.* He doesn't need it.

Debt creates financial bondage and keeps you from focusing your attention on the kingdom. Stay out of debt and never cosign a loan for anyone.

When you cosign any loan, you become an enabler and are promoting entitlement and sociopathy in an abuser who isn't yet wise enough to know he is one.

How long will you slumber, O sluggard? When will you rise from your sleep? A little sheep, a little slumber, A little folding of the hands to sleep—So shall your poverty come on you like a robber, And your need like an armed man.

—PROV. 6:8–11

The number one cause of financial bondage is laziness. We are all lazy in one way or another: spiritually, emotionally, or physically. Laziness is a deceptive sin, because we all have it but seldom know that we do.

I can't tell you how many people I have met, for example, who feel "called" by God to go into their own individualized "full-time Christian work." They honestly believe it. I heard about a man who raised support to pray full-time (and read his Bible) forty hours a week. That was his whole ministry. And people fell for it. He ended up getting divorced and basically ruining his life. Laziness was calling him, not God.

I support full-time Christian workers who work for reputable organizations that make them accountable and won't let them be lazy. The other extreme also needs to be avoided, where a Christian organization forces them to work so hard they have to sin by ignoring their families. Balance is needed.

Dear Lord, whenever I feel "called" to be lazy, will you please remind me somehow that it isn't You that's calling me?

> *He who deals* with *a slack hand becomes poor, But
> the hand of the diligent makes* one *rich.*
> —PROV. 10:4

Solomon had a flair for being blunt. He didn't beat around the bush. He freely pointed out his own folly and he just as freely points out yours and mine.

Solomon says if you are lazy you will probably be poor, and if you are poor you are probably lazy. There are, of course, exceptions to this.

If you are lazy, you want basic things but don't have them unless some enabler comes around and promotes your laziness by giving those things to you. You are both equally sinful.

If you are wise you will gather in the summers of opportunities and save for the winters of low supplies. Wise financial advisors recommend saving 10 percent of each paycheck (10 percent of take-home pay) and giving it to yourself as a gift by putting it in a bank. Don't touch it unless there is an absolute life or death emergency.

Do this until you have enough savings to live on for about six months with no salary. Only then should you start a separate savings account to use for potential safe investments.

You will have financial emergencies. You will have career setbacks. God's goal for you is Christ-likeness, not wealth.

Starting with my next paycheck, I will save some of my take-home pay each pay period. If I owe people money, I will pay them back first, *then start saving.*

The generous soul will be made rich, And he who waters will also be watered himself. The people will curse him who withholds grain, But blessing will be on the head of him who sells it.
—PROV. 11:25–26

Some of the wealthiest Christians I know are very generous people. They are careful who they give God's money to, but they are, nevertheless, very generous.

Some of the poorest (financially and otherwise) Christians I know are the type who will nickel and dime you to death. They will go out to eat, get decent service, and instead of giving the customary 15 percent tip that the waiters and waitresses depend on, they will give a gospel tract and 5 or 10 percent—or even a tract alone.

I hate to eat with them. If they are planning on giving less than the customary tip, they shouldn't give the waiter a tract. They will turn people away from Christ. Solomon said that a person who is offended will be harder to win to Christ than it would be to defeat a strong city in battle.

People will curse them and their God if they "withhold grain." They will want to know us and our God if we sell at a reasonable price and are reasonably generous in our financial dealings.

Lord, help me in my financial dealings to obey Your golden rule.

> *He who trusts in his riches will fall, But the righteous will flourish like foliage.*
>
> —PROV. 11:28

We need to have only three goals for each day of life:

1. *Become more Christ-like today.* In Romans 8:29, Paul said God's goal for you was to be conformed to the image of His Son.

2. *Serve Christ today.* Matthew told us (see Matt. 6:33) to seek first (primarily) the kingdom of God—not things of the world.

3. *Stay out of trouble today.* Matthew, in 6:34, continues by implying that if we adequately handle the troubles of each day and stay out of trouble each day, we will be doing quite well.

If these are our goals, then money is not our goal. It's fine to earn money. It is even fine to get rich if that's what God wants. But we will live for Christ, not money.

If we live for money, then God will be jealous. He doesn't want money to be our god. *He* wants to be our God. He will see to it that we fall flat on our faces sooner or later, one way or another. If we live for Him, we will flourish in many ways.

If money is our primary goal for today, the God who loves us will take it away.

Lord, please forgive me for the times I have based my self-worth on my net worth.

He who tills his land will be satisfied with bread,
But he who follows frivolity is devoid of
understanding. —PROV. 12:11

It costs a lot to feel important. You have to have the right car, the right house, the right clothes, the right country club, the right friends, and the right schools for your children. You also have to give to the right charities, attend the "right" church for business advantages, and give money to the right political action committees.

What is really sad is that after you have done all this, you find out it doesn't work anyway. How much money does it take to make you feel significant? Just a little bit more than you will ever have. When you finally discover this (if ever), you get really furious at yourself for wasting all those years of time, effort and money to buy something that is free. True significance comes only from God, not money.

The Hebrew word for frivolity in today's passage implies the frantic pursuit of vain, worthless fantasies. I remember a patient who had been driven by the frivolous, frantic pursuit of materialism, and it worked for a while. He had everything this world had to offer, including misery, meaninglessness, and suicidal ideation. Trusting Christ was a significant part of his recovery.

Lord, please help me find significance in You rather than in frivolous, frantic, trivial pursuits.

> *Wealth* gained by *dishonesty will be diminished,*
> *But he who gathers by labor will increase.*
> —PROV. 13:11

According to various national polls, about 75 percent of businessmen and businesswomen in America would cheat in business if they thought they wouldn't get caught. Does that surprise you?

If it does surprise you, it is probably because you are such an honest person. Honest people assume that others will be honest. They assume others will be fair.

Cheaters in business are abusers. Financial abuse can be just as devastating as verbal or physical abuse. When I have felt financially abused by "friends," I was crushed—not by the loss of money, but by the loss of the valued friendships.

If you keep friends who borrow and don't return, let you pay for meals at restaurants, mooch off you, then you have a mental illness known as codependency. Read *Love Is A Choice* (Thomas Nelson, 1989) to find out all about it. Break out of it. Protect yourself.

A majority of people are basically dishonest. Protect yourself from them and don't be one yourself. If you are dishonest, God's discipline will be severe. If you are honest, fair, and work hard, your wealth and self-worth will increase.

Lord, when I am tempted to be dishonest in any financial dealings, please remind me of how much a clear conscience and godly self-concept are really worth.

A good man *leaves an inheritance to his children's children, But the wealth of the sinner is stored up for the righteous.* —PROV. 13:22

The sociopathic personality is extremely self-centered. He deserves everything. Every good idea was his idea and he should be paid for telling you so. He deserves 110 percent of billing for his commission. He deserves a better mate too.

He demands immediate gratification. He is impulsive and wants to buy all the pleasure he can get right now. He uses and abuses everyone, even the members of his immediately family—even his own children.

He also lets his friends pay for the meal. He borrows as much as he can from them with no intent to pay it back. He wants to rent your apartment so he can mooch and stay there until you kick him out.

The wise, mature believer is the opposite. His money habits reveal his good character. He is hard working, frugal, yet reasonably generous. He helps those who are legitimately poor. But he saves enough money to leave a good inheritance to his children and his grandchildren. He lives for God, not to get rich. His wealth accumulates gradually because he lives by God's financial guidelines.

I will start planning today how I can leave an inheritance for my responsible children and grandchildren. I will also leave them a spiritual inheritance that is worth trillions more.

> *Better* is *a dinner of herbs where love is, Than a
> fatted calf with hatred.*
> —PROV. 15:17

I have had many millionaires come to my office. Many told me they considered suicide the night before, but decided to get help instead.

Some were suicidal because they had lived worldly lives in the fast lane. They tried sex, power and money and were left so empty they wanted to die. They ignored their children until their children grew up, then when they finally realized the enormous value of a close fellowship with one's own children, it was too late. Their children were too busy for them.

Some of the millionaires were committed Christians who lived moral lives but still felt extremely suicidal. When you are acquiring wealth, you feel like you are driving—like you have power. But once you get wealth, it drives you and you are driven. We recently wrote a book about this sort of perfectionism called *We Are Driven* (Thomas Nelson, 1991). With wealth come constant bills, constant beggars, constant "investors," social pressures, getting conned by business associates, and general burnout.

Better to live reasonably and have time to love and be loved, with peace, than to have great wealth with no personal freedom.

Lord, please give me a dinner of herbs with friends and family who love me, rather than caviar and lobster with codependents who abuse me.

He who has pity on the poor lends to the LORD,
And He will pay back what he has given. He who
gives to the poor will not lack, but he who hides his
eyes will have many curses.

—PROV. 19:17, 28:27

There are two kinds of poor people: those who are poor because they are lazy and those who are poor for valid reasons. It is very important to differentiate the two, because we are out of God's will if we don't somehow help the valid poor if we ignorantly enable the lazy to keep sinning.

Socialism doesn't work. Russia proved that. If you pay people the same for being non-productive as they get for being productive, then laziness will usually win out.

But there are literally scores and scores of verses on how much God loves the validly poor. He wants us to develop plans to help them. This may involve a little financial support, but usually it will mean providing them with better jobs and wise counsel to help them become as self-sufficient as possible. That's what the validly poor would want anyway. The validly poor don't want handouts. They are insulted by them. The lazy poor only want handouts. That's a good way to differentiate between the two.

If a poor person only wants money, I won't give him any. If a poor person only wants advice, I will give him a little money and a better job.

> *He who loves pleasure* will be *a poor man; He who
> loves wine and oil will not be rich.*
>
> —PROV. 21:17

The sociopath is impulsive. He wants whatever his heart desires right now. That's why he is always broke. Whatever money he has, he spends.

He loves to be the big shot. He demands constant pleasure. He craves constant excitement. He is prone toward drugs to get high quickly without the natural highs that come from loving and being loved by God and others.

He loves fancy wines and can tell you which kinds are from which vineyards in which countries. He loves gourmet foods. He loves the jet set and the fast lane. His motto is "You only go around once in life, so I have to get all the pleasure I can get."

I asked a group of college students what their goals in life were. Some had never thought about it. Others said, "to have as much pleasure as I can today." Many nodded in agreement. The true believers had clear-cut, long-term goals—the Lord willing. But guess which students will get admitted to the graduate school of journalism, media, psychology, and medicine? The believers tend to get weeded out. But God makes them rich anyway—if not financially, then in many other ways.

If you live for pleasure you will be poor in many ways. If you live for God, you will have many kinds of pleasure—forever.

Lord, I choose to live for You rather than for constant pleasure.

*A good name is to be chosen rather than great
riches, Loving favor rather than silver and gold.*
—PROV. 22:1

You have a choice of being a billionaire with a lousy reputation or middle-class financially with a godly reputation. Which do you choose?

The billion dollars? Then repent!

The Bible says when we get to heaven we will know each other as we were known. We will be judged at the judgment seat of Christ for all good and bad deeds, even though we cannot lose our salvation. Our reputations will follow us for eternity, but we will still love each other. God also says when we get to heaven He will wipe away all tears. Maybe God will help us forget the bad and remember only the good. I have no idea how He will balance all this, but I know He has a great plan.

My family went out to eat and the restaurant forgot to charge for one of the meals. I realized it in the parking lot, walked back in, and paid what I owed. The waitress was amazed; I said I would rather have self-respect than the money. Back in the car, one of my younger children asked the same question. Our family discussed today's passage, and my children learned the valuable lesson it teaches. A good reputation is worth millions. Loving and being loved by honest, respected family members and friends is worth billions.

Is money really worth the pain of low self-esteem and a poor reputation with others? It's not even close!

> *. . . And the borrower* is *servant to the lender.*
> *Owe no one anything except to love one another,*
> *for he who loves another has fulfilled the law.*
> —PROV. 22:7b, ROM. 13:8

The Bible says when you owe money, you are a slave of whoever you borrowed from. We should owe only love.

Financial advisors interpret this Romans passage in different ways. Some say no debt for any reason. I like that concept; it would be a safe way to live. But the Greek for "owe no one anything" is in a tense that implies "don't keep on owing anything." I think it is saying to pay off your debts—keep paying them down, and avoid new debt.

Our financial counseling book, *The Money Diet* (Baker Book House), contains lots of advice on avoiding slavery to debt. If you do borrow money on a car, borrow less than you could sell it for immediately in an emergency. If you buy a house, realize that its value may go down by 40 percent or more in various real estate cycles. So don't borrow more than 60 percent of its current appraised value. Don't use credit cards unless you pay them off each month. Learn to live on 80 percent of your take-home pay, with 10 percent going to your local church and 10 percent to your savings. Pay off your debts and don't borrow more.

Lord, I really want to be your slave, so help me to get out of financial bondage and stay out of it no matter how You want me to interpret Romans 13:8.

He who has a bountiful eye will be blessed,
For he gives of his bread to the poor.
—PROV. 22:9

Some poor people need money itself. We said earlier that if a poor person *only* wants money without personal responsibility, don't give him any. But if a poor person wants advice on how to be responsible, give him some money, some advice and a better job.

But a third of the world is currently starving to death. Many devout missionaries live on less than fifty dollars per month. Many of them are discouraged because their families have to go several days each month with no food at all and most other days on primarily a rice diet.

Did you know that almost half of all money spent on missions in the world is going to TV evangelists? Some are godly men who live frugal lives. Others are not.

The Bible doesn't specifically say how much New Testament believers should give or to how many causes we should donate our money. But the early church brought money weekly. Paul said the pastor-teacher should be a full-time paid position. We recommend that 10 percent of your take-home pay given to your local church is a good place to *start*. Give extra money to reputable, organizations that are *accountable*. Don't let Satan siphon your missionary dollars.

Lord, give me a generous heart today.

> *Do not rob the poor because he is poor, Nor oppress the afflicted at the gate; For the LORD will plead their cause, And plunder the soul of those who plunder them.* —PROV. 22:22–23

If you don't give some of your time, effort and money to help poor people in some way, then you are out of God's will for your life. But if you rip off poor people, you are in *major* trouble, because you are ripping off God's children—future kings and queens in the messianic kingdom.

If you oppress the valid poor and rip them off or treat them as though they are less important than you are, God Himself will be their lawyer. He will plead their cause. He will plunder your soul for plundering their money. Even when you give money to help the poor, you had better not be condescending. Treat them with the dignity and respect they deserve as joint-heirs with Christ. Help them to help themselves.

Many people in the world are starving to death because their corrupt leaders are robbing them blind. They will answer to God for that. Our government used to send food to third world countries, only to find out that the local officials would sell it to the poor. Now our government is doing wiser things like sending farmers to teach the poor how to grow bigger and better crops.

Lord, in this world of abuses, help me to genuinely care about the sufferings of the legitimate poor.

A little sleep, a little slumber, A little folding of the hands to rest; So your poverty will come like a prowler, And your want like an armed man.
—PROV. 24:33–34

Ted was brilliant but lazy. He got Bs and Cs throughout his school years, which would have been great for most people. But he did that with no study whatsoever.

He was accepted at a state college and went to as few classes as possible. People recognized his brilliance, though, so he was offered an executive position after his third year of college.

He took the job, quit college, and earned great pay for a couple of years, but then got fired. He was lazy. His brilliance was sometimes helpful, but his laziness hurt the morale of the whole division. His bosses kept prodding and encouraging him, but he refused to mature. They finally gave up on him.

That was twenty years ago, and Ted is still unemployed, mooching off his wife. When they get kicked out of their apartment, they go to another one that doesn't require references and pay a month, then live there without paying until they get kicked out.

He does odd jobs now and then. He won't go back to college because he has already been an executive and he is too proud. He won't take a regular job because he has already been an executive. When asked why he has been chronically unemployed, he replies that he is waiting for an executive position to open for him. Are there any rescuers/enablers out there?

Lazy people get what they deserve—nothing!

> *Whoever falsely boasts of giving Is like clouds and wind without rain.*
> —PROV. 25:14

God loves you. He wants you to feel clean and moral and significant. God declares your significance in many passages throughout the Bible.

God gave you lots of freedom to create your own giving strategy, but He also gave you a few boundaries and recommendations. Here are some of them.

Give generously to pastor/teachers so they can devote a reasonable amount of time studying God's Word for sermon preparation and still do the other work of a pastor. They should be paid at least the average annual income of the families in their church.

Give primarily to your local church.

Give whatever you can give with a cheerful heart. We are no longer under the Old Testament tithe system, but I think 10 percent of take-home pay is a good place to start.

Give secretly, not to get attention and recognition.

Don't give to wolves in sheep's clothing. There are many sociopaths in full time Christian work.

Give to help the genuine poor, widows, and orphans. See if your local church has such a program already set up.

Don't boast about what you will give. It's better to pledge little then give much than to pledge much and give little.

Today's passage says making a pledge and not delivering is like seeing promising clouds fly by in the wind but disappointing us by not dropping any rain on our dry lawns.

The sluggard is wiser in his own eyes Than seven men who can answer sensibly. —PROV. 26:16

It took thirteen years of higher education to become a psychiatrist. One of the main things we studied in all those years are the forty defense mechanisms.

Those are the primary ways that we deceive ourselves. As psychiatrists our goal is to listen well to each patient but to read between the lines. Study body language. Look for self-deceit. Point out the truth to our patients. We leave it up to them what to do with the truth when they learn it, but encourage them to choose biblical options.

One of the greatest sins of mankind is laziness. It causes us to deceive ourselves. If we put our mouths on an imaginary *automatic pilot* of truth, every time we were lazy in one of those three areas, our lips would say, "I'm doing this (or not doing this) because I am lazy." We would be awfully embarrassed. Instead we deny, rationalize, project, use sarcasm, use prejudice, repress, displace, isolate our feelings, etc. We do all these things because we are too lazy to look at the painful truth and overhaul our lives, with God's help, to become real people.

Lazy people are only wise in their own eyes.

> *Be diligent to know the state of your flocks,* And
> *attend to your herds; For riches* are *not forever, Nor*
> *does a crown* endure *to all generations.*
> —PROV. 27:23–24a

Most of my close friends are very diligent people. I hope some more of it rubs off on me. I have one close friend who is a business consultant. He used to buy businesses that had gone broke, applied biblical principles to that business, fired the lazy employees, promoted the diligent ones, then sold the businesses for a profit.

His goal is not to make money. He and I pray together often that he will have opportunities to be a witness for Christ in his secular business environment. He is diligent in his pursuit of Christ's Kingdom while at work.

Our passage for today was written by Solomon, another man who was diligent in his business once God got hold of him. Solomon said to be diligent and to know what is really going on in our business. I think this applies to our children and our church as well, but it is primarily addressing diligence in our careers. Our relationship with God and with our immediate family are far more important than our careers, but God also wants us to work as though *He* is our boss at work. He wants us to be an example of diligence with our time, with our effort, with our spending, with our loyalty, and with our respect of company property.

I will be an example of diligence at my job today whether I run a corporation or run a home.

*One who increases his possessions by usury and
extortion Gathers it for him who will pity the poor.*
—PROV. 28:8

The sociopath loves to have no boundaries. He loves
to lie and steal. He will often lie merely because lying
is more fun to him. He cheats people even when it
would be just as easy for him to get the same amount
of money the old fashioned way—earn it!

The reason for this is because both the fear of getting caught and the challenge to get away with it pro-
duce adrenaline rushes. He likes the way it feels to
cheat people, especially if they remind him of the parents who spoiled and overindulged him and taught
him he was entitled and should have no boundaries.

He will also employ "usury," or excessive interest on
loans he makes, because of his sense of entitlement.
The sociopath does live in constant anxiety from his
fear of being caught. God sends him severe consequences.

My father always taught me not to trust anyone financially until I had eaten enough meals with him to
use up a bushel of salt, and make sure the meals are
dutch treat. I wish I had listened sooner.

---

*Lord, please protect me from those who would exhort, and give me
insight into any unfair financial practices I may accidentally be a
part of.*

A man with an evil eye hastens after riches, And does not consider that poverty will come upon him.
—PROV. 28:22

When you are thirty years old, you worry about what people think about you. When you are forty, you no longer care what they think. And by the time you are fifty, you realize no one was thinking about you in the first place.

Youth and idealism go hand in hand. When you are thirty you believe your thinking is so superior that you can create a way to get rich quick. By age forty, you hope to gradually get rich, and by fifty, you're thankful to keep up the payments on your medical bills.

God never promises financial wealth either quickly or slowly. The Proverbs are not promises. They are general sayings that are accurate but have exceptions. Not all wise men have gray hair. Not all children who obey their parents live to a ripe old age. And not all who work hard get rich.

But in general, tilling your land will net you plenty of bread. Following get-rich-quick frivolities usually results in poverty. Faithful men and women will be blessed, for sure, and people who try to get rich quick will be punished by God in some way, someday, for sure.

It is practically impossible to get rich quick without ripping people off. Wealth should not be your goal anyway; serving Christ should.

———————

Lord, in my financial dealings please give me the wisdom to work hard, be faithful to follow Your principles, and to be patient.

*Remove falsehood and lies far from me; Give me
neither poverty nor riches—Feed me with the food
You prescribe for me; Lest I be full and deny You,
And say, "Who is the LORD?" Or lest I be poor and
steal, And profane the name of my God.*
—PROV. 30:8–9

Don't become a Christian just because you think God
will owe you a favor and you will be able to manipulate
God to make you rich.

Even if you are rich when you trust Christ, there is a
good chance God will knock you down to bring about
humility—one of His prime goals in me and you.

Today's passage calls for middle-class values and finances. Keep me honest. Supply my basic needs. Help
me please not to get rich, because I am afraid that if I
get rich I will get arrogant and say, "Who needs You,
Lord?" Help me please not to become poor, because if I
am hungry enough, I know I would steal food to survive. Please help me to be middle class, where there
are enough well-fed but humble people that I can asso-
ciate with those who share my goals and values.

It's not a sin to be rich or poor, but it is a sin to be
arrogant, to live for money, and to steal. If we can be
humble and rich, I hope God blesses us with whatever
we can handle and, most of all, whatever will make us
the most effective for Christ.

---

*Lord, please determine how much wealth to give me based on what
amount will motivate me the most to focus on serving You.*

> *When God gives any man wealth and possessions,*
> *and enables him to enjoy them, to accept his lot*
> *and be happy in his work—this is a gift of God.*
> —ECCL. 5:19 NIV

This is a great passage for wealthy believers. I used to live in Chicago—a busy, hard-working city I still love. In Chicago, though, some believers were so obsessive-compulsive (perfectionistic) that they taught that all believers should live at the poverty level and give away all the rest of their earnings to help charity. The members of these groups were nearly always young, idealistic but well-meaning and zealous Christians who grew up in wealthy families.

Then I moved to Dallas. My friends in Dallas enjoy having lots of good, clean fun. In Dallas, there are large groups of Christians who think the more spiritual you are, the more wealth God will give you. If you are poor, you must be out of God's will.

Now I live near Los Angeles, where people don't care if you are rich or poor, as long as you stay out of their way on the California freeways! Rich is cool. Poor is cool. Middle class is cool. I'm OK. You're OK.

Solomon says if God has blessed us with great wealth, He will also give us the power to enjoy it and enjoy our career as well. Our wealth is a gift from God. We should not feel guilty about it. We will also not have time to obsess about the brevity of our lives because God will keep you busy serving Him.

If I am wealthy, I will realize it is God's money. I won't waste it, but I will enjoy it because God wants me to.

*"But when you do a charitable deed, do not let
your left hand know what your right hand is doing,
that your charitable deed may be in secret; and
your Father who sees in secret will Himself reward
you openly."*
                                        —MATT. 6:3–4

At Christmas time, what do you enjoy more—opening a present a friend gave you, or watching your child's big, bright eyes light up when he gets the toy he was hoping for?

It is genuinely much more blessed to give than to receive. Sociopaths who impulsively blow all their money on self-indulgence and drug highs have no idea what kind of genuine highs they are missing out on by not thinking of creative ways to give good gifts and to help people who genuinely need it.

When the Pharisees put money in the temple treasury, they would sometimes hire a trumpeter to blow his long trumpet so everyone would see how much he was giving and applaud. They got their reward.

The Bible says to enjoy giving. Give with a cheerful heart. Give creatively.

If you brag about a gift you just gave, then that is your reward. The reward you would have gotten at the judgment seat of Christ for that one gift is lost. So decide each time you give which reward you would rather have. God leaves *that* up to you, too.

Lord, please help me when I give, to give to You.

> *Command those who are rich in this present age*
> *not to be haughty, nor to trust in uncertain riches*
> *but in the living God, who gives us richly all things*
> *to enjoy.* Let them *do good, that they be rich in*
> *good works, ready to give, willing to share.*
>
> 1 TIM. 6:17–18

Paul gives some good advice to rich believers in to-day's passage.

Paul seems to be warning that the primary *curse* of wealth is the arrogance (being haughty) that it causes. People treat you special when you are rich—most of it is pure manipulation to get bigger tips or privileges or "class by association."

Even churches tend to treat you better if you are rich. A pastor may pay you more compliments because you are rich because he wants your donations.

If you "buy your own press," then arrogance will raise its ugly head. Have a good self-concept, but don't be arrogant. Don't *trust* in your riches but enjoy them and trust God. Secretly, do good works with your riches and your talents. Then you can benefit from your wealth in this life as well as in the Millennium.

If people are impressed with you *because* of your wealth, your insecurity and inferiority feelings are what will tempt you to believe you are somehow superior.

Lord, please keep me from the primary curse of the rich: arrogance.

The LORD is King forever and ever; The nations have perished out of His land. LORD, You have heard the desire of the humble; You will prepare their heart; You will cause Your ear to hear, To do justice to the fatherless and the oppressed, That the man of the earth may oppress no more.
—PS. 10:16–18

This book was *especially* designed for some very special people in the hearts of Dr. Minirth and myself—adult children of abuse.

We have seen the pain in their faces and the joy of their breakthroughs into emotional health when they felt free to forgive. We will spend the next three and a half weeks looking at the sometimes painful topics of self-protection from the unnecessary suffering that comes from being victimized.

Today's passage begins with a promise that some day in the future abusive people will be eliminated, as well as abusive nations. God allows victimization on earth right now. But God hears the cries of victims. Some day men of the earth will oppress and abuse no more.

I don't really know why God allows innocent children to be abused by sociopathic adults or older siblings. I do know that He hates abuse and ultimately punishes abuse.

Thank You, Lord, that some day soon You will put an end to the abuses of the fatherless and oppressed.

> *The LORD lives! Blessed be my Rock! Let the God of my salvation be exalted. It is God who avenges me, And subdues the people under me; He delivers me from my enemies.*
> —PS. 18:46–47

God is not dead. He is your Rock. He is the God of your salvation. And God is the avenger for victims of abuse.

God is a God of vengeance (see Rom. 12). He is a professional at it. He can subdue entire nations at will.

He will deliver you from your abusers by teaching you common sense ways to deliver yourself from your abusers.

Thank Him for his promise. Praise Him for His love. Your body is the temple of the Holy Spirit. You are God's very own child.

Protect the Holy Spirit's temple. Don't let the abuse continue even one more hour. Call the police if crimes have been committed against you recently. Get a court injunction if you need to. Realize that you may be so used to being abused that you erroneously think that you deserve it, and thus find ways to trap yourself into another abusive situation. Study codependency. Study *Love Is A Choice* (Thomas Nelson, 1989).

God will hear your humble cry and show you ways to courageously protect yourself with His help.

Dear Lord, please be my Rock, my salvation, my avenger, and my deliverer. I will give thanks to You and praise Your name.

Mark the blameless man, and observe the upright;
For the future of that man is peace. But the
transgressors shall be destroyed together; The
future of the wicked shall be cut off.
—PS. 37:37–38

You may not have had much peace growing up. You may have been the innocent victim of emotional, physical or sexual abuse. But remain committed to Christ; there is a future for you.

God can help you scrape out those emotional pus wounds from the past and bring you peace for the first time in years. He also promises eternal peace after you join Him in heaven.

God will destroy unrepentant abusers. They have no future but hell. When you are in trouble and feel frightened and victimized, God wants to be your strength.

God will help you deliver yourself. It won't be easy. It will be hard work. It will take courage. When you are lost at sea, you pray to God but row toward shore. When you pray to God, remove yourself immediately from the abusive situation. God will save you from it if you trust Him and do your part.

You can do all things, including freeing yourself from an abusive situation, through Christ, who strengthens you so you can do the hard work it will take.

Lord, be my strength and deliver me from further abuse and from further pain from past abuses. Give me the strength and patience to work through the difficult task of forgiving my abusers.

> *Revive me, O Lord, for Your name's sake! For Your*
> *righteousness' sake bring my soul out of trouble. In*
> *Your mercy cut off my enemies, And destroy all*
> *those who afflict my soul; For I am Your servant.*
> —PS. 143:11–12

King David knew what it was like to be the victim of abuses. He was attacked by bears and lions as a youth. He was attacked by Goliath, a nine foot giant whose growth hormone never quit. He was attacked by King Saul. He was attacked by the Philistines. He was attacked by other nations. And he was attacked by his own son, Absalom. All those attackers were not trying to *abuse* David, they were trying to *kill him*. David can understand your pain. He has been there.

David asked God to deliver him from his enemies. God was David's shelter. David was willing to do God's will. God's Holy Spirit was good to David, encouraging David and inspiring David to write much of the book of Psalms.

David sought God's guidance into "the land of uprightness." David not only wanted deliverance, he wanted spiritual *revival*. God's reputation was at stake. David called on God to be his "Holy Hit Man"— "destroy those who afflict my soul: For I am Your servant." David wanted deliverance from abuse, vengeance on his abusers, and personal holiness.

God is my bodyguard and His reputation is at stake. I will trust Him to deliver me from abuse and to punish those who abuse me while helping me forgive them.

VICTIMIZATION – *October 2*

*Do not enter the path of the wicked, And do not
walk in the way of evil. Avoid it, do not travel on
it; Turn away from it and pass on. For they do not
sleep unless they have done evil; And their sleep is
taken away unless they make* someone *fall.*
—PROV. 4:14–16

Did you ever see a sign on a front lawn that said "Beware of Dangerous Dogs"? I have. When I was an ele-
mentary school child I sometimes cut across people's
yards to get home.

When I saw that sign I didn't know if the people were
lying about the dogs and just hated kids or whether
there really were dangerous dogs nearby. I decided not
to take a chance and I walked home the long (and
proper) way.

This passage is God's "Beware of Dangerous Jerks"
sign to you. Don't enter their path. Don't walk in their
ways. Avoid it. Don't even travel on it. Turn away from
it. Pass on around it.

Could God possibly be any more blunt? *Avoid jerks!*
They are sociopathic. They get bored easily. They
can't even sleep at night until they have sublimated
some of their rage by hurting someone. Misery loves
company. They want you to fall morally so you will be
like them. Are you codependent on them because one
of your parents was one?

You can't change a sociopath but you sure can stay
away from one.

*Lord, help me not to be a masochist. Help me instead to responsibly
stay totally out of the path of abusers.*

> *Do not be envious of evil men, Nor desire to be*
> *with them; For their heart devises violence, And*
> *their lips talk of troublemaking.*
>
> —PROV. 24:1–2

Earlier in this devotional book we discussed Psalm 1:1–3, where David warned believers to avoid walking, standing or sitting with sociopaths who abuse and use people. It is better to spend our valuable time meditating day and night on God's Word and bonding to kind, loving people.

Solomon, the son of David and Bathsheba, gives advice similar to his father's. Solomon tells us not to be jealous of the sociopaths. Don't desire to hang around with them. In the depths of their unconscious, they are driven by violent rage.

It is ironic that David sexually used Solomon's mother Bathsheba out of wedlock. Bathsheba was married to Uriah, whom David murdered. But David repented. God hates abuse, but loves and wants to save all abusers. Now David, a former abuser, and his son, Solomon, team up under God's inspiration to warn future generations about avoiding abuse.

Lord, please help me to take the inspired advice of an abused former abuser (David) and his son (Solomon) by staying as far away as possible from sociopathic abusers.

But those who rebuke the wicked *will have delight,*
And a good blessing will come upon them.
                              —PROV. 24:25

There is a common tendency in adult children of abuse to not want to turn criminal abusers in to the police. They fear reprisals—possibly even getting killed by the abuser if they turn him in. Some don't trust the police to do anything because some of their friends turned in abusers and nothing happened.

When a criminal abuser is the victim's father or mother, the tendency is to excuse the abuse and exaggerate the good in that parent. The victim bases too much self-concept on the opinion of the abusive parent and fantasizes that the parent will surely repent some day. The other parent usually knew about the abuse and was passive and allowed the protection of the family secret too.

But the Bible says to turn in the criminal abuser—rebuke him. Don't let him get away with crime.

In Proverbs 26:17, Solomon also says to be very careful. Don't meddle in quarrels between sociopaths that don't involve you or you will get hurt, like grabbing a pit bull by the ears.

———————

Lord, please give me the discretion to rebuke and turn in abusers to protect future potential victims from them.

A prudent man foresees evil and hides himself; The simple pass on and are punished.
—PROV. 27:12

Sociopathic jerks are hateful and manipulative. They can really sound like good people. They not only deceive themselves, they try to con us. If we voted on who is most popular in the social subgroups of people, the sociopaths would normally rank near the top. They have charisma and hide many of their evil motives.

If your father ignored you when you were growing up and you are a female, you will have a hole in your soul that will make you more prone to jerk-addictions.

You don't really want sex, you want to hear "I love you" from a male because of your father-vacuum. The sociopath has no love for you and no interest in love from you. He only wants sex. So he says, "I love you"— a phony boloney "I love you" at that!

Be prudent. See through his evil. Don't be simple-minded, or your own naiveté will make you a victim once again.

If you are a male and your mother ignored or abused you growing up, watch out for the same things from female sociopaths. They can be equally subtle. Remember that psychiatric research shows there are equal numbers of male and female sociopaths.

Get smart. *Don't trust con men or con women,* especially *if your own parent of the opposite sex was one.*

He who blesses his friend with a loud voice, rising early in the morning, It will be counted a curse to him.
　　　　　　　　　　　　　　　　　—PROV. 27:14

While we are on the subject of avoiding jerks, let's talk for a little while about how to avoid being one. There are some well-intentioned people I have known over the years who simply lack social skills. Some are too passive. Others are too aggressive.

Today's passage is about the overly aggressive type. He's the type who wakes up at 5 A.M., jumps out of bed, and shouts loudly at his sleeping college roommate, "Wake up, Jim, my friend! Don't you want to go jog with me?" He or she butts into your private conversations or sits at your table unwanted when you are on a date and even dominates the conversation. He may even pray long, loud, attention-seeking prayers at a meal or at a church gathering.

You feel like belting him in the face, but you don't want to be un-Christlike. Crossing your boundaries—your right in this case to sleep until *you* wake yourself up—is sociopathic. It comes from a sense of entitlement. Sometimes it is also a correctable inherited chemical imbalance (some form of bipolar disorder).

A basic rule of thumb for avoiding *being* a jerk is to go by the golden rule. Do unto others as you would have them do unto you. Stop and ask yourself whether you are being overly aggressive or expecting too much in each social situation. Be teachable.

There is some jerkiness in all of us. The golden rule will help us grow out of it.

October 7 – VICTIMIZATION

Though you grind a fool in a mortar with a pestle along with crushed grain, Yet his foolishness will not depart from him. —PROV. 27:22

One of the *main* reasons why so many adult children of abuse remain in another abusive situation, is that they *cling* to the fantasy that they are powerful enough to change their abuser into a good person. Some think their passive mother should have changed dad into a good person, but since mom didn't do that, I will marry someone just like dad and change *him*.

They may be a minority, but there are some neat people who would enjoy loving you as a friend and being loved by you. You don't need your mom or your dad. You don't need a substitute abuser. Bond to healthy people. Your abusers probably will never change and never come through for you.

If they do, consider that an unexpected bonus in life. God wants them to change too, and God could easily change them. He doesn't want to force anyone to change, though. He doesn't want robots. They have to allow Him into their lives, and most refuse. That's why the Bible repeatedly says that the road to destruction is broad and the road to righteousness is narrow.

Give up on the assumption that your abuser will change. Give up on God forcing him to change. Grieve the loss of your fantasy. Bond to healthy believers instead.

Whoever causes the upright to go astray in an evil way, He himself will fall into his own pit; But the blameless will inherit good things.
—PROV. 28:10

My older brother, Dr. Richard Meier, was a great brother to me when I was growing up—and he still is. He was a golden gloves boxer in high school and was very athletic and strong. Yet he was very loving and gentle with me. He let me tag along with him and his friends even though I was younger than him.

I felt safe around Richard. He wouldn't fight my battles for me, but I knew he was there if I needed him. I knew if anyone messed with me, my big brother would clobber him. His loyalty has never been in doubt. We have always prayed for each other's best interest.

God is like that, too. God loves you. He gets *furious* when someone uses you, abuses you, or causes you to sin and go astray. God will punish that person severely. God will "clobber" him. He will make him fall into his own pit. God's loyalty to you is always 100 percent, even though it doesn't always feel that way.

But God will bless the committed believer. He will inherit many good things, both in this life and in the Millennium. His loyalty to you includes many creative ways of blessing you with love and joyful experiences throughout eternity. God is a friend who sticks even closer than a loyal brother.

If anyone leads you astray, God will clobber him.

> *A man burdened with bloodshed will flee into a pit;*
> *Let no one help him.*
> —PROV. 28:17

A murder occurs every few minutes in America. Many go unsolved. I have had patients who hired mafia hit men to kill someone, only to change their minds in the nick of time. The ultimate sense of entitlement is the rationalization that you have the right to snuff out the life of another human being—a right only God has—just because you are angry at him.

Many victims of abuse feel like committing murder. It's normal to feel that way in that type of situation. But it's not normal to do it. It is obviously one of the worst sins a person could possibly commit. Many innocent victims fear they will commit murder, so they redirect their rage on themselves and either kill themselves or keep hurting themselves. What a tragic loss for those who are so enraged at their abusers that they kill themselves. Suicide is murder. Only God has the right to terminate human life, including your own life. When a believer kills him or herself he or she is murdering one of God's own children and crossing a boundary that God does not want anyone to ever cross.

Solomon said a murderer will fear punishment so he will flee, but fall into a pit. Don't help him out of the pit. Turn him in to the authorities so he can be punished and society can be protected. But again, be very careful to protect yourself from that murderer. Each murder gets easier to commit, and you may be his next target.

Life and death are God's business.

*Whoever robs his father or his mother, And says,
"It is no transgression," The same is companion to
a destroyer.*   —PROV. 28:24

We have talked a great deal about parents who have
verbally, physically or sexually abused their children.
All of us, as parents, have probably been slightly abusive at one time or another, in one way or another. But
even great parents make occasional mistakes and say
things they regret later.

If you had imperfect but decent parents who loved
you, disciplined you, tried to be an example to you,
and tried to be consistent and fair, then consider yourself very fortunate. Some people put their parents on a
pedestal and think they were perfect. That is wrong.
But it is also wrong to think that they were all bad unless they really were. We tend to be black or white
thinkers—either all good or totally abusive. We need to
appreciate the good things our parents have done for
us.

Don't rob your parents of the respect they deserve
for the good things they have done. Don't destroy their
reputation by criticizing them publicly. Be honest with
your therapist about all parental faults, to help you *forgive* them. Determine to unconditionally love your parents even if their love for you seems conditional.

*Lord, help me not to be a destroyer of my parents' reputation, or their
peace of mind, or their financial security. Give me opportunities to
thank them for what they did right and forgive them for their sins of
abuse.*

> *Whoever is a partner with a thief hates his own*
> *life: He swears to tell the truth, but reveals nothing.*
> —PROV. 29:24

In today's brief passage, Solomon says to stay away from any thief. That seems pretty simple and to the point. You think to yourself, that's easy, I'll stay away from bank robbers and burglars.

But let's take a closer look at who is a thief, so you won't accidentally be a thief's partner and destroy your own life in the process.

People who have sex before marriage are thieves. He or she is using someone's daughter or son just for selfish pleasure. People who cheat on tests are thieves. People who borrow and don't repay are thieves. Adulterers are thieves. All overly controlling people who steal your right to self-determination are thieves. All religious persecutors and discriminators are thieves. All drug abusers and alcoholics are thieves in many ways. Rescuers and severe codependents are thieves, robbing freedom and hindering those dependent on them from maturing.

People who harbor vengeful motives and plans are thieves because they are stealing God's job. People who miss work and say they are sick when they aren't are thieves.

Lord, this job of staying away from thieves is a lot more complicated than it sounded at first glance. Not being a thief sounds pretty hard, too. Lord, please help me to see the truth and behave accordingly.

Do not give what is holy to the dogs; nor cast your pearls before swine, lest they trample them under their feet, and turn and tear you in pieces.

—MATT. 7:6

"**S**wine" and "dogs" in the days of Jesus' ministry on earth were out-and-out sociopaths who were nonbelievers. Jesus loves to save them, but most refuse Him. The Bible says the Holy Spirit will convict these sociopaths of their need to trust Christ, especially if people are praying for them. The Holy Spirit will also bring catastrophic circumstances in their lives to wake them up to their need of a Savior.

If a catastrophe happens to an abuser you are praying for, look at the positive side of things. The Holy Spirit may be using that catastrophe to win him or her to Christ. We should always keep praying.

If you care about a jerk, or you are related to one, or you are married to one that you care about, then pray for him. Model Christ-likeness to him. Show unconditional love, but make him respect you by being assertive and protecting yourself from any abuse.

Don't preach to him. Let your life preach to him. Don't throw Bible verses at him. Only share as many Bible passages as he is willing to hear, or he will trample you and tear you to pieces.

Dear God, please help me to be a good, but very careful witness to the sociopaths I cannot avoid.

> *Beware of false prophets, who come to you in*
> *sheep's clothing, but inwardly they are ravenous*
> *wolves. You will know them by their fruits.*
> —MATT. 7:15–16

We couldn't rightfully talk about sociopathic abusers and how to protect yourself from victimization without covering phony religious leaders.

When I was in high school, I worked as a stock boy and bagger at a grocery store. Another classmate from my school worked there too. He was a real jerk. Every other word was a swear word, he was abusive toward women, and he stole beer from the back of the store until he got fired. But he wanted to become a minister.

Sociopaths love the ministry for the ability to hide laziness, the vulnerable women they can seduce—and the pay in many denominations is pretty good, too. Only 20 percent of pastors polled in a huge council of churches even thought people have spiritual problems. They deny the deity of Christ, the inerrancy of Scripture, the virgin birth, and Christ's substitutionary atonement. Pastors who believe these basic things are weeded out of many major denominations.

Some wolves *act* like they *are* Bible-believing evangelicals, though. Their time will come at death, and again on judgment day. They will ask Jesus, "Why am I in hell burning like this? Didn't I cast out demons and prophesy in your name?" Jesus will say, "I never knew you."

Beware of wolves dressed in robes like sheep. Don't be victimized by them. Protect yourself.

But he who is greatest among you shall be your servant. And whoever exalts himself will be abased, and he who humbles himself will be exalted.
—MATT. 23:12

This passage is another confirmation of yesterday's theme of wolves in sheep's clothing—nonbelievers who are full-time Christian workers—or in some cases, sociopathic believers who are full-time Christian workers. Jesus said never call your religious leader or pastor "Rabbi" so and so, or "Father" so and so. God is your "Rabbi" (scholarly teacher) and "Father" (your heavenly Father).

The Bible says a genuine pastor will be your *servant*, not lord it over you. A good pastor is worthy of great honor and decent pay (see Gal. 6:6). A local church should be run by the deacons or elders. The pastor should get one vote, like any other elder, but his leadership, experience and Bible-knowledge should be respected.

I would never join a local church whose pastor is not accountable to a board of elders in that church. Even a good man will eventually fall without accountability. I also believe in rehabilitating good pastors who do fall into serious sin. King David did quite well after his rehabilitation by Nathan. Each case needs to be examined individually by the elders of that local church. Long-term therapy and accountability are a must.

You have great dignity and should not allow yourself to be victimized or controlled in any way by a religious leader. God called them to humbly serve you the way Jesus served His disciples.

> *If anyone defiles the temple of God, God will*
> *destroy him. For the temple of God is holy, which*
> *temple you are.*   —1 COR. 3:17

You have heard of the "child within"? Well, the Bible says we all also have "a jerk within"—our sinful nature, our unconscious, our depraved motives.

When we become a Christian, the Holy Spirit instantly fills us and seals us until the day of redemption in heaven (Eph. 1:13–14). We instantly become a temple for the Holy Spirit to dwell in. We don't need any good works to earn salvation (Eph. 2:8–9), but if there are no good works, that proves you never trusted Christ in the first place (see entire book of James).

When we do good works (with the help of the Holy Spirit), we are laying up treasures in heaven and in the messianic kingdom. Each good work will be rewarded. But when we defile the temple of the Holy Spirit by openly rebelling against God, refusing to repent and come back to God, then God will destroy that temple— the body. The person will still be saved and go to heaven, as this passage clearly indicates. But he will lose out on the rewards he could have gotten if he were serving God during that time of rebellion.

God will make him or her die and go to heaven, so that person could also have lived longer on earth and earned more rewards and helped more people if he or she had repented.

Dear Lord, please help me to take you seriously and to beware of potential victimization by my own "jerk within."

*Beware of dogs, beware of evil workers, beware of
the mutilation!* —PHIL. 3:2

There are so many different kinds of jerks in the
world, it's hard to keep track of them all to protect ourselves. Yesterday we even discussed the "jerk within."
My "jerk within" is the jerk I fear the most.

Today's passage warns us, though, about some
"jerks without" rather than "within." Paul asks for forgiveness for warning us over and over about not getting victimized by various jerks.

Paul said to avoid being victimized by "dogs"—
sociopathic abusers who want to use you and abuse
you. Don't be victimized by "evil workers"—liberal
religious leaders who try to deceive you for selfish motives. And don't be victimized by "the mutilation"—
believers who are legalistic. "Mutilators" in Paul's days
on earth were believers who trusted Christ for salvation, but also believed you should be circumcised if you
were a male.

If your religious leader tells you that you have to be
circumcised, baptized using certain words to be saved,
or if he tells you that you have to belong to his denomination to be saved, then he is a "mutilator"—a legalist.
Mutilators hate practical applications of Scripture because biblical psychology liberates believers from the
mutilators' control.

---

*It's hard to find the best local church for your family—one that be-
lieves in inerrancy and is also not into the "mutilation" of your freedom in Christ.*

> *But know this, that in the last days perilous times will come: For men will be lovers of themselves, lovers of money, boasters, proud, blasphemers, disobedient to parents, unthankful, unholy, unloving, unforgiving, slanderers, without self-control, brutal, despisers of good, traitors, headstrong, haughty, lovers of pleasure rather than lovers of God, having a form of godliness but denying its power. And from such people turn away!*
> —2 TIM. 3:1–5

The apostle Paul led a young man named Timothy to Christ. He trained him to become an excellent pastor-teacher. Timothy was a good man, but still wet behind the ears. Paul loved Timothy and prayed for him often.

Paul wanted to be sure Timothy didn't get victimized by any jerks, so Paul warned Timothy to watch out for the following: narcissistic, self-centered sociopaths; lovers of money; braggers; proud people; children who live in rebellion against their parents; unthankful gripers; unholy sociopathic people; unloving, heartless people; bitter people; gossips; people without self-control; brutal people; despisers of good morals; traitors; stubborn people; condescending people; people who live for pleasure rather than living for God; people who use religion to justify their sinful behavior but deny the *power* of Christ and the Bible.

Lord, help me to "turn away" from these abusers to protect myself. Help me to also turn away from allowing my own sinful nature from exhibiting sociopathic behaviors.

But avoid foolish disputes, genealogies, contentions,
and strivings about the law; for they are
unprofitable and useless. Reject a divisive man
after the first and second admonition, knowing
that such a person is warped and sinning,
being self-condemned. —TITUS 3:9–11

Some people tell me they refuse to go to any local church because local churches are imperfect and have hypocrites in them. I ask them if they ever go into grocery stores, since grocery stores also have hypocrites in them. Then I explain to them that if they found a perfect local church, they couldn't join it, anyway, because it wouldn't be perfect any more. I guess that's why people call psychiatrists "head shrinkers"—we try to help some people enjoy life more by reducing their swollen egos (as we hopefully also work on our own).

In today's passage, Paul tells Titus how to decrease the hypocrite level in his local church. Paul told Titus that sociopathic abusers love to stir up trouble. They love arguments to relieve their boredom. They love pitting one person against another. They are arrogant and legalistic. Paul said to warn them once, then a second time, then on the third warning, kick them out of your church.

We have a responsibility to weed them out if they won't repent after two warnings. Don't be victimized by them.

Dear Lord, please protect me, my loved ones, and my local church from the abuse of self-righteous legalists.

> *Shepherd the flock of God which is among you,*
> *serving as overseers, not by constraint but willingly,*
> *not for dishonest gain but eagerly; nor as being*
> *lords over those entrusted to you, but being*
> *examples to the flock.* —1 PETER 5:2–3

I would never join a local church whose pastor is not accountable to a board of elders in that same local church. As a Christian psychiatrist, I have seen *many* believers suffer as a result of victimization by domineering pastors who have great charisma but lord it over the flocks.

I have also seen many excellent, dedicated seminary graduates who are hired by churches that don't make that pastor accountable. They want that pastor to run their church like the owner of a private corporation.

I believe in human depravity even in fine, dedicated believers. Each of us *will* fall eventually into a variety of serious sins if we are not accountable.

In our passage for today, the pastor is told to tend, feed, care, serve, and guide. Overseers are elders. The pastor is one of the elders.

Pastor accountability helps prevent the sheep from being victimized by their own shepherd. It also helps prevent good shepherds from being victimized (and often having their careers ruined) by their own "jerk within."

Lord, give me the wisdom to find a healthy, loving church with a godly imperfect pastor who is accountable to a godly imperfect board of elders. Show Your grace by being our Chief Shepherd and helping us all to help each other.

> *But there were also false prophets among the*
> *people, even as there will be false teachers among*
> *you, who will secretly bring in destructive heresies,*
> *even denying the Lord who brought them, and*
> *bring on themselves swift destruction.*
> —2 PETER 2:1–2

In yesterday's passage the apostle Peter told us what a good pastor would be like. We also discussed how to help good pastors stay that way—by accountability.

In today's passage, Peter warns us as local church members not to be victimized by phonies who call themselves "prophets"—claiming to have prophetic powers, and phonies who call themselves Bible teachers but really aren't.

Their messages will be brought in secretly. They will teach things or prophesy things that are *obviously true,* but sneak in a little falsehood alongside the truth to disguise the falsehood. It is believable that way.

Their messages will be close to the truth, but just far enough to differ philosophically from Christ's original intent. These sociopaths exploit church members with deceptive words.

Satan wants to destroy practical Christianity that *works,* so he uses religious, paranoid sociopaths to do his dirty work. Some of them are naive believers, or nonbelievers who think they are believers. Others are open sociopaths who *know* they are deceiving you for selfish gains. It's a human tragedy.

Dear Lord, help me not to overlook subtle abuses by those who sneak falsehood alongside many of your good truths.

Whoever transgresses and does not abide in the doctrine of Christ does not have God. He who abides in the doctrine of Christ has both the Father and the Son. If anyone comes to you and does not bring this doctrine, do not receive him into your house nor greet him; for he who greets him shares in his evil deeds. —2 JOHN 1:9–11

The apostle John warns us in today's passage that our world is full of religious, liberal deceivers. One test is to ask them if Jesus Christ eternally existed as God, but took on a human body to die and rise again to pay for our sins. That's the gospel in a nutshell. Satan hates the gospel. Satan motivates religious deceivers, so when you ask that specific question, that's where you will usually find variances.

John says don't follow these deceivers or you will lose out on many exciting rewards you could have earned by being active in a solid, biblical local church. If you follow these leaders who do not have Christ, you will be out of fellowship with Christ, so don't do it. Don't even let these abusers into your home when they come door-to-door. Don't witness to them. Don't greet them in a way that implies you approve of what they are doing. Many of them are good people who are being victimized by their cults. I weep for them. But don't rescue them. Pray for them to see the truth and be liberated.

When these cult members come to your door to explain the "truth" to you, just say no!

*Do not be wise in your own eyes; Fear the LORD
and depart from evil. It will be health to your flesh,
And strength to your bones. The fear of the LORD
prolongs days, But the years of the wicked will be
shortened.*　　　　　　—PROV. 3:7–8, 10:27

Many years ago, a surgeon general of the United States estimated that about 80 percent of the illnesses presented to a family doctor's office are *primarily* the result of lowered resistance from psychological stress.

A few years ago I did two radio broadcasts with Dr. C. Everett Koop, the former surgeon general of the United States. I asked him privately about this relationship and he agreed. I respected his opinion because I know how much he keeps up with the research out of his genuine love for helping people.

Solomon said basically the same thing three thousand years before there was any medical research to back him up. He said to quit deceiving yourself. Fear God. Look at the truth about your depravity and depart from evil. Spiritual health will result in better physical health. You will probably live longer. People who practice sinful habits die much younger. Even the life and health insurance companies know that and base their rates on it.

———————

Job suffered a physical illness totally unrelated to sin. Others do too. But in general, your spiritual health has a profound effect on your physical health.

> *The merciful man does good for his own soul, But*
> *he who is cruel troubles his own flesh. A sound*
> *heart is life to the body, But envy is rottenness to*
> *the bones.*   —PROV. 11:17, 14:30

In our passages for today, Solomon said that evil motives like jealousy and vengeance cause trouble to your body and wise attitudes promote good physical health.

Now, we know that the stress of intense negative emotions like bitterness, grudges, envy and vengeful motives cause a series of physiological changes in the body.

A stimulating factor is released from the hypothalamus in your brain which causes a hormone (ACTH) to be released from your pituitary gland and into your blood stream. ACTH reaches your adrenal glands (above your kidneys) and causes them to release excessive stress hormones. Eventually, you have fewer antibodies because your white blood cells are suppressed. Then you come down with colds, flu, bronchitis, yeast infections, pneumonia, or even cancers. Those negative emotions also cause serotonin and norepinephrine depletions from the brain, resulting in clinical depression. The wages of sin is more than just eventual eternal spiritual death in hell—it is also the physical death of your body.

_____

Don't judge people unfairly. Not all diseases are the result of sin
(Job's wasn't, for example), but some are.

Hope deferred makes the heart sick, But when the desire comes, it is a tree of life.

—PROV. 13:12

Another way we can improve our physical health is by developing realistic expectations. You would be surprised, but expecting too much of ourselves, or our mate, or our children, or our church, or our place of employment, or even the world in general can literally kill you.

Expect to be human. *Expect* occasional failures in yourself and others. Don't expect others to meet all your needs. Go meet your own, using a variety of sources. Unrealistic expectations are the result of idealism and arrogant pride. Every good thing that happens to you is a bonus of grace (undeserved favor) from God.

Solomon said when your expectations get deferred, your emotional heart gets sick. In reality, your psychological and physical hearts can both get sick. A spirit broken by unmet expectations, "dries the bones."

In contrast, a merry heart does good, just like proper medicines. Christians who refuse to take appropriate medications for their illnesses are being foolish, are expecting God to do something quick and cheap about their illnesses—another unrealistic expectation that causes death. Even Jesus said they that are sick need a physician. God is the Creator of *common sense* as well as the universe.

A realistic set of expectations would be to have almost none.

> *"Behold, I set before you today a blessing and a*
> *curse: the blessing, if you obey the commandments*
> *of the LORD your God which I command you*
> *today; and the curse, if you do not obey the*
> *commandments of the LORD your God, but turn*
> *aside from the way which I command you today,*
> *to go after other gods which you have not known."*
> —DEUT. 11:26–28

With God, some things are unconditional and some are conditional. That's the way God operates.

God's Word tells us in many places that eternal salvation is unconditional—except for the one condition of putting your trust in Christ's atonement. He loves you unconditionally. But certain blessings in our lives are also conditional upon certain behaviors and attitudes.

In today's passage, Moses was speaking on Mount Ebal, in 1405 B.C., about thirty-five miles north of Jerusalem near the city of Shechem.

Moses was teaching the nation of Israel that: God sets before Israel and Gentile believers a blessing and a curse. Obey God's commandments and you will get the blessings. Disobey God's Commandments and you will get the curse (suffering in the form of discipline or even disease). God specifically warns about the dangers of worshiping other "gods" in our lives.

I have a choice. I can obey and receive blessings along with some necessary suffering, or I can disobey and receive quite a bit of unnecessary suffering.

> *Then the Angel of the Lord came up from Gilgal to*
> *Bochim, and said: "I led you up from Egypt and*
> *brought you to the land of which I swore to your*
> *fathers; and I said, 'I will never break My covenant*
> *with you. And you shall make no covenant with the*
> *inhabitants of this land; you shall tear down their*
> *altars.' But you have not obeyed My voice. Why*
> *have you done this? Therefore I also said, 'I will not*
> *drive them out before you; but they shall be thorns*
> *in your side, and their gods shall be a snare to*
> *you.'"*
>
> —JUDG. 2:1–3

The New Testament says the "Angel of the Lord" in the Old Testament was Christ Himself.

Gilgal is where the Israelites first camped after crossing the Jordan near Jericho. Jesus spoke to the children of Israel and promised them that He would never break His covenant with them, and He won't. Jerusalem will be the capital of the world for the one thousand years of the messianic kingdom some day. Jesus told them *not* to make any covenants with the evil people of that land at that time. The Holy Spirit had given up on those various peoples because they were so resistant to God's convictions.

But Israel disobeyed God's condition by making peace treaties with some of the people God wanted them to annihilate. As a result, Israel has had a great deal of suffering down through the ages from the people whose lives they spared.

───────

Sometimes God's conditions seem harsh, but we can trust God. He knows what He is doing.

> *And Samuel said to Saul, "You have done foolishly.*
> *You have not kept the commandment of the LORD*
> *your God, which He commanded you. For now the*
> *LORD would have established your kingdom over*
> *Israel forever. But now your kingdom shall not*
> *continue.*
>
> —1 SAM. 13:13–14a

King Saul was a tall, proud man with paranoid and sociopathic tendencies. Once in a while he was godly but he was immature.

God gave Saul a golden opportunity. If Saul had made pleasing God his goal, then Saul would have been a great king. God would have made his descendants rule over Israel forever. Saul would have been the apple of God's eye and a man after God's own heart.

Saul could have blown it sometimes, if his heart attitude had been right and he would have repented genuinely. But Saul remained rebellious and arrogant most of the time.

Therefore, Saul's kingdom was cut off by God and given instead to David, a man after God's own heart. David made terrible mistakes, too, but he had a great overall attitude and *usually* obeyed God enthusiastically.

———————

Dwight L. Moody made the statement: "The world has yet to see what God can do with a man whose heart is totally *turned toward Him."*

> *And Solomon said: "You have shown great mercy*
> *to your servant David my father, because he walked*
> *before You in truth, in righteousness, and in*
> *uprightness of heart with You."*
> —1 KINGS 3:6

King Solomon was about twenty years old when he succeeded his father, King David. Solomon acknowledged his own immaturity. He needed God's wisdom.

In today's passage Solomon was talking to God in prayer, discussing his father David. Solomon knew that his father earnestly sought after the truth. David prayed often that God would even show him his *secret,* unconscious sins. David was righteous most of the time. He wanted to do what was right. His mind, emotions and will were upright—he had a great overall attitude. That's why God was so merciful to David when David did impulsively blow it on a few occasions, even though David committed adultery and murder.

Saul blew it. David blew it. Saul was conditionally rejected. David was accepted. Why? Because God looks like an X-ray machine right into the depth of our hearts and sees our *intent,* our drives, our motives, our spiritual struggles, our genuine grief when we fail Him. That's why. It was all conditional.

Most of God's conditions that affect our blessings and suffering have more to do with *who we are* on the inside than on *what we do* on the outside.

Lord, search my innermost being and help me to walk before You in genuine truth, righteousness, and uprightness of heart.

*Behold, I have done according to your words; see, I
have given you a wise and understanding heart, so
that there has not been anyone like you before you,
nor shall any like you arise after you. And I have
also given you what you have not asked: both
riches and honor, so that there shall not be anyone
like you among the kings all your days. "So if you
walk in My ways, to keep My statutes and My
commandments, as your father David walked,
then I will lengthen your days."*

—1 KINGS 3:12–14

In Matthew 6:33, we were told that if we dedicate our
lives to furthering Christ's kingdom and give up sex,
power and money; God will turn right around and give
us a good marital sex life, godly power to use in various areas of authority, and a variety of material blessings.

Solomon could have asked God for things. By age
twenty, Solomon had already tried most of those
"things." He made more blunders, even *after* God gave
him wisdom, including allowing pagan worship of the
"gods" of his pagan wives. But Solomon had a very
wise and good heart most of the time. He prayed for
wisdom to rule God's people well. That was a great attitude. That met God's condition to bless Solomon's life.

*Lord, give me an understanding, wise, insightful heart so I can serve
You better.*

And Elisha sent a messenger to him, saying, "Go and wash in the Jordan seven times, and your flesh shall be restored to you, and you shall be clean." But Naaman became furious, and went away and said, "Indeed, I said to myself, 'He will surely come out to me, and stand and call on the name of the LORD his God, and wave his hand over the place, and heal the leprosy.'"   —2 KINGS 5:10–11

If there is one major theme that I see throughout the Bible from Genesis through Revelation, it is the theme of humility versus pride. God, throughout human history, has resisted and sent extra suffering to the proud, and blessed the humble.

In today's true story, Naaman was the commander of the army of Ben-Hadad II of Syria, about 850 B.C. He was dying of leprosy.

Naaman heard Elisha's God would heal anything, so he went to Elisha. He thought Elisha should feel honored to heal a man of Naaman's caliber. He thought Elisha would wave some sort of magic wand and cure him instantly.

Elisha told him to jump into the muddy Jordan River seven times and he would be healed. Naaman was outraged and was ready to keep leprosy and death rather than meet God's condition of humility and obedience. However, his servant talked some sense into Naaman, and he obeyed and was healed.

Humility heals a host of hurts!

> *So his fame spread far and wide, for he was*
> *marvelously helped till he* became *strong. But when*
> *he was strong his heart was lifted up, to his*
> *destruction, for he transgressed against the LORD*
> *his God by entering the temple of the LORD to burn*
> *incense on the altar of incense.*
> —2 CHRON. 26:15–16

Uzziah illustrates once again the theme of humility versus pride. He became King of Judah at age sixteen and reigned for fifty-two years. He was a humble young man when he took the throne.

He studied God's conditions and "did what was right in the sight of the LORD." His father, Amaziah, was a godly king and was a friend of the prophet Zechariah.

Because Uzziah was humble, God made him prosper more and more as time went on. His fame from military victories and the invention of new weapons spread far and wide on earth.

Like lots of believers, Uzziah could handle wars, but he *couldn't handle success,* one of the biggest stresses known to mankind. Sadly, this humble man for so many years now became proud and arrogant and gave himself the credit for his successes rather than God. He even broke God's sacred temple rules. Like Naaman, Uzziah got leprosy. Unlike Naaman, who humbled himself and dipped in the Jordan River, Uzziah kept his leprosy until it killed him.

Be proud of what you and God can do together (see Gal. 6:4), but realize you can do nothing without His help.

> *For You, O LORD, will bless the righteous; With
> favor You will surround him as with a shield. Who
> is the man that fears the LORD? Him shall He teach
> in the way He chooses. He himself shall dwell in
> prosperity, And his descendants shall inherit the
> earth.* —PS. 5:12, 25:12–13

David had his good times and his bad times. He knew
when God blessed him with special blessings and he
knew when he suffered much unnecessary pain made
necessary by his own sins.

In today's passage, David listed some of those conditions that he noticed.

Righteousness—When David was righteous, God
surrounded his life with a shield of protection.

Fear of the Lord—When David had a reverential
trust in the Lord, He taught David His ways. God promised David that his descendants (especially the Messiah
Himself—David's offspring) would inherit the earth (referring primarily to the messianic kingdom).

Trust the Lord—The result is various blessings from
God.

---

*Dear Lord, surround me today with a shield of protection, teach me
Your ways, and give me a taste of Your love for me.*

> *Blessed is he who considers the poor; The LORD*
> *will deliver him in time of trouble. The LORD will*
> *preserve him and keep him alive, And he will be*
> *blessed on the earth; You will not deliver him to the*
> *will of his enemies. The LORD will strengthen him*
> *on his bed of illness; You will sustain him on his*
> *sickbed.*
> —PS. 41:1–3

We have mentioned that the humility versus pride theme is repeated literally hundreds of times from cover to cover of the Bible. A related theme that is also mentioned over and over is the theme of caring for those *special* groups of people that God especially values but proud humans often ignore:

1. The poor
2. The abused
3. Widows (including single parents or psychologically abandoned mates)
4. Orphans (including "psychological orphans" whose fathers are alive but ignore or abuse them)

David said that creatively considering ways to help the poor is a *condition* for God to bless you. David was inspired by God to list the blessings that will come to those who help the poor. The Lord will respond when we minister to those around us.

How can you meet some needs of poor people somewhere—possibly poor missionaries, or poor people in your local church, or the starving, or the homeless?

If I regard iniquity in my heart,
The Lord will not hear.

—PS. 66:18

I read this verse as a teenager and it hit me between the eyes like a sledge hammer. I have thought about it thousands of times since then. It's a very short and simple condition, but obeying it will have a profound effect on your life.

We all deceive ourselves. We live with our depravity. Our unconscious matures as we become sanctified over the years. We gain more control over it.

But this verse has nothing to do with everyday unconscious sins. It has everything to do with conscious, willful sins—the kind we know we shouldn't do but we do anyway sometimes.

When we willfully sin, we need to ask God to forgive us—not for salvation, but to restore fellowship and for answered prayers. But if I am planning on committing the same willful sin tomorrow or any time in the future, God won't hear my prayers. I start the time clock of habitual willful sin. No one knows how long that time clock clicks. It's probably different for each person. Sometimes it leads to our physical death. We still go to heaven, but we miss out on a lot of golden opportunities on earth. Habitual, willful sin always leads to severe, unnecessary suffering sooner or later unless we repent of it and give it up.

Lord, I will search my life honestly today to see if I find any habitual, willful sins. I will give them up immediately.

> *For the LORD God is a sun and shield; The LORD*
> *will give grace and glory; No good thing will He*
> *withhold From those who walk uprightly.*
>   —PS. 84:11

Yesterday we discussed the important condition of giving up habitual, willful sin. In today's passage, David continues a related theme: walking uprightly. If we walk uprightly, God's blessings include:

Giving us insight, guidance, and biblical principles;

He will be our shield, helping us protect ourselves from the sociopathic abusers of this world;

He will give us undeserved favors;

He will give us glory now and in the future;

He won't withhold any good thing that we legitimately need.

Walking uprightly involves no habitual willful sins in our plans, meditating on God's Word day and night, obeying His principles, striving for humility, living for His kingdom, putting family before career, and *forgiving* our abusers, among other things.

No one is perfect. Living uprightly is an internal attitude with a determination to eliminate all negative addictions (habitual, willful sins).

Lord, be my sun and shield today. Help me to live by faith. Thank You for the dignity and glory You bestow upon me.

> *Whoever secretly slanders his neighbor, Him I will
> destroy; The one who has a haughty look and a
> proud heart, Him I will not endure.*
>
> —PS. 101:5

We have been looking at some positive conditions for
obtaining blessings from God. In today's passage,
David also shares with us some negative conditions
that will result in unnecessary suffering.

I have spoken unkind words about people many
times, hundreds of times since I became a Christian. I
don't ever intentionally lie about my neighbors, but
you can slander someone by saying the negative truth
about him to someone who is not part of the problem
or part of the solution. It would be better to pray
quickly, turn vengeance over to God, confront the person tactfully, and forgive.

I have to fight a haughty look and a proud heart too.
In a sense, all sins involve arrogance, pride and entitlement.

We must concentrate on removing arrogance in our
attitudes and on having a godly tongue today and
every day. God will physically destroy verbal abusers.
He will not endure unrepentant pride.

*Dear Lord, please keep my subtle pride and vengeful motives from
slipping me into the sin of slander.*

November 6 – SUFFERING AND BLESSINGS

> *"But when his heart was lifted up, and his spirit was hardened in pride, he was deposed from his kingly throne, and they took his glory from him. Then he was driven from the sons of men, his heart was made like the beasts, and his dwelling was with the wild donkeys. They fed him with grass like oxen, and his body was wet with the dew of heaven, till he knew that the Most High God rules in the kingdom of men, and appoints over it whomever He chooses."*
>
> —DAN. 5:20–21

Six hundred years before Christ, the world was ruled by Nebuchadnezzar, King of Babylon. He was standing in his castle one day, bragging he had single-handedly taken over the world, killing many to do so. So God "goofed up" his dopamine, a brain chemical. When dopamine is blocked, we become *psychotic*—out of touch with reality. Major tranquilizers can usually correct this chemical imbalance if it has been going on six months or less.

Nebuchadnezzar was psychotic for seven years, thinking he was a bird. Then God brought him back to his senses and he trusted God now that he was humble. He even wrote a beautiful letter about God for the whole world to read. Daniel recorded it.

This story gives us insight into the importance God places on humility. When we are proud we turn our backs on God. But when we are humble, He embraces us and brings us back to His side.

Be humble today. Remember that it is not by your strength that you serve God, but by your faith in Him.

Then the word of the LORD came by Haggai the prophet, saying, "Is it time for you yourselves to dwell in your paneled houses, and this temple to lie in ruins?"
—HAG. 1:3

Another negative condition God insists that we avoid is *materialism*. God does not want us to love money.

Some people misunderstand this and think it is a sin to be rich. While it is sinful to be rich if we are consumed by those riches, there are also poverty-stricken people who are obsessed with money. There are lazy, poor people who are bitter and jealous and obsessed with grudges toward the wealthy. The *attitude* is sin.

Sometimes the most humble and devout believers of each era were also the wealthiest men on earth. In general, though, the Bible makes it plain that most rich people are arrogant and many poor are humble.

In 520 B.C., in Judah, the people of Israel were so obsessed with materialism that they all wanted to have big houses with wood paneling on the walls. The temple of God went to pot because hardly anyone donated enough money to keep it up. So God said He would ruin their vineyards and crops and flocks and put holes in their pockets for their money to fall out.

Are you living for money? If you live for money God will put "holes in your pocket." If you live for God He will give you many blessings, which may or may not include money.

> *"If you then, being evil, know how to give good
> gifts to your children, how much more will your
> Father who is in heaven give good things to those
> who ask Him!"*
>
> —MATT. 7:11

God has blessings He wanted to give you in your life-time but wouldn't because you didn't ask. God *can* do anything He wants to, but He has clearly stated that we *have not* because we ask not. Some adult children of abuse hate to ask God for good things. They feel false guilt when they do. But God loves to help you.

So a major positive condition for receiving all sorts of psychological, spiritual and physical blessings from God is asking Him for prayer requests. If we try to live the Christian life on our own, God lets us fall flat on our faces. If we wait around for Him to live it through us without the hard work of self-discipline, insight, psychological work, Scripture meditation and prayer, God will still allow us to fall flat on our faces.

God wants teamwork! He wants us to do all things through Christ who gives us the strength to do them (see Phil. 4:13). So He makes His blessings conditional on our prayers. He gives us what we ask for if it is in our best interest. He listens to the *words* of our prayers, but also, more importantly, to the *intent* of our hearts.

It's quite simple. No prayer life—No blessings. Don't be afraid to ask.

> *Do not be deceived, God is not mocked; for whatever a man sows, that he will also reap. For he who sows to his flesh will of the flesh reap corruption, but he who sows to the Spirit will of the Spirit reap everlasting life.* —GAL. 6:7–8

We all tend to develop positive and negative habits. I started reading my Bible every day when I was ten years old. I crave God's word. It's spiritual food. I would feel a sense of withdrawal if I went several days in a row without it. But I have negative tendencies too. Even though I used to be trim and played sports in college, in medical school I had to study eighty to one hundred hours each week. Snacking, studying, and no sports became a negative habit and I became overweight. I have been gradually losing weight for six years now and still need to lose more. We discussed food addictions in our book *Love Hunger* (Thomas Nelson, 1990).

Paul said if we feed fleshly drives, we will yield to fleshly addictions. If we feed the spirit, we will yield to positive spiritual habits and blessings. Paul told us not to be deceived. Do not turn up your nose at God. Do good deeds for people and especially for fellow believers.

All negative addictions in believers are habitual, willful sins. With each negative addiction you have, quit feeding it; ask God for power, fill the particular vacuum that was driving it, and develop a plan for not falling back into it.

> *Children, obey your parents in the Lord, for this is*
> *right. "Honor your father and mother," which is the*
> *first commandment with promise: "that it may be*
> *well with you and you may live long on the earth."*
> *And you, fathers, do not provoke your children to*
> *wrath, but bring them up in the training and*
> *admonition of the Lord.*   —EPH. 6:1–4

The Greek word interpreted "children" here means young children. Paul gave a condition for young children living at home. They should obey their parents (unless, of course, their parents told them to disobey the Bible. The laws of God are always higher than the laws of man). Paul said that, in general, obeying parents tends to result in a meaningful life and a long life.

Paul gives two conditions to us fathers too. I've violated this first one a few times, as my teenagers will freely tell you. But I strive not to provoke my children to anger. The second condition for fathers has two parts to it. God wants us to provide for their physical and spiritual needs and to "train" them, especially in spiritual things.

If children obey their parents, they will have a more meaningful life and probably live longer. If fathers avoid provoking their children and provide for them and train them spiritually, they will almost always have a more intimate fellowship with their mature, adult children some day.

> *But without faith it is impossible to please Him, for he who comes to God must believe that He is, and that He is a rewarder of those who diligently seek Him.* —HEB. 11:6

Faith must be a fairly important condition for blessing, since without it we would all go to hell for eternity. Sounds pretty important to me! Without faith, we cannot please God. We can't be saved from hell unless we believe Christ is God, the promised Messiah, who died on the cross, shedding His blood for our sins. He rose again and ascended to heaven. Faith is the *only* condition for salvation (see Eph. 2:8–9).

Intimacy with God has another positive condition, however. If we want it, we must *diligently seek Him.* There goes that hard work theme again that we lazy Christians hate to see. God loves you unconditionally, but fellowship with Him is conditional on diligent bonding efforts on our part.

Faith in Christ for salvation means to believe He is God and depend on His death on the cross to save you from hell (the penalty for your sins) just like you depend on your chair to hold you off the floor. We also need faith for daily living, the "working out" of our salvation with fear and trembling and diligence in seeking intimate bonding with God.

Lord, please increase my faith in You and my diligence to work on who I am.

> *There is sin leading to death. I do not say that he*
> *should pray about that. All unrighteousness is sin,*
> *and there is sin not leading to death.*
>
> —1 JOHN 5:17

A lot of Christians don't like to think about this passage. But remember, if God makes some tough rules, He is God—the rule-maker! We had better learn them.

This passage is popularly (or unpopularly) known as "the Christian Death Penalty." I have seen cases where this appeared to be quite obviously occurring. A Christian denounces God because he is angry for some tragedy. He lives in prolonged, willful sin, the condition for the Christian death penalty. A year later he dies. He goes to heaven, but loses out on some good opportunities to help people on earth.

Willful sins that are not prolonged habitual sins are not punished by death. But James tells us (see James 1), that lust from our own sinful nature, if we meditate on it, becomes a habit and leads to death. In the book of Acts, Ananias and Sapphira were believers who were killed by God. They were setting a bad example of hypocrisy in their local church so God kept them from continuing that.

Remember that we see life as being all-inclusive. God sees our lives here on earth as a very brief prelude to an eternal masterpiece.

Blessed is he who reads and those who hear the words of this prophecy, and keep those things which are written in it; for the time is near.
—REV. 1:3

I would like to end this section on conditions on a positive note. Every book of the Bible is important. Every time you read any portion of God's Word, you will be blessed. It will accomplish in you whatever God hoped it would accomplish. What you accomplish with it, of course, depends on the condition of your cooperation with God. But there is only one book in the whole Bible that promises very special blessings to all who read it, hear it, and heed it: the book of Revelation.

In our passage today, John says the time is near. The Greek word used here for time is *kairos,* which means "the time of the end." I have loved the book of Revelation since hearing childhood sermons on it.

Relative to God's IQ, mine is just a notch higher than a dumb donkey's. But if you hang a carrot in front of a donkey's face, he will keep plowing your field by continually walking toward it. I long for the Rapture, Second Coming, the messianic kingdom, the new earth. Those are the "carrots" hanging in front of this "donkey" that keep me motivated. Maybe that is one of the special blessings John was talking about when he said to read, hear and heed Revelation.

Be sure to read through the book of Revelation at least once a year. Get the Dallas Theological Seminary's Bible Knowledge Commentary *(Victor Books) to assist you.*

> *God said to him: "Because you have asked this thing, and have not asked long life for yourself, nor have asked riches for yourself, nor have asked the life of your enemies, but have asked for yourself understanding to discern justice, behold, I have done according to your words; see, I have given you a wise and understanding heart, so that there has not been anyone like you before you, nor shall any like you arise after you."* —1 KINGS 3:11–12

We looked at part of this passage earlier, but I want to introduce another important concept. Solomon had no idea what God would teach him. He just knew he wanted God's wisdom.

God made Solomon the wisest man who ever has or ever will live (apart from Christ who was God and man). God did this by teaching Solomon the truth. The ugly, unadulterated truth.

Truth is terrible and wonderful. Truth makes you sad and happy. Truth causes pain and relief from pain. Truth takes the fun out of sin but sets you free. Truth makes you tense but cures anxiety. Truth deflates your pride and gives you self-worth. Truth moves you to become God's slave but sets you free from the slavery of your own depravity. Truth is addicting but frees you from addictions. Truth reveals the outrage and rage of the innocent victim of abuse, but provides the *freedom to forgive.*

———————————

Dear Lord, I fear but desire the truth in my inward parts. Please give me truth even though I resist it.

THE PURSUIT OF TRUTH – *November 15*

A wise man will hear and increase learning, And a man of understanding will attain wise counsel. Give instruction to a wise man, and he will be still wiser; Teach a just man, and he will increase in learning.
—PROV. 1:5, 9:9

If you are a wise person, you will crave truth and knowledge. You will listen to advice but be skeptical and check it out for yourself. The only absolute truth you can check anything with is the original Greek New Testament or Hebrew Old Testament.

If you are wise you will increase your learning and become even wiser. If you have understanding you will obtain wise counsel. That may mean a wise pastor who has studied the original languages well. That may mean a great commentary that holds to biblical inerrancy. That may mean a Christian therapist to professionally help you scrape out old emotional wounds from your past with his wisdom of experience.

Wise men become wiser and just (fair) men keep learning. Point out the truth to a fool (or immature person) and he will hate you for the temporary pain it causes.

The world wants sex, power, and money in a vain quest for significance they will never find. Truth sets you free from the rat race and free to serve and love.

Dear Lord, help me to hear the truth, pursue the truth, tell the truth, and live the truth.

The fear of the LORD is the beginning of knowledge,
but fools despise wisdom and instruction.
—PROV. 1:7

The fear of the Lord is another repeated theme in the Bible. It means respect, worship, awe, submission to. But let's be honest, the fear of hell is part of what motivates us to become Christians.

Immature people hate instruction because they are operating their whole lives on self-deceit, and the truth scares them. They live for pleasure and think the only source of pleasure is sin. Then they are disappointed when they suffer the natural consequences of their sins and don't understand why life is so meaningless.

Job said *departing* from sin shows that you are smart. Sin hurts you; it hurts others. God says that it is not worth it, even though it is momentarily pleasant.

Why is it whenever Moses or Abraham or Isaiah came face to face with God they literally fell on their faces? How can I obtain enough of the truth to periodically do the same thing with the same "fear" of God? Coming face to face with God somehow gave these men a glimpse into their own depravity compared to the holiness of God.

Dear God, give me a healthy fear of You without losing touch with Your intimate love.

For the LORD gives wisdom; From His mouth come knowledge and understanding; He stores up sound wisdom for the upright; He is a shield to those who walk uprightly; He guards the paths of justice, And preserves the way of His saints. Then you will understand righteousness and justice, Equity and every good path. —PROV. 2:6–9

I went to graduate school to learn human physiology—but that's not wisdom. That's just facts. I went to medical school to study diseases, but that's not wisdom. I went to psychiatry residency to learn about brain chemistry, defense mechanisms, phobias and personalities, and it was closer to wisdom and it was exciting. All real truth is God's truth.

Wisdom comes from God, our source of divine truth, and knowledge, and understanding of things. God limits what He teaches us by our own cooperation. He uses our mate, our children, our friends, circumstances, the Holy Spirit and His Word to teach us truth. He uses truth, knowledge and His own divine intervention to be our shield from pain and abuse. He guards our paths and shines His light on our decisions in life. He helps us comprehend the stupidity of sin and the human rat race 90 percent of us are running in. He teaches us about "life after life." He is our source of truth, and God is truth.

If you want to really pursue truth and knowledge at the University of Heaven, you had better really get to know The Professor.

Let not mercy and truth forsake you; Bind them around your neck, Write them on the tablet of your heart, And so find favor and high esteem In the sight of God and man. —PROV. 3:3–4

God has a merciful and loyal *love* for us. We need to develop that kind of merciful, humble, and loyal love for Him and for each other. If we learn the truth together, we will feel unity as we develop the mind of Christ together.

Somehow, God allows us to keep our unique personalities even though we are all growing toward Christ-likeness. He wants to keep our basic personality patterns. He doesn't want millions of robots. But He wants each of us to become more Christ-like in our attitudes and behavior patterns.

The ancient Jews used to put passages of Scripture on wood or clay tablets and hang them around their necks, over their hearts, even on their foreheads. They would nail them to the doorposts and walls of their houses. They taught their children these principles.

Solomon said that if you apply these wise principles in your heart (mind, emotions and will), you will not only please God, you will be highly regarded by men of wisdom.

———

Don't be surprised when immature people hate the truth. Wise people will love you for it.

By pride comes only contention,
But with the well-advised is wisdom.
                                                            —PROV. 13:10

Foolishness and psychological immaturity are the same thing. You will notice from our passage for today that foolishness and false pride go hand-in-hand. Wisdom and humility go hand-in-hand.

The fool doesn't want any advice. He already knows everything. His ways are all the right ways. Everything that goes wrong is someone else's fault. Can you see how all these self-deceiving lies protect his ego?

The truth would hurt, so he believes his own lies. A wise person also hurts when he hears the truth, but he is humble and realizes how joyful he will feel once he has applied biblical principles to work through that brief pain.

Hostile confrontation is a sign that there is at least one fool present. The humble and wise feel free to disagree. They don't demand that their mate and friends all agree with them on everything.

Scoffers make fun of people. They put others down so they can feel one-up. In contrast to those with humility and understanding, God's truth and knowledge make sense. It seems like utter foolishness to those who are perishing.

Dear Lord, make me humble enough to love myself the way you love me, by seeing the truth about who I am in Your eyes.

> *Listen to counsel and receive instruction, That you*
> *may be wise in your latter days. As in water face*
> *reveals face, So a man's heart reveals the man.*
> —PROV. 19:20, 27:19

Wisdom comes from God, but He won't give it to us automatically. It takes hard work.

In our passages for today, Solomon gives us the following practical advice for pursuing truth and knowledge:

Listen to counsel. Sometimes I need the spiritual counsel of my pastor; sometimes the psychological counsel of a Christian professional therapist; sometimes the legal counsel of a Christian lawyer; sometimes a business consultant; sometimes a medical family doctor; sometimes an understanding friend (see Prov. 19:20).

Receive instruction—moral correction and discipline. Be accountable.

Proverbs 27:19 teaches us that our innermost thoughts reflect our personality.

Get revelation (the kind of insight a prophet would give you) (Prov. 29:18).

Lord, help me to be humble enough to seek wise counsel, to be accountable, to improve my unconscious thoughts, and to see through the deceit of riches.

*For in much wisdom is much grief, and he who
increases knowledge increases sorrow.*
—ECCL. 1:18

My wife and I bought a poster a number of years ago
that showed a cartoon woman with her head and arms
squeezing through the wringer of an old wringer
washing machine, with anguish in her face. The cap-
tion read: The truth will set you free—but first it will
make you miserable! When our patients come to one of
our hospital units, we bombard them with truth daily
as we uncover it. We warn them that they have to feel a
little worse before they can recover and feel great. The
truth really does hurt.

When Solomon prayed for wisdom, God taught him
the truth about human psychology, his own depravity,
codependency, the stupidity of the human rat race, the
vanity of illicit sex and of power and money, unconscious secret sins and motives, and the value of serving
God as the *only* way to obtain meaning in life.

How would you feel if you learned all this overnight?
Solomon was overwhelmed. The truth made him temporarily miserable. Much wisdom brought Solomon
much grieving and weeping to do. His increased
knowledge caused him increased sorrow (mental anguish). His joy came after the grief from the revelation.
He became a twenty-year-old Ph.D. in Christian psychology with God as his Major Professor.

*The truth does hurt, but the long-term joy is worth the short-term
pain.*

> *I said: "Woe is me, for I am undone! Because I am*
> *a man of unclean lips, And I dwell in the midst of*
> *a people of unclean lips; For my eyes have seen the*
> *King, the LORD of hosts." Also I heard the voice of*
> *the Lord, saying: "Whom shall I send, and who will*
> *go for Us?" Then I said, "Here am I! Send me."*
> —ISA. 6:1, 5, 8

The year Uzziah died, Isaiah the prophet was given the rare privilege of seeing the Lord (Jesus in a pre-birth body) sitting on His throne majestically. Seeing the Lord in His majestic state in heaven produced awe, reverence, fear and an overwhelming sense of his own depravity in Isaiah.

The word "woe" implies judgment. It was as though Isaiah was saying, "Oh No! You and I both see me as I really am! I am a man of unclean attitudes, actions and words, and the people I live with aren't any better. I have just seen God!"

Then the Lord showed His compassion for people, wanting them to be committed believers. He asked Isaiah, "Whom shall I send, and who will go for *Us* (the Trinity)?" And Isaiah said those famous words we should all say to the triune God, "Here am I! Send me."

Are you ready, like Isaiah, to stand spiritually naked before the Lord and change your lifestyle by rededicating your life to furthering Christ's Kingdom, saying, "Here I am, Lord. Please send me."?

Dear Lord, I pursue the truth and knowledge about Your will for my life. Please guide me.

*I say to you, love your enemies, bless those who
curse you, do good to those who hate you, and
pray for those who spitefully use you and persecute
you.*
                                        —MATT. 5:44

When we look at the truth, our whole life experience
can be seen from a different perspective. Let's assume
some people have abused you in your past. You find it
difficult to forgive them because the truth is they don't
deserve it. The truth is God hated those abuses and
continues to smolder with rage toward the abuser until
he either repents or burns forever in hell. Your abusers
are definitely your enemies, and that's the truth, too.

Now Jesus is somehow saying not only should you
forgive your undeserving abusers, you should love
them, bless them, do good to them, and pray for them.
At the same time, you have a God-given responsibility
to protect yourself from them.

Once you forgive your abusers, turn vengeance over
to God. Then choose to love them in the sense that
loving someone is wanting what is best for him, which
would be to repent, be saved, and grow toward Christ-
likeness. They probably won't repent or change. But
once in a while they do. Pray for that to happen to your
abusers. It's rare but it happens.

Praying for them may actually help you forgive
them.

Try to see the truth about your abusers from God's perspective.

> *Now one of them, when he saw that he was healed,*
> *returned, and with a loud voice glorified God, and*
> *fell down on his face at His feet, giving Him thanks.*
> *And he was a Samaritan.* —LUKE 17:15–16

If you really, genuinely pursue truth and knowledge, you will become ever increasingly aware of how much God has done for you and through you. We will be shocked someday when we get to heaven and God reveals to us the thousands of incidents in our lives that we assumed were accidents that were really God nudging us along in the right direction or protecting us or disciplining us. He loves us.

When I was a young, idealistic medical student, I felt like I could rescue the whole world and I saw myself arrogantly as God's gift to mankind. Now, at the ripe old age of forty-five, I am absolutely amazed that God would even use me. I feel like Isaiah did when King Uzziah died of leprosy.

In today's passage, Jesus saw ten lepers and had compassion for their eternal destiny. He healed them and they all ran off, delighted, without even a "Thanks, Jesus."

But one, a Samaritan, came back to thank Jesus. In the process, he also put his faith in Christ for salvation and went away cleansed from leprosy on the outside and from the consequences of his sin on the inside.

Think of the seven main things you are thankful to God for, in order, right now, then thank Him for them.

Then Jesus said to those Jews who believed Him,
"If you abide in My word, you are My disciples
indeed. And you shall know the truth, and the truth
shall make you free." —JOHN 8:31–32

One very good reason why we should pursue truth and knowledge is because it frees us from anxiety and depression.

One of the most important steps for both anxiety and depression is discovering the *truth*. The truth truly sets people free if they deal with it biblically, so as therapists, we attempt to reflect truth back to our patients as we become aware of it.

People seldom know the truth about what underlies a depression or anxiety disorder. We take a detailed history, make some logical guesses, and talk with the patients about areas we suspect. When we hit on the right one, they have a nervous system response. Their pupils dilate quickly. Their skin blotches. Their arms cross defensively. They look down. And they often deny whatever you just said that triggered the response. We home in on that topic until they get in touch with it.

When enough truth has been looked at and dealt with, there is no longer a fear of finding out the truth, so the anxiety is gone. And if the grudges are gone, so is the depression.

Discovering the painful truth, even about child abuse, and dealing with it biblically, truly does heal anxiety disorders and depressions.

*O Timothy! Guard what was committed to your
trust, avoiding the profane and vain babblings and
contradictions of what is falsely called knowledge.*
—1 TIM. 6:20

Wordly knowledge is sometimes true and sometimes
false. But knowledge is doubling in the world at a rate
of about once every five years. It used to be once every
thousand years. Daniel said that would happen in the
end time.

Since God's Word is perfect, every lick of good scientific research will agree with Scripture, and it does. Scientific evidence done objectively using the scientific
method has never and will never contradict the Bible.
All truth is God's truth. Only scientific theories contradict the Bible, not proven facts.

Scientific *opinions* in every area of science and psychology often contradict Scripture. Nonbelievers simply hate the idea that the Bible may be correct because
it would make them accountable to God.

Ask God often for wisdom, but also study all of God's
truth, both from the Bible and from scientific research.
Pray for scientific research. It can only bring more
people to Christ, even though worldly "knowledge" includes many opinions that contradict Scripture.

---

*Dear Lord, please help me to sort out scientific theories from scien-
tific facts, so my faith in Your Word can grow.*

*But each one is tempted when he is drawn away by
his own desires and enticed. Then, when desire has
conceived, it gives birth to sin; and sin, when it is
full-grown, brings forth death.*
—JAMES 1:14–15

Another area we really need to know the truth about
is the area of temptations. There are two sources of
temptations: our own sinful lusts and demonic temptations.

Nonbelievers are moving more and more into many
New Age beliefs that were common in ancient
Babylonia—astrology, calling on "spirit guides," crys-
tals. Bible prophecy predicts this and warns believers
not to practice any of these things. God hates them and
will punish all who practice them.

When nonbelievers get passive in trance states and
call on "spirit guides," they are becoming increasingly
possessed by demons. Most people have no idea that
their "spirit guides" are demons in disguise.

Christians cannot be demon-possessed according to
the Bible. The Holy Spirit is stronger than Satan. But
Christians can be strongly tempted by demons and by
their own lusts. If we dwell on our temptations, they
become sin. If we keep sinning we develop negative
addictions or habitual willful sin.

We must not only resist temptation, we must become accountable, and get whatever counsel we need
to figure out which vacuum that sin was filling.

*Lord, when I am tempted allow me the wisdom to see the ways of
escape and the courage to pursue them.*

> *All Scripture is given by inspiration of God, and is profitable for doctrine, for reproof, for correction, for instruction in righteousness.* —2 TIM. 3:16

Do you want to pursue truth and knowledge? The best place to look is God's Word.

The apostle Peter said the prophets never wrote down their own private thoughts. They wrote what they wrote as they were *moved* by the Holy Spirit.

Jesus said not even the punctuation points (jots or tittles) are wrong in Scripture. The apostle Paul said that *all* Scripture is *inspired* (*theopneustos*—God-breathed). He added that every bit of Scripture is profitable for us to learn Bible doctrines (like salvation by grace through faith), for reproof (convicting the course of our lives and the causes we stand for), for instruction in correct living habits. If we do this, we will become mature (not perfect as some English Bibles erroneously state).

Life without a Bible would be like being lost in the middle of the Amazon jungles without a compass and a map. Our ability to do productive psychotherapy would be drastically limited without the insights from God's Word on human thoughts, feelings, motives, and behaviors. Secular psychiatrists are getting better at helping people every few years because psychiatric research is revealing what works and what doesn't work. What works is truth, and truth is biblical in every case.

Thank You, Lord, for "moving" the authors of Your love letter to us.

Beloved, I pray that you may prosper in all things and be in health, just as your soul prospers. For I rejoiced greatly when brethren came and testified of the truth that is in you, just as you walk in the truth.

—3 JOHN 1:2–3

John wrote this passage to his good friend Gaius, but God inspired John to write this for you and me as well. God wants you and me to prosper in every area of our lives. Jesus said (see John 10:10) that He came that we might have life and have it more *abundantly*.

If we will walk in the truth—the truth about ourselves, about God, and about His principles—then we will tend to be in health (physical, mental and spiritual health). Again, there are no guarantees because even godly Job suffered for spiritual reasons.

John said there is nothing that makes him happier than to see fellow believers walking in the truth. Isn't that a beautiful statement? We are part of a very unique family. We look at the truth in ourselves and others. We speak the truth in love to each other. We confess the truth about our faults to each other with accountability both individually and in small groups. We study the truth in Bible studies and devotional books like this one. We believe the truth about ourselves, so we can see ourselves as God sees us. No wonder that you can go to any country in the world and if you find any true believers they excitedly welcome you with open arms. We are united by bonds of love and truth.

We are a unified, loyal family of truth!

> *I have seen all the works that are done under the*
> *sun; and indeed, all is vanity and grasping for the*
> *wind. And I saw that all labor and all achievement*
> *spring from man's envy of his neighbor. This too is*
> *meaningless, a chasing after the wind.*
> —ECCL. 1:14, 4:4 (NIV)

According to national polls, the three greatest fears humans face are failure, abandonment, and death. That's why so many people have a mid-life crisis. It takes that long to give up the idealism of youth and face the truth!

We all feel abandoned to some extent if we have any kind of insight into human nature. By mid-life, we realize how many people we thought loved us were really selfishly using us.

And then there is death. By mid-life we have nearly all lost someone whom we really did care about. We grieve their unwilling abandonment of us, but also are reminded of how little control we have over health or death.

The fear of failure, our number one fear, is really a fear of the pain that we all experience from realizing our insignificance, humanly speaking. And nothing we do in life seems to help for more than a moment. We compete for significance, but it is like chasing the wind—we never catch it.

If we join the kingdom-team, we will conquer all three fears—we will succeed, we will love and be loved, and we will conquer eternal death.

That which has been is what will be, That which is done is what will be done, And there is nothing new under the sun.   —ECCL. 1:9

When a patient comes to a Minirth-Meier clinic, that person is the "identified patient" in his or her family. But our therapists directly or indirectly treat the whole family system. If people don't break their repetitive co-dependency cycles and patterns, the "cure" will be short-lived.

I have taught hundreds of future pastors and experienced pastors over the years. Sometimes they are afraid to begin pastoral counseling. They are well prepared to create a powerful sermon but afraid they won't know what to say to someone who is being forced into a divorce or someone who just found out his child has leukemia.

I tell them that once they see one hundred people in counseling, once a week for several months each, they will never see a new problem. Each person is unique and significant, but the same behavior problems have been cropping up over and over again since Adam and Eve.

A daughter of an abusive alcoholic will marry an abusive alcoholic 85 percent of the time. That's just the way it is. In psychiatry, we see these codependency patterns over and over again.

We can control our patterns and be different from the 90 percent of humans who don't. But it will require God's help and lots of insight and the will to break with family traditions.

> *Where* there is *no wood, the fire goes out; And*
> *where* there is *no talebearer, strife ceases.* As
> *charcoal* is *to burning coals, and wood to fire, So* is
> *a contentious man to kindle strife.*
>
> —PROV. 26:20–21

Life seems meaningless at times when you find out people you thought were your friends "bad-mouth" you and exaggerate or lie about you. It can be devastating. A gun can kill a body but a tongue can kill a reputation.

Solomon said a good reputation is rather to be chosen than great wealth. Your reputation is important to you, and it should be. God's reputation is important to Him, too.

In our passage for today, Solomon said that fires burn where there is wood, and strife "burns" wherever a talebearer is present. Sociopaths—the abusers of this world—love to "kindle strife." They love to pit one person against another. They misuse their tongues to do evil.

They often do it just to relieve their boredom. Sometimes they do it to sublimate their rage toward authority figures from their past. Seldom do they have any insight whatsoever as to why they are doing what they are doing. Seldom would they care even if they did know. They are loyal to no one but themselves. They will burn in hell themselves for the fires they have put men through with their tongues.

Dear Lord, help me to guard my own tongue and protect myself from the tongues of disloyal people.

Whatever my eyes desired I did not keep from them. I did not withhold my heart from any pleasure. . . . And indeed all was vanity and grasping for the wind. There was no profit under the sun.
—ECCL. 2:10–11

Before Solomon matured, he experimented with *everything!* He had great wealth, was a connoisseur of fine wines, was the most powerful political figure of his day, and had one thousand wives and concubines.

He had everything this world had to offer. He tried to get all the gusto he could get out of life.

But he was miserable. Many millionaires have come to our Minirth-Meier offices who "had it all" like Solomon, but had held a gun to their heads the night before because their lives were meaningless. They changed their minds at the last second and decided to give therapy a try.

Solomon said all his work, sex, wine, money and power were absolutely meaningless. He still felt insignificant. Grabbing for significance is like grabbing for the wind. You know it must be out there somewhere—you can "feel" it—but you can't quite get hold of it.

Solomon hated life. He had restless nights of insomnia—until he developed personal faith in the coming Messiah. When he got out of the rat race and into the service of the King of Kings, then he found life, meaning, joy, and significance.

There is only one way to find true significance. Trust *Christ.*

> *Do not love the world or the things in the world. If*
> *anyone loves the world, the love of the Father is not*
> *in him. For all that is in the world—the lust of the*
> *flesh, the lust of the eyes, and the pride of life—is*
> *not of the Father but is of the world.*
>
> —1 JOHN 2:15–16

Demas was a believer. He worked hand-in-hand with the apostle Paul and is mentioned favorably and fondly in Colossians 4:14 and Philemon 2:4.

But Demas never licked his codependency. He was addicted to the world. He fought it for awhile but never filled the holes in his soul. His unconscious cravings and vacuums sucked him right out of Christian work and back into the worldly rat race.

The world has three major categories of temptation.

Lusts of the flesh—illicit body appetites, including illicit sexual fantasies, pornography, fornication, affairs, food addictions, drug or alcohol addictions, etc.

Lusts of the eyes—materialism, or the desire to buy everything in sight to feel significant—houses, cars, jewelry, people, things.

Lusts of life or pride of life—power struggles, the desire to control people, the craving for prestige at work or politically.

If the rat race doesn't work anyway, why try it?

> *"Lord, make me to know my end, And what is the measure of my days, That I may know how frail I am. Indeed, You have made my days as handbreadths, And my age is as nothing before You; Certainly every man at his best state is but vapor.*
> —PS. 39:4–5

Together, we will reflect from today until Christmas—on topics related to Christ's First or Second Coming or the brevity of our human lives in between those two comings. It should help us experience our most meaningful Christmas season ever.

King David determined in his own mind to really concentrate on the shortness of his own life to motivate himself. He especially yearned for a godly perspective after it dawned on him that even though much of his pain came from abusers, much of it also was due to his own sins.

David had his share of being betrayed by those he was personally loyal to. He saved Israel by defeating Goliath and became Saul's loyal musician, only to have Saul throw spears at him and attempt to kill him in fits of jealous rage. But David's greatest pains came from his own sins. To get life in perspective, David had to forgive his abusers and himself. Concentrating on the brevity of life here on this planet helped him do so.

Life is so short there is not enough time to hold grudges and get personal vengeance.

> *Teach us to number our days, That we may gain a heart of wisdom.*
> *Do not boast about tomorrow, For you do not know what a day may bring forth.*
> —PS. 90:12, PROV. 27:1

God looks trillions of years back and trillions of years forward, then glances at human history on earth as though He was reading a brief newspaper article in the middle of the day. Fortunately for us, we are a very significant part of His future, even though we only average seventy brief years on earth.

Seventy years isn't much when one thousand human years seem like one God-day. Apart from trusting and serving Christ, humans grow up, eat, sleep, work hard, grieve over their losses, and die. It's a very quick rat race without God.

I realized once again how brief my own life is on November 15, 1989, when a car hit mine head on so hard that mine flipped into the air and landed upside down on the roof. The two cars looked like folded accordions but no one had a scratch.

I was listening to the Psalms during the accident, and I listened to them the next day. Verse 12 really stood out to me so I memorized it. I learned a few days later that my godly mother-in-law claimed that verse all that week, even before my accident, and had been praying daily for my safety.

David encouraged us to count our days so we will realize that each day is significant and may be our last. Only God knows if we will be on earth tomorrow.

Come, and let us return to the LORD; For He has torn, but He will heal us; He has stricken, but He will bind us up. After two days He will revive us; On the third day He will raise us up, That we may live in His sight. —HOSEA 6:1–2

The prophet Hosea shared a very interesting puzzle for us to think about. I think it has a dual meaning.

Hosea prophesies that Israel will be torn up by permission of God the Father, but later healed by Him.

The Father will heal Israel on the third day after they have been severely torn up. It seems logical to guess that God may be talking about "God-days," one thousand human years each. Prophetic years have always been Jewish years, three hundred sixty days each.

Israel was most severely torn up and scattered in A.D. 70 by Titus and the Roman legions. Millions were killed and the nation of Israel ended for awhile—a couple of God-days. Then in 1948 they were a nation again. But two thousand 360-day years won't be up for a few more years. *If* this passage happens to be referring to the great A.D. 70 destruction, one significant implication may be drawn: Christ's Second Coming could easily take place in the 21st Century. The Rapture could happen any day.

We are living on borrowed time between the first Christmas "two days ago" and the messianic kingdom.

> *Therefore He shall give them up, until the time that
> she who is in labor has given birth; then the
> remnant of His brethren shall return to the children
> of Israel. And He shall stand and feed His flock in
> the strength of the LORD, in the majesty of the name
> of the LORD His God; and they shall abide, for now
> He shall be great to the ends of the earth.*
>
> —MIC. 5:3–4

We *are* living on borrowed time. We'll live eternally with God but life on earth is very brief. When I was growing up in Saginaw, Michigan, our local newspaper had printed in it daily: "Only one life, twill soon be past. Only what's done for Christ will last." That left a helpful impression on me.

God had a near future and distant future schedule in mind when He told Micah to pen these words. The Messiah picked the humble town of Bethlehem to be born in, and chose a manger for His first cradle.

Christ will rapture us soon, then return with us years later to the Mount of Olives in Jerusalem to establish a one thousand year messianic kingdom. Israel has been "in labor" for two thousand years now and will give birth from 1948, when Israel began the regathering of His brothers, until the messianic kingdom officially begins. Jesus will reign with King David and shepherd His flock.

If you have put your faith in Christ, you are part of His eternal victorious plan. In the meantime, your life here on earth is short—it will soon be over. Only what is done for Christ will last.

*"The glory of this latter temple shall be greater
than the former," says the LORD of hosts. "And in
this place I will give peace," says the LORD of hosts.*
—HAG. 2:9

Like Micah the prophet, I keep watch for the Lord (see
Mic. 7:7). Except I watch for the Rapture and Micah
was looking for political deliverance. I am waiting for
God my Savior.

I am longing for Christ's return. It's *not* that life on
earth is so terrible I want to hurry up and get it over
with. I have my family, my friends, a great church, and
a meaningful lifestyle. But I feel horrible when I see all
the pain in the world. I want it to end right now.

The passage from Haggai is also a reminder that we
are living on borrowed time. Solomon built a beautiful
temple three thousand years ago. A rebuilt version of it
was destroyed in A.D. 70 by the Romans. A temporary
temple will probably be rebuilt in our lifetime, because
the Antichrist will defile it half-way through the seven
year tribulation period. But a beautiful temple of peace
will be built in Jerusalem during the messianic kingdom that will surpass all of them.

The life of serving Christ in a practical way, putting
family above career and all, is an abundant and wonderful life. But it is nothing in comparison to the exciting events of our near future.

*Dear Lord, when I feel self-pity for the pains I have suffered here on
earth, I know You pity me even more than I do. Remind me, Lord,
that the pain is short in comparison to eternal joys.*

> *And this shall be the plague with which the L*ORD
> *will strike all the people who fought against*
> *Jerusalem: Their flesh shall dissolve while they*
> *stand on their feet, Their eyes shall dissolve in their*
> *sockets, And their tongues shall dissolve in their*
> *mouths.*
>
> —ZECH. 14:12

Zechariah was a Levite, but was born in Babylon. He was also a priest. Zechariah's name means *Yahweh remembers*. He wrote his prophetic book around five hundred years before Christ's birth. And yet he perfectly describes nuclear warfare 2500 years before it was invented. It can't be anything else. What else would cause human flesh to melt before the skeleton has a chance to fall to the ground?

The time is the battle of Armageddon and the Gentile armies surrounding Jerusalem at the end of the Tribulation. You and I will be with Jesus during those seven years, but we'll descend with Him on the Mount of Olives as God's angels destroy all who refuse to trust Christ as Messiah. God will give mankind one more chance.

The soldiers of the Gentile nations will experience nuclear warfare, either directly from God or from each other. Their eyes and tongues will melt out of their sockets before their bodies have time to fall to the ground.

We are living on borrowed time. World War III will be a nuclear war. It will occur.

> *"Now learn this parable from the fig tree: When its branch has already become tender and puts forth leaves, you know that summer is near. So you also, when you see all these things, know that it is near, at the very doors. Assuredly, I say to you, this generation will by no means pass away till all these things are fulfilled."* —MATT. 24:32–34

The fig tree symbolizes the nation of Israel in many instances in the Bible. What does it mean for the fig tree to bud forth its branches and leaves? I think it refers to Israel "budding forth" its branches to its historical boundaries by regaining land (especially Jerusalem) in the 1967 war.

But I'm a scientist, a realist and—believe it or not—very skeptical—it could mean a lot of different things. But whatever it means, the young people living at the time of the *budding forth* will live to see all the terrible events of the Great Tribulation unless they are believers prior to the Rapture and "disappear" from earth in the Rapture. That generation living during the "budding forth" will experience the Second Coming of Christ to earth (after the seven year tribulation) to set up His messianic kingdom. Many nonbelievers now will end up trusting Christ after the Rapture. Many of them will be killed during the Tribulation and join us in heaven somewhere in their new bodies.

Israel is already "budding forth," the new Roman Empire (European unity) is happening before our very eyes, and Babylon is being rebuilt in Iraq as you read this page. We're living on borrowed time.

> *Jesus said to her, "I am the resurrection and the life. He who believes in Me, though he may die, he shall live."*
> —JOHN 11:25

Have you lost any loved ones to death? I have seen friends and relatives die. I have also watched people die in hospitals of heart attacks, cancer and other causes. The memories never leave you.

I remember one heart attack patient who appeared to be recovering. I talked to him quite a bit and really enjoyed getting to know him. He was a committed Christian. But his heart failed and we kept pumping his dead heart hoping to resuscitate him. He remained conscious.

Finally, I told him we could not save him. I told him to prepare to be with God. I let go as he looked up with a big smile on his face and died.

My grandfather died the same way, with a smile and his hand pointing to the ceiling and a Bible clutched in his other hand. My wife's grandmother died the same way, with a Bible open on her lap, and peace all over her face. The death of nonbelievers is different.

Christ's death *and resurrection* made this all possible. Jesus Christ said *He is* the resurrection. *He is* the life. Whoever trusts *Him* for salvation will keep on living when he or she "dies."

Perfectionists like myself hate to think about death. It makes me feel out of control. If I do die, I hope it will be with a Bible in one hand, my finger pointing to the sky, and a peaceful smile on my face.

But why do you judge your brother? Or why do you show contempt for your brother? For we shall all stand before the judgment seat of Christ. For it is written: "As I live, says the LORD, every knee shall bow to Me, and every tongue shall confess to God." *So then each of us shall give account of himself to God.*   —ROM. 14:10–12

God created and owns the universe. He is the potter. I am the clay. He designed my genetic makeup. I am His creation. We are fearfully and wonderfully made, and some day each of us will stand in judgment before that Creator.

The Bible tells us there are two judgments. There will be a judgment for believers, called the judgment seat of Christ, later a judgment *only* for nonbelievers, called the Great White Throne judgment.

When anyone dies who is old enough and mature enough to have *rejected* the Holy Spirit's call to trust Christ's death and resurrection for eternal salvation, that person goes immediately to hell for eternity. At the end of the messianic kingdom, Christ will call all nonbelievers out of hell to somehow explain to each one why they are suffering as much as they are, then send them back to hell (which may be in the center of the earth) for eternity. Tomorrow we will look at the other judgment—for believers.

Why would a loving God create an eternal hell? I don't know, but I'm smart enough not to argue with Him too much about it!

> *For we must all appear before the judgment seat of*
> *Christ, that each one may receive the things* done *in*
> *the body, according to what he has done, whether*
> *good or bad.*
> —2 COR. 5:10

Paul said that the moment our body dies, if we have trusted Christ, we appear before Christ in our new body. He tells us elsewhere that we will know people when we get there, as we were known on earth. Our tears are wiped away.

At the Rapture, Jesus will "collect" all believers who have died and gone to heaven and also all "alive" believers from earth together. He will hold the *judgment seat of Christ.* It has nothing to do with salvation (see Eph. 2:8–9), because salvation has nothing to do with our works—only His work.

Christ will somehow judge each of us for every motive and deed. He will wipe away all tears. Some say we will only see the good things, but I think heaven will be better if, for one time in our lives, we all face the truth about our depravity and goodness, and see the truth about each other. None would be so arrogant as to reject another after that. Together, we would hug each other and cry tears of joy for belonging to God and to each other for eternity.

> *When we've been there ten thousand years,*
> *Bright, shining as the sun.*
> *We've no less days, to sing God's praise.*
> *Then when we'd first begun.*

For the grace of God that brings salvation has appeared to all men, teaching us that, denying ungodliness and worldly lusts, we should live soberly, righteously, and godly in the present age, looking for the blessed hope and glorious appearing of our great God and Savior Jesus Christ.
— TITUS 2:11–13

The Rapture is my blessed *hope*. I think about it often. When my wife and I go to the Pacific Ocean to watch the sunset, I think about the "Son-Rise" I will witness some day. If I die before the Rapture, I'll be there anyway (1 Thess. 4:13–18). If I live until the Rapture, I'll be there.

But in the meantime, even though we are experiencing "the abundant life" here on earth. We are living on borrowed time. Our life is very brief.

Our financial savings mean nothing. Our business successes mean nothing. Our favorite athletic teams mean nothing.

Only three things will last forever—God, His Word, and people. That's why God wants us to give up on worldly lusts and popularity. Stay sober and live right in this present age.

Look for the Rapture, but keep doing good deeds— not to get to heaven, but to obey God, and to help people. We are His "special people" if we are committed believers.

The world is very appealing whenever I get my eyes off of God's true eternal perspective.

> *These all died in faith, not having received the*
> *promises, but having seen them afar off were*
> *assured of them, embraced them, and confessed*
> *that they were strangers and pilgrims on the earth.*
> —HEB. 11:13

In Hebrews 11, God listed (through the apostle Paul) a hall of fame for faith in Him. It includes Abel, who was killed by Cain. It includes Enoch, who had so much faith God allowed him to go to heaven without experiencing death.

Noah is in the hall of fame, and so are Abraham and Sarah, in spite of all their faults. Isaac and Jacob weren't perfect either, but they made it to the "hall."

Also listed were Moses and his parents, Joshua, Rahab the prostitute who lied for God to protect His spies, Gideon, Barak, Sampson, Jephthah, David, Samuel, and God says there are many more not listed yet.

Paul said these all died—in faith. Their great faith was related to their *perspective*. They considered themselves to be strangers and pilgrims on this earth, living on borrowed time. They put off immediate worldly gratification for delayed, heavenly gratification.

They had faith in God to keep His promises. They had faith that there would be "eternal payoffs" for the sacrifices they made to obey God.

May God grant us the wisdom to see ourselves as visitors on a strange and evil planet, with a mission to love and help others.

*Therefore gird up the loins of your mind, be sober,
and rest your hope fully upon the grace that is to
be brought to you at the revelation of Jesus Christ;
as obedient children, not conforming yourselves to
the former lusts, as in your ignorance; but as he
who called you is holy, you also be holy in all your
conduct, because it is written, "Be holy, for I am
holy."*
—1 PETER 1:13–16

In biblical times, men wore long robes that they could walk in but not run in. When they needed to go at a faster pace, they would "gird up their loins" or tie the bottom of their robe to their waist.

Peter tells us to be prepared to concentrate and work hard for Christ during this brief borrowed time we call "life." The Greek word for sober, *nēphontes*, is used figuratively here, implying freedom from psychological or spiritual "drunkenness" or addictions. When passive we are controlled by outside circumstances and temptations. When assertively "sober," we are in control (with God's strength).

We hope fully on the grace we will receive at the Rapture. Peter had already referred four times to Christ's return for motivational reasons.

As we prepare to celebrate Christ's first coming this Christmas season, may we also "gird up the loins of our mind" in preparation for His second coming.

> *And if you call on the Father, who without*
> *partiality judges according to each one's work,*
> *conduct yourselves throughout the time of your*
> *sojourning* here *in fear; knowing that you were*
> *not redeemed with corruptible things, like silver*
> *or gold, from your aimless conduct received by*
> *tradition from your fathers, but with the precious*
> *blood of Christ.*
>   —1 PETER 1:17–19a

Most child abusers were abused as children. The innocent victim becomes so enraged inside that he or she develops into an explosive persecutor. The family tradition continues.

Not only do all humans inherit a basically sociopathic nature that must be lovingly nurtured away from its natural inclination, we also have the misfortune of modeling our behavior off of imperfect parents.

As committed believers, we renounce all of our aimless types of conduct passed on by codependent family traditions. Instead, we think about the beauty of life, considering ourselves sojourners. We live in "reverent fear," or a desire to please God, and guilt when we displease Him.

The blood of Christ, our Lamb-Messiah, has redeemed, (paid a ransom for) us. Don't take that lightly. Salvation is *free* for us, because the Lamb paid the price.

Lord, I find myself in warfare with my own unconscious lusts and
desires, pulling me to "settle in" to my worldly "family traditions."
Help me break that cycle now.

*Having been born again, not of corruptible seed
but incorruptible, through the word of God which
lives and abides forever, because* "All flesh is as
grass, And all the glory of man as the flower of the
grass. The grass withers, and its flower falls away,
But the word of the LORD endures forever." *Now
this is the word which by the gospel was preached
to you.*   —1 PETER 1:23–25

The apostle Paul said that the Word of God will last
forever, but your current body won't! It grows. It looks
pretty for a brief moment of time. It withers and gets
wrinkled and dry. It dies.

If there wasn't so much natural evidence that God is
real, I would be depressed. If Old Testament prophecies didn't absolutely amaze me, I would be in despair.
Life without Christ is absolutely meaningless.

All my good feelings of love and hope and significance are wrapped up in one hope—the hope that
Jesus Christ is Who He claims to be and that I can
count on the promises of God's Word. I'm depending
on Christ's shed blood to pay the penalty for my sins
and His resurrection for the power to resurrect into my
own new, eternal body with Him.

---

*Some day I'm going to trade in this old "Edsel" for a brand new Fer-
rari Testerosa. In the meantime, I will keep chugging along, helping
whoever I can along the way.*

> *But the end of all things is at hand; therefore be serious and watchful in your prayers. for so an entrance will be supplied to you abundantly into the everlasting kingdom of our Lord and Savior Jesus Christ.*
>
> —1 PETER 4:7

Peter wrote that "the end of all things is at hand" a couple of thousand years ago to get it in perspective. Only God knows the Rapture date. Whatever God's date is, it's about two thousand years closer than it was when Peter wrote this. God doesn't want us to know the exact date or He would have told us. What He does want is a proper perspective.

We are important to God. He decided it was worth Christ's pain and death and resurrection in order to save us and fellowship with us eternally. Peter says just knowing this is true will strengthen us or firm us up.

Peter knew he must soon die. He wanted to make his time productive. He used it to teach principles of Christian living as well as about our bright futures in eternity.

We are borrowing a temporary "tent" before entering eternity. To devote our lives to it would be a waste. To neglect it—since it is the temple of the Holy Spirit—would also be a sin.

*Therefore, since all these things will be dissolved,
what manner of persons ought you to be in holy
conduct and godliness, looking for and hastening
the coming of the day of God, because of which the
heavens will be dissolved being on fire, and the
elements will melt with fervent heat?*
—2 PETER 3:11–12

My wife and I love to travel. The mountains of Switzerland, Alaska, and Colorado take our breath away. But none of them compare to walking on Mt. Ararat in eastern Turkey and meditating on our "roots" from Noah.

We enjoyed watching the hustle and bustle all around Brussels, Belgium, as its citizens clean the city so Brussels can be a beautiful, proud capital of the budding new Roman Empire (the EEC).

We tend to spend too much time worrying about what our own house and yard look like. There is nothing wrong with enjoying the beautiful sites of the world or working on your house and yard. An ugly yard would be a poor testimony for Christ.

But once again we must keep an "eternal perspective." This world will be burned up after the messianic kingdom. Only believers will enter the new heavens and the new earth God will create. The people will all be beautiful then too—on the *inside* in particular. Our depraved parts die when our body dies (or at the Rapture).

I will praise the Lord for His beautiful evidences of creative genius throughout the world. I will invest my life in God, His Word, and people, starting with my own mate and children.

> *And I looked, and behold, a white horse. And he*
> *who sat on it had a bow; and a crown was given to*
> *him, and he went out conquering and to conquer.*
> *And I will give power to my two witnesses, and*
> *they will prophesy one thousand two hundred and*
> *sixty days, clothed in sackcloth.*
>
> —REV. 6:2, 11:3

In the "near" future Europe will be ruled by a charming prince. He will take over without war by political intrigue. He will be a charming, but chauvinistic, sociopathic politician with power as his goal, but will be so intelligent that I'm afraid I would accidentally vote for him.

He will "ride a white horse" and be everyone's hero. He will bring great economic prosperity to the entire world until the Great Tribulation begins. It appears that he will be heavily dependent on OPEC oil. He will resent Babylon's (Iraq's) clout.

The European president will be considered a "prince" of peace. He will even sign a seven-year peace treaty with Israel. The signing of this peace treaty will let new believers figure out that he is the Antichrist.

Two witnesses will be sent to earth to cause the plagues of the Great Tribulation three-and-a-half years before the Second Coming of Christ.

Reading the daily newspaper becomes exciting when you study Bible prophecy and stay active helping serve in His kingdom now.

> *Then I saw another angel flying in the midst of*
> *heaven, having the everlasting gospel to preach*
> *to those who dwell on the earth—to every nation,*
> *tribe, tongue, and people—saying with a loud voice,*
> *"Fear God and give glory to Him, for the hour of*
> *His judgment has come; and worship Him who*
> *made heaven and earth, the sea and springs of*
> *water."* —REV. 14:6–7

What better time than Christmas to meditate on the Lamb-Messiah turning into the Lion-Messiah? The prophets say in many places that when the Lion-Messiah descends on the Mount of Olives at His Second Coming, He will *roar* and His believing children will come *trembling* but rejoicing from all over the world to join Him—even American believers from the distant coastlands—even Jewish believers who were hiding in caves from the Antichrist.

The Lion-Messiah and the Lamb-Messiah are one. His angels of death will slay all nonbelievers, but before they do that, the Lamb-Messiah part of the nature of Christ will send angels around the entire globe giving people one last chance to repent, trust Christ, and enter the Millennium alive and well.

Does the Christmas season bring back sad memories of past abuse? Keep forgiving and keep in mind the billions of happy Christmases to come.

> *Then a mighty angel took up a stone like a great*
> *millstone and threw it into the sea, saying, "Thus*
> *with violence the great city Babylon shall be*
> *thrown down, and shall not be found anymore.*
> *The sound of harpists, musicians, flutists, and*
> *trumpeters shall not be heard in you anymore."*
> —REV. 18:21

God loves Arab believers. In heaven there will be no distinction between male, female, or any race.

But there are evil Arabs just like there are evil people among every group. Evil Arabs will rule Babylon and OPEC during the Tribulation. They will promote materialism throughout the world. Their oil will make them rich. Their religion then will be contaminated by "spirit guides," astrology, mind-altering experiences.

Most believers see Babylon as symbolic. But I have a very "profound" proposal: Could Babylon be Babylon? I think so! Watch it grow—and soon. In fact, it is already happening. Even its ancient gardens are being restored.

But God will "nuke" Babylon before the Millennium.

A star hovered over Bethlehem as a sign of the Messiah's First Coming. Perhaps the death of communism, Babylon being rebuilt, oil prices skyrocketing, and a temple in Israel, will serve as "stars" on the horizon of Christ's Second Coming.

*"Who shall not fear You, O Lord, and glorify Your
name? For You alone are holy. For all nations shall
come and worship before You, for Your judgments
have been manifested."*
                                    —REV. 15:4

Nearly two-thousand years ago, the angels sang
"Happy Birthday" to the Lamb-Messiah as He was
wrapped in swaddling clothes and lying in a manger. I
wish I had a recording of that angelic choir as they
sang and chanted with joy and pride.

In today's passage, the millions of Jews who trust
Christ sing songs to the Messiah, hoping for His Second
Coming to end their persecution and annihilation.

I can imagine small groups of them, hiding together,
singing traditional Jewish-tunes with new words:

> *Jesus, He's the Messiah,*
> *The Son of David,*
> *The Great "I Am,"*
> *He's my God! Hey!*
> *We are His chosen lambs,*
> *Chosen from all the lands,*
> *We'll live eternally*
> *With Christ from above, Hey!*
> *We are His chosen lambs,*
> *Chosen from all the lands,*
> *We'll live eternally*
> *With joy, peace and love. Hey!*
> —Paul Meier

---

*This Christmas I am extremely grateful to be a Gentile dog eating
crumbs from the banquet table prepared for the Jews. Some day we
will be equal brothers in Christ.*

> *Commit your works to the LORD, And your thoughts will be established. For whom He foreknew, He also predestined to be conformed to the image of His Son, that He might be the firstborn among many brethren.*
> —PROV. 16:3, ROM. 8:29

Every morning, when I wake up—before I even get out of bed—I dedicate each day to three daily goals: becoming more like Christ; serving Christ; staying out of trouble today.

These three goals prepare me for anything that could possibly go "wrong" that day. In fact, with these biblical goals, "things" can only go "right" in the long run.

In Proverbs 16:3, the Hebrew word for "commit" literally means to "roll" your works over to the Lord so He can influence your thinking to help you deal with them correctly.

In Romans 8:29, the apostle Paul teaches us that God—thousands of years ago—could look into the distant future and see our lives. He knew us intimately. He knew who would trust Christ as Savior and who would refuse. Those whom He "foreknew" would choose Christ, He predestined to make Christ-like in our behavior, so Christ could be the firstborn among many godly brothers and sisters.

If Christ-likeness in my life has been God's long-term goal for me, then I should cooperate and make it my own daily goal.

Better is the poor who walks in his integrity Than one perverse in his ways, though he be rich. Let us hear the conclusion of the whole matter: Fear God and keep His commandments, For this is the whole duty of man. For God will bring every work into judgment, Including every secret thing, Whether it is good or whether it is evil.
—PROV. 28:6, ECCL. 12:13–14

My second goal each day is to serve Christ in a balanced way. I could wake up in the morning like many humans and fantasize ways to acquire sex, power and money—and "significance." Or, I can wake up each morning, think about how stupid and worthless the rat race is, and dedicate that day to serving Christ instead.

Solomon did not withhold from himself any pleasure. He found it meaningless. He still felt insignificant.

But when God gave Solomon wisdom, Solomon concluded that serving God was the whole duty of man, especially since God will eventually bring into judgment every good or evil work we have ever done, even in secret.

I fantasize ways I can serve Christ each morning—with my mate, my children, my friends and with others, in that order.

Serving Christ or being a slave to the rat race of sex, power and money are the only two alternatives. If you refuse to serve Christ, you cannot avoid being a slave to the rat race.

> *"But seek first the kingdom of God and His righteousness, and all these things shall be added to you."*
>
> —MATT. 6:33

The rat race offers you three exciting things, but they all will lead to your destruction eventually: sex—the illicit kind, sexual fantasies, pornography, affairs, and other lusts of the flesh like food addictions or drug/alcohol addictions; power—the desire to control as many people as possible in order to feel significant; materialism—the desire to buy everything in sight in order to feel important—significant.

Instead, Christ calls us to give up illicit sex, power and money. Give them to Jesus. Live instead to serve Jesus Christ and you will have meaning and a sense of significance in Him. He'll give you a good sex life with your mate, power to use your leadership abilities in a Christ-like constructive way, and material blessings in a quantity that is best for your spiritual welfare.

This verse revolutionized my own life when I was a thirty-year-old Christian workaholic, "burning out" for Jesus. As a result of this verse, I slowed down, quit doing many external good deeds, took care of my own mental health, spent time with my wife and children, served Christ in easy ways daily, and lowered my career to number 6 on my priority list.

Live for "things" and you'll get the wind. Live for Christ in a balanced way and He will bless you with new and better "things."

*For as we have many members in one body, but
all the members do not have the same function,
so we, being many, are one body in Christ, and
individually members of one another.*
—ROM. 12:4–5

Many believers have looked me right in the eye and
sincerely said they felt like they were worthless to
Christ and with no talents to offer in His service.

I tell them that one of the most worthwhile and
meaningful talents I have is the ability to be a loving
lap for two- and three-year-olds from broken homes.
My wife and I have periodically taught Sunday school
for two- and three-year-olds. She is a former school
teacher, so she tells the Bible story lesson. I sit there
and the kids take turns climbing on my lap to get a hug
and a little attention.

The children with two loving parents climb rapidly
on and off. Their love tanks are already full. The "orphans" climb on my lap and don't want to leave. Their
love tanks are empty.

It doesn't take four graduate degrees to fill an orphan's love tank, just a little love and compassion—and
Christ even gives you that. God designed each of us to
have our own unique psychological talents and spiritual gifts. He created them so we would use them to
help others.

_____

*In the New Year, ask your friends what your gifts and talents are and
use them in simple ways, doing Christ's easy yoke of chores. He'll
bless you in many surprising ways for doing so.*

> *Do not let your heart envy sinners, But in the fear*
> *of the LORD continue all day long; For surely there*
> *is a hereafter, And your hope will not be cut off.*
> *Honor all people. Love the brotherhood. Fear God.*
> *Honor the king.*
> —PROV. 23:17–18, 1 PETER 2:17

It is so easy to look at the "cool" people, the "in crowd," the "jet set," the "rich and famous" and then to tell yourself, I think I could do that! Worldly people can be very appealing. It is easy to be jealous. That is what happened to Demas, the believer who worked with the apostle Paul for awhile. The "call of the wild" got to him and he abandoned his commitment to Christ.

Solomon said to keep serving Christ. Surely there is a hereafter, so don't give in to "the call of the wild." "Honor all people," advises the apostle Peter. Serve the brotherhood. Help your brothers with their overburdens and crises, and allow them to help you with yours. Love them with a deep, genuine, loyal love. Think about the fact that they will be your friends forever. Fear hurting God's feelings. Try to please Him. Love Him. And honor your president and your country. Serve your country and keep it free. Get involved politically and fight for biblical issues. Make the committed Christian vote count.

Lord, give me the strength and courage to follow you one day at a time, one deed at a time, and one thought at a time.

> *"Therefore do not worry about tomorrow, for*
> *tomorrow will worry about its own things.*
> *Sufficient for the day is its own trouble."*
> —MATT. 6:34

It is New Year's Eve, and there is a natural tendency on this particular day for *many* people to reflect on the previous year.

We make scores of New Year's resolutions that we cannot possibly keep. Then comes guilt. And the cycle runs us deeper and deeper into the pits.

I never make any New Year's resolutions. I set the same three goals every morning of my life. My first goal is to become more like Christ that day, which is also God's goal for me. In Matthew 6:33, Jesus told us to seek first to serve His Kingdom and He will give us all the other things we sincerely need. So I choose to serve Him that day as my second goal.

In Matthew 6:34, Jesus said that if we *just stay out of trouble today,* we have had a pretty good day: "Sufficient for the day is its own trouble." This verse also implies that God will only send you as much trouble as you can handle with His help that day. So my third goal each day is to handle that day's troubles and stay out of trouble by guarding my thoughts and motives.

I remember as a child learning this hymn:

> *Some golden daybreak, Jesus will come.*
> *Some golden daybreak, battles all won.*
> *He'll shout the victory, Break through the blue—*
> *Some golden daybreak, for me and for you.*
> *Keep Watching! Happy New Years!*
> *(Micah 7:7)*

About the Authors

Paul Meier, M.D., received an M.S. degree in cardio-vascular physiology at Michigan State University and an M.D. degree from the University of Arkansas College of Medicine. He completed his psychiatric residency at Duke University.

Frank Minirth, M.D., is a diplomate of the American Board of Psychiatry and Neurology and received an M.D. degree from the University of Arkansas College of Medicine.

Dr. Minirth and Dr. Meier founded the Minirth-Meier Clinic in Dallas, Texas, one of the largest psychiatric clinics in the world, with associated clinics in various cities around the USA.

Both Dr. Minirth and Dr. Meier have received degrees from Dallas Theological Seminary. They have also co-authored more than thirty books, including *Happiness Is a Choice, Worry-Free Living, Love Is A Choice, Love Hunger* and *We Are Driven*.